When God Speaks

Life is a journey filled with decisions, but God's pathways do not always travel in a straight line.

Through Meri's personal testimony and life experiences she imparts a fresh revelation on how to find God's purpose for your life. "Find your Purpose and you'll find your Passion" is one of her key life phrases. Her ministry is to challenge and encourage the Body of Christ through the gifts of the Holy Spirit and the teaching of God's Word.

Join Meri Crouley as she takes you through the hills and valleys of her walk with God, through the painful moments as well as the incredible joys of her youth, marriage, and ministry. Share her trials and triumphs as she learns to follow the faithful footsteps and listen to the still small voice of the world's greatest guide, God Almighty.

Don't miss *"When God Speaks"*, a facinating read that reveals the real woman behind the successful youth ministry "Youthwave Explosion Foundation" and the "Now Is The Time" television ministry.

Read on to discover "When God Speaks",
the most awesome release of the year!

When God Speaks

From Glory to Glory
One Womans Story of Faith

Katrina,
To a pure
woman of
God who is
called a
leader in
the body
of
Christ
Mary
Morley

When God Speaks

Published in the United States by deeperPublishing, an imprint of deepercalling media inc

Cover design Copyright © 2004 Sharon K Gilbert. Cover photograph Copyright © 2004.

All enquiries regarding this publication and Meri Crouley may be made to:

    deepercalling media inc

    web: www.deepercalling.com

    email: info@deepercalling.com

    ISBN 0-9726135-9-5

04 PHX 1

All scripture quotations, unless otherwise noted, are taken from the *Holy Bible*, King James Version.

DEDICATION

To my husband, Rick, who has been my inspiration and help mate throughout all of my journeys. Through Rick I learned what it was to step out by faith and trust God. Rick taught me about adventure and taking chances with God.

Secondly, I want to dedicate this book to my wonderful parents, Joe and Pat Jensen. My parents have always been my role models and inspiration. My dad has always shown me tenacity and perseverence through his life-long love of pitching baseball. Turning 75 years old this year, he is still pitching hard ball baseball and won the most valuable player in the world series for seniors this last year. He has been an example to me in that he has never lost sight of his dreams no matter what age he is. My mother has always shown me the loving characteristics of what a true woman of God is. Without her example in the Christian faith and the prayers she and my father have prayed, I would not probably be here to tell this story of my journey. Thank you for being the wonderful parents that you are. I love you!

Lastly, special thanks to Sharon Gilbert for capturing the essence of my book with a fabulous cover design, to Sandy Greene and Norma Morand, for their editing talents, and finally to Bill Goodyear and Merridee Book at deepercalling media, my publisher, for believing in my testimony and encouraging me with the book.

CONTENTS

CHAPTER 1

IN THE BEGINNING

Life is a Journey. As I sat there in the hospital bed not knowing whether I would live or die, I suddenly turned introspective. Recently, I had been diagnosed with a brain tumor and was scheduled for surgery. Life can take a sudden twist of events. As I thought back throughout the course of my life, I realized God was always in control. I knew that life was a journey and God was leading the way. As I waited for the doctor to put me asleep before removing the tumor, I thought about the past and how far I had come. I started to get sleepy, but the picture was still clear to me.....

My parents are wonderful people. They have been married for over 43 years and are an inspiration to me! They met when they were both in a mutual friend's wedding. My mother was a bridesmaid and my dad a groomsman. When they laid eyes on each other they knew there was something special; and that something has not left their hearts to this very day.

My dad is an avid sportsman. He especially loves baseball. He played sports all through high school and college and even played semi-pro baseball. My mother loves people and has many friends. She eventually went on to work for a major airline in reservations. When they met at the wedding it wasn't too long after that they were seriously involved. My dad proposed to my mother; and they had a large wedding in St. Paul, Minnesota at St. Luke's Catholic Church.

They first lived in St. Paul, Minnesota, in a cozy apartment. Their first son, Jack, was born during this time. Then they moved to a little home in the suburbs of Minneapolis called Bloomington. This is where I was born. It was a wonderful time and we lived in this house for about five years. I had many happy memories, from playing with my best friend, Noel Villacorta, to my neighborhood friends, all outside playing in the backyard swimming pool.

When I was five years old my parents started looking for a larger home. The family had been expanding as of late and there was not room enough at our home in Bloomington any longer. In addition to my older brother, Jack, I now had another sister, Therese, and two more brothers, Joe and Mark.

As my parents started looking for a house, they had to put their existing home on the market to sell. They found a wonderful home in St. Paul, Minnesota, on Portland Avenue. It had five bedrooms and was a beautiful two-story home with a basement - complete with an apartment in it. They put an offer in on the home in St. Paul and just believed their home in Bloomington would sell.

It was over two months and the home in Bloomington had not sold yet. They were starting to get nervous! They decided to pray and ask the Lord to help sell the house. The next week - after they started praying together - the Lord miraculously sold their home in Bloomington and they were able to make preparations to move into the home in St. Paul.

I remember moving day so clearly! Even though I was just five years old, it was so exciting to see the moving truck pull up to the house and have these big men come in and remove the furniture in my room to take to the new house. We were moving from the suburbs to the city and it was a big change for me. All of my other siblings were excited as well!

I will never forget the first night at the new home as my mother tucked me into bed. I shared a room with my sister, Terry. My mother said prayers she told us that God was watching over us. I could feel that He was there somehow and felt secure in that knowledge. I always felt God had given us angels to watch over us as we were growing up.

The first day of elementary school came so quickly. It was such a frightening day as all of the other children and their mothers got together for the first time with the new kindergarten teacher. It was frightening, but a new adventure as well. What new journeys was God going to take me on today?

I remember one time when I was going to school. We had guards crossing at the corner that helped walk us across the street. We would all line up at a certain time and the guards would help us across the street. I was a little late that day and when I got there everyone had already crossed the street and I was left all alone. I remember running home to my mother and telling her that they had left me. There would be many more times growing up when I would feel like that lost little girl running home to mother saying they had all left. But when we feel that God has left, He will make His presence known to us and tell us "I will never leave you nor forsake you."

Life was always hectic around the Jensen household, but it was a family filled with love and I was very happy growing up. Some of the only bad memories I had were the fact that I had an extreme overbite. After I lost my baby teeth and my permanent teeth started growing I noticed that they were bigger than my baby teeth and they stuck out. I was starting to look like a gopher and was told so on a regular basis by kids in the neighborhood. Children can be so cruel sometimes! I remember walking home from school and having some kid I never met look at me and stick out his teeth and laugh. Then they would run away and called me "Bucky Beaver" or some other expletive that didn't make me feel very good.

In the sixth grade I thankfully got braces and thought I was starting to look and feel normal again. It started to make a huge difference in my self-esteem and how I felt about myself.

I went to a Catholic Parochial school all throughout grade school. I remember going to mass and feeling so close to God sometimes. I would go and look at the statues and hope God was listening to me when I prayed. I didn't realize this, but God has always had his hand on my life and on my family's life. The road ahead would get rocky but God would never take his hand off of us.

By the time I reached eighth grade I was going through typical teenage stuff. I had gotten my braces off by this time and remember looking in the mirror and thinking about how big my teeth looked. It was such a shock! But basically I was starting to be pretty pleased with my appearance. It was during this time though that Satan started to make inroads in my life.

I graduated from Immaculate Heart of Mary Grade School and was accepted into an all girl Catholic School called Our Lady of Peace High School or O.L.P. for short. All the girls had wonderful nicknames for these initials such as Old Ladies Penitentiary. I had a couple of wonderful years at O.L.P. We would get in so much trouble! Sometimes we would have food fights in the cafeteria. When the nuns would come in to see what the commotion was, the perpetrators would always hide. I was always one of the ones hiding. I didn't get caught very often. I guess it was because I had such an angelic face!

I recollect one incident when one of my best friends, Donna Kahnke, was trying to pretend that she was going to hit the fire alarm. She had the little hammer out as she called out to me, "Meri, watch me hit the fire alarm." She only wanted to tease me. She had meant to hit the wall but in her hurry she actually hit the alarm and it broke causing this huge noise to sound throughout the school. I will never forget her face as she took off running down the hall for who knows where. The school had been in the middle of a huge dress rehearsal for a play that was going on that weekend and everyone had piled out onto the lawn and the sidewalks. The fire engines came not realizing it was a false alarm. Donna got in big trouble not only with the school but also with her parents. I thought it was extremely amusing.

Life definitely was a journey and I wanted to ride it for all it was worth! It was during this time that I started making choices that were not the best for me or for my walk with God. Even though I had been raised in church and went to a private school, I did not know Christ personally. I started to hang out with kids that were not the best examples and that were doing things that I know my parents would not like.

I remember the first time I was offered drugs. I had been at a party at the Mississippi River in St. Paul. I lived off of Summit Avenue not too far from the river. On sunny days during the spring some of us would walk or ride our bikes down to the river. You then had to walk down some paths to get to the sand. It was on one of these nice, sunny days in the spring that it happened. There were about nine of us just sitting around when one of the kids in the group who I had never met, pulled out a joint and started passing it around. I told them I did not want to smoke it. It kept going around but as it came to me again, the leader of the group started taunting me that I should try it. His name was Tony and he had made a big impression on my other girlfriend. Eventually I relented and smoked it. All I remember was that the first time I started coughing and it wasn't all that great.

That is the way it is with sin. When you first do it, it isn't all that great. But the more you do it the more you get accustomed to it. Then it becomes a habit - a habit hard to break for many people. I know it led me into a life that in a few years I would not believe the things I would do.

I wasn't all that impressed with smoking pot after this first episode. But the more that I went down to the river and started hanging with a group of kids that my parents had no idea of what I was doing, the easier it became. The Bible says, "Bad company corrupts good morals." It is so important to watch who our kids are associating with and who their friends and influences are. My parents had not been raised in the drug culture and were not even aware of the signs to look for.

In addition to the parties at the river, we would go to school dances called "mixers." Since I went to an all-girls Catholic school we would have these dances either at our school or at one of the all-boys schools in the area. These dances were another place where we would choose to get wild. Some of the girls would buy a bottle of wine and we would drink it before we went in. I was not particularly fond of wine at this time, especially since it was the good old "Boone's Farm" wine. The dances seemed tame enough, but the combination of the wine and pot made some of the kids get out of control.

At the end of my sophomore year at O.L.P., the school was forced to close because of not enough funding by the Catholic diocese. My family had decided that it was time to move again after living in our home on Portland Avenue for over eight years. Our family had now expanded to a whopping seven children. Two new additions had been added, my sisters Jane and Karen.

My parents found a great lot in Bloomington, a suburb of Minneapolis, and decided to build a home. They had put our home in St. Paul on the market and felt by the time the home sold on Portland Avenue the new home would be built and we could all move in. Basically, that is what happened and I was enrolled in a new school. Only this time it was not a private school, but a public high school called Kennedy Senior High.

I will always remember the summer we moved. We had sold our home in St. Paul and the house in Bloomington was completed. It was a little scary because I had lived in St. Paul since I was four years old and was going to have to make all new friends in a new school and new city. The only good thing was that I was forced to attend a new school due to the closure of O.L.P.

It was exciting moving into a brand new house! It was a four-bedroom house and there were seven of us children so we had to share rooms. The house was a beautiful two-story, white home with black shutters. It was on a very large lot located on the end of a cul-de-sac. There were enormous oak trees in our back yard and all over the neighborhood.

Moving day was a thrill for us! We arrived at the new home and I ran to the room that I had chosen. I looked around and was excited about the new adventures that I would discover in this house. I was looking forward to going to a new school and making friends.

A lot of the neighbors came around on moving day to welcome our family. There sure were a lot of us to welcome! It was probably quite a sight seeing seven kids and my parents moving all of the possessions that we had accumulated over 15 years into a new home.

The end of the summer had come and it was time to start school. I was going to be entering my junior year in high school. I had gone to private schools all of my life, but now my parents had decided I should go to a public school. It was a very large school and went from the 9th to 12th grade. There were about 5,000 kids in attendance.

The first day of school for me was both exciting and frightening. I remember waiting on the corner for the school bus to pick me up. I had never taken a school bus before because in

St. Paul I had always walked to school. But now, since I lived in the suburbs, things weren't so close together as in the city.

As I walked into Kennedy High School on the first day of school, I remember walking down the halls going from one class to another. I had always worn uniforms at the private schools that I went to before. Now everyone was dressed in a variety of clothing. There were many kids that had long hair and wore jeans and jean jackets.

I felt very lonely walking from class to class not knowing a soul. But it was also exhilarating because I always liked a challenge and this definitely was one. I soon found out that there were two groups of clicks at our school. You were either a freak or a jock. A jock was someone who was into sports and went to many of the school functions. You were also considered a jock if you were a cheerleader or on one of the dance squads. A freak was someone who avoided jocks and liked to party all the time.

I started gravitating toward the freak crowd. I remember going into the bathrooms at school between periods and hanging out. This was the best way I found to socialize with other kids. Kids would be in the bathroom smoking and talking. I had started smoking a little bit when I lived in St. Paul. I really didn't like it much but I thought I was cool when I did it. So I started smoking cigarettes in the bathrooms at Kennedy to meet other kids.

It's sad that the devil deceives kids so much into thinking that it is cool to smoke cigarettes. There's nothing cool about it. It's definitely a stepping stone to other drugs. This is how it started with me. Smoking cigarettes led the way to smoking pot. And pot then was the gateway to other drugs that I soon started to take.

In the bathroom I started making some new friends. They were girls that were part of the freak group. Sarah Ferguson was one of the first girls at Kennedy to accept me into her click. It was very hard coming into a new school during my junior year. Many of these kids had been to school with each other since kindergarten and they didn't always open up to new kids.

Sarah was a very pretty girl with long, wavy brown hair and big brown eyes. She was not very tall and had a very good figure. She invited me to her house that weekend to hang out with her and some of her friends. I went over to her house and went up into her bedroom. It was through Sarah that I started getting introduced to some of the darker things of life.

The devil never shows you the end of the journey at the beginning. He always tries to make it look so glamorous and exciting until he gets you to a point where you're addicted or caught in a trap that you can't get out of. I have heard that if you put a frog in boiling water, of course the frog will jump right out. But if you place the frog in lukewarm water and turn up the heat very slowly, eventually the frog will cook to death. Slowly the devil was turning up the heat in my life.

I thought Sarah had a really cool room. There were pictures of rock stars hung all over her walls. She had long beads that went from the top of her door to the floor so when you entered the room you had to move the beads aside to enter. She also had incense burning as rock music blared from her stereo speakers.

Sarah opened me up to a whole new world of drugs and music. We started going to concerts of our favorite rock stars. Before we would go to these concerts we would smoke pot or get high on some other drug. Up until this point the only drug that I had done was marijuana. But eventually I started taking speed and downers once in a while. It all seemed so exciting and that we had the world by the tail.

Eventually I started making more friends that were part of the freak group. During the weekends we would have a whole list of parties to choose from. I was one of the main partiers in the group and would always know where the best parties were. People would call me for the list of parties. It was really amazing! We would go from party to party on weekends having the time of our lives.

So between the concerts and the parties I was a busy girl. Unlike many of the girls I knew at this time, I didn't have one steady boyfriend. I liked to play the field and try to set up a couple of dates a night and then choose the one I felt like going out the most with. I was on a fast track but going downward fast.

My two years at Kennedy Senior High were a blur. I basically stayed on the B honor roll without even opening up a book. The classes I chose weren't that hard and it was easy to get through. I was also enrolled in the student work program so after going to school for half the day, I would then go to a job where I would work the other half and get credit for it at school.

The job I was given was at an advertising agency called "Chuck Ruhr Advertising." It was located not far from Kennedy in a beautiful colonial mansion that was made into an office building. They were a fairly new company but were growing and had some of the best media and advertising executives in the business. I was chosen to be the girl Friday around the office. I basically opened mail, did filing, and other miscellaneous tasks for the vice-president of the company.

It was a great job and I loved it! Everyone around me was so creative that I thrived in the environment. I couldn't wait to go to work in the afternoon. My day was something like this: I would wake up and get ready for school; from 8:30 until 12:00 I was at school in my various classes and then from 1:00 until 5:00 I went to Chuck Ruhr advertising and worked part time.

Between school, work, and partying the time just flew by. Before I knew it the time had come for graduation. I remember graduation day and how we were excited about all of the parties that were going to take place that night. I was all ready to go in my blue cap and gown, when my dad told me he wanted me to look outside in the driveway. My dad had bought me a car for my graduation present. It was so beautiful to look out and see this shiny blue car sitting in the driveway with my brother Jack behind the wheel. I started to cry and ran out of the house. It wasn't a brand new car, but to me it was. It was a Rebel Rambler. I felt that this somehow fit my life at this time....the rambling rebel.

I remember getting my diploma that night. As I walked on that stage after my name was called and then walked off that stage, I felt proud. I thought this was only the beginning of great things for me. You see I always felt that I had important things to do in this life. I just didn't know at that time that I was feeling the calling of God on my life. God had called me from the time I was in my mother's womb. He knew that I would be rebellious and stray from His ways. But He also knew the future and what choices I would make.

The summer after I graduated I had decided to take a trip to California with a good friend of mine from high school, Lynn Terrance. We decided to drive her car and make a sightseeing trip out of it across the country. A boyfriend I used to date but had broken up with a year prior also decided to go along with us for protection. It was through this trip to California that I first started to see the hand of God working in my behalf.

We planned the trip to first go through the Black Hills of South Dakota and see Mount Rushmore. It took us a day to drive to Mount Rushmore from Minneapolis. Once we got there we went to a bar to listen to some music. At this bar we ran into a guy who sold us some pot. We were having a great time and spent the night in Mount Rushmore and the next morning we proceeded on our trip.

We made our way across the country and passed through Las Vegas. The lights of Las Vegas were really exciting to see at night. It's amazing how the bright lights of the world can attract so many people to them. It does not even compare to the Light of the World, Jesus.

As we continued on into California we started getting really excited. First we were on our way to San Francisco to see a good friend of Dan's named Mickey. He was singing in a band called the Elvin Bishop group, which was fairly famous at the time. Dan knew Mickey when he used to live in Georgia for a short time. We were driving through Sacramento on our way on to San Francisco when an unexpected stop happened.

We had all been taking turns driving Lynn's car and I was at the wheel. I had the music on full blast and was really enjoying myself listening to the music and looking at the scenery as I was driving. Dan was in the back seat asleep and Lynn was in the front seat dozing as well. All of a sudden I heard a police car tell me through the speaker to pull over immediately.

Little to my knowledge there had been a police car following me for five miles with his lights on trying to get me to pull over. I was enjoying myself so much that I was totally oblivious to the fact that he was trying to pull me over. Dan woke up immediately and sat up in the seat. Lynn was startled awake and everyone started getting paranoid. We had the pot in our glove compartment that we had bought in Mount Rushmore.

The police officer had us all get out of the car and started looking in our vehicle. He noticed an empty beer can in the back that Dan had been drinking earlier in the day. Because of that beer can he had the right to search the vehicle as well as our purses. He went through my purse but only found some make up and a brush. When he searched Lynn's purse he found some speed in a little plastic bag.

I will never forget the smirk on the policeman's face as he looked at Lynn. I knew he was going to bust her. Then, to our dismay, he looked in the glove compartment. He pulled out the bag of pot and Dan immediately told the policeman that the pot was his.

The policeman looked at Dan and said, "So you want to play the hero huh?" He knew that by Dan saying the pot was his that only he would be charged with possession of marijuana. It seemed like I was living a dream at this point. I was so excited about going to see San Francisco and all of the things we were going to do. All of a sudden my bubble was instantaneously burst.

The policeman looked at us and told us that he was putting Dan and Lynn under arrest. He told me that I would have to follow them to the police station where they would be booked and sentenced. I would then find out how much their bail was and possibly get them out. I remember following the police car with Dan and Lynn in the back seat. I felt numb wondering how all of this happened. Just an hour ago I was so excited about going to San Francisco and now my two friends were arrested

As I followed them over in Lynn's car I prayed silently under my breath, "Dear Lord, please get me out of this one." My parents would totally freak out if they knew that my two friends were in jail and I had nowhere to go. I could not call them so I just drove on wondering what would happen when I got there. I thought maybe they would be released on their on recognizance.

Once I got to the jail and parked my car, I made my way to the division where you find out how much bail is and what the procedures are to get someone out of jail. I walked into a very sterile looking room with many people with sad faces sitting in chairs. There were some people to my right who were very vocal about what was going on. The one was shouting that he had never even received anything in the mail about a warrant that he had just gotten taken in on. I thought to myself, "This seems like the beginning of a long night!"

I stood in line and waited to find out how much bail was for my two friends. When I got to the window and told their names the woman at the window said to me, "Lynn is booked under a felony with possession of an illegal drug and her bail is $5,000 and Dan's bail is $1,200." My mouth dropped open and I was in total shock. I could not believe that the bail that they wanted was this much. I only had about $200 on me and I wasn't about to call Minnesota and ask for the money. My parents would have been in total shock and grounded me for the rest of my known existence.

I told the woman at the window that I wasn't sure about what I was going to do because I did not have that kind of money. She told me they would be arraigned in front of a judge sometime in the next few days and that I should sit tight and that sometimes the judge would drop the bail or greatly reduce it. That answer did not give me the encouragement I needed.

I asked her how would I find out when the arraignment would be and she answered that I should just call the courthouse and they would let me know the time. I turned away from the window bewildered, not knowing what I was going to do. I was in a strange city and I did not know one soul in it. Who was I going to call and where was I going to stay that night? It was already about 3:00 p.m. in the afternoon and with only $200 on me that wasn't a lot to last a long period of time.

There were two guys standing to the left of the window that I just turned away from. They had overheard some of what was going on. They must have saw the dejected look on my face and asked me what was going on. I proceeded to tell them my plight and within a few minutes was being offered a place to stay at their home. Normally I would not even consider such an offer but I was desperate and these people looked safe enough so I told them yes.

I remember following them over to their home in the heart of downtown Sacramento praying that God would protect me. As I pulled up to their home I was strangely comforted. The house that they were staying in was an older, two- story traditional home with a flower bed in the front. It reminded me of homes in the area of St. Paul where I grew up. I pulled in their driveway and got out and made my way to the front door. The two guys names were Dave and Paul. Paul was a shorter guy who was around 22 years old. He had longer, brown hair with a beard and mustache. Dave was a lot more conservative looking with shorter, blonde hair and no facial hair. They had known each other since grade school and had recently moved into the house together as roommates.

They didn't have a whole lot of furniture since they were young guys who had just recently moved out. Dave offered that I could sleep in his room. There really was no other choice since there was only the floor and they didn't have any bedding to put me up with.

I found out that Dave was a practicing Scientologist. Scientology is a religion founded by L. Ron Hubbard that basically brainwashes you into thinking what they want you to. It is a cult and many of the members go through a process called Auditing involving classes. Once fully "audited" you are pronounced "Clear". I was totally unaware at this point that this was a cult and listened to Dave as he intently tried to tell me about Scientology and what it had done for him.

Dave had a double bed in his room and I remember looking at it before I was to go to sleep for the first time since arriving at their home. I was totally exhausted from the day's events and just wanted to crash and not wake up for a week or so. I remember the glean in Dave's eyes, thinking that he was going to be able to get somewhere with me that night. I looked at Dave and very sweetly told him that I had a boyfriend and he was in jail (not true, but it sounded good), and that I was trying to get them out by the next few days so we could continue on our adventure. He looked disappointed, but I knew by his look that he was safe and would not do anything against my will. I thanked the Lord silently again.

I slept like a rock that night and woke up the next morning to the birds chirping with the sun beaming through the windows. I was excited, thinking my friends would be released today and we could get on with our merry adventure that had been detained by a freak of unfair circumstances. Little did I realize that God was trying to get my attention.

Dave got out of bed and walked over to the wall where he had a big, posted chart. He then explained to me that this was a Scientology chart and that it let him know how he was to proceed that day in the decisions that he made. I remember looking at him and thinking that it sure was a weird way to make your decisions for the day by waking up and looking at a poster on the wall. God really protected me from not getting involved in this cult. It wasn't even of the slightest bit of interest to me.

Dave and Paul went to work and I was left all alone in the house wondering what I was to do first. I got out the yellow pages and proceeded to call legal aid in the phone book. There was a place not too far from the house I was staying at that offered free legal advise, so I ripped the page out of the yellow pages and drove to their offices. When I got to the legal offices it was not what I was expecting. It basically looked like a run down home and a lot of hippies were running it. The attorney who met with me was not all that comforting about my situation. He painted a pretty bleak picture about what to expect and I could feel my spirit sinking.

I drove away from their offices praying, "God, if you're out there please get me out of this situation." I have never bargained with God before, but at this stage of my life I was willing to try anything. I prayed to God and told him that if He would get my friends out of jail that I would turn my life over to Him and serve Him. Little did I know that when you make a bargain with God He expects you to keep it.

I then drove by the courthouse to see if I could find out any information on my two friends. The court clerk told me that they were scheduled for arraignment sometime within the next few days, but the court docket was extremely full and they weren't guaranteed an exact time. I thanked the woman for the information and walked back to Lynn's car.

For the next few days I was on pins and needles wondering what was going on with my friends at the jail. Every time I went down to the courthouse to get information I couldn't find anything out. Dave and Paul were supportive and tried to make light of everything. They were great guys and really were concerned for my situation.

I woke up the following morning and remembered looking out the window and thinking, "Something has got to break today!" I decided to walk to the courthouse instead of taking the car and having to deal with the hassle of parking. As I was walking the ten blocks to the jail I remember meditating and thinking about my friends. I then again said a silent prayer to the Lord and asked Him to please take care of the situation. I reminded God of my bargain I had with Him and asked the Lord to please answer quickly.

As I rounded the corner to the jail I saw something that almost made me do handstands. My friend, Lynn, was standing on the corner and was looking around. I yelled her name and came running over to her and hugged her harder than I have ever hugged anyone before. I asked her where Dan was and she told me he was getting finished with the processing for him to leave jail and would be out within the hour. I was overjoyed! God sure knew what He was doing.

Lynn told me about the horrors of jail life. She told me that she was strip searched and then given jail clothes to wear. For two days she had to wait until her arraignment that morning. She didn't know how to get hold of me and didn't want to call home either. At the arraignment that morning the judge had mercy on them and let them out on their own recognizance if they would do a drug treatment therapy when they got back to Minnesota.

I was amazed at the fact that God had spared me of the ordeal of having to spend time in jail. After everything Lynn told me about what had happened, I was sorry for them but greatly relieved at not having not experienced that horrible situation. God sure does take care of His children's children. My mom and dad had been praying for me and I know it was because of their faithfulness that God spared me and protected me of all the possible dangers that could have happened.

We all had a joyful reunion when we finally saw Dan and went over to Dave and Paul's house to retrieve our belongings. Then we continued on our way up to San Francisco to visit the band that we were originally going to see.

It's amazing how when we are in trouble the first thing we will do is call out to God for help. But once we are out of the situation that we were praying about how easily we forget our promises that we have made to Him. Such was the case with me. Once we were back on the road again I fell back into my old habits and the partying life. Eat, drink, and be merry was the way I was feeling; and I was glad that the past was behind me and looking forward to new and exciting adventures ahead of me.

The next few weeks were a blur of seeing different cities, concerts, and doing as much as we could in a short amount of time. We went to San Francisco and stayed there for a few days. We then went down to Southern California and visited many of the beach cities. We were at the ocean every day just catching a few rays and meeting new friends.

When it was finally time to leave to return to Minnesota it was hard to go. We had all enjoyed ourselves except for the brief jail incident. The Bible says that sin is fun for a season but we will eventually reap what we have sown. In the not too distant future I would start seeing that life wasn't just all one big party after all.

Chapter 2

GETTING SAVED

Once I got back from my trip to California, the summer sped by quickly for me. I had enrolled at a school in downtown Minneapolis called Minnesota School of Business. Some people from the school had come during my senior year at Kennedy and explained about a career in Court Reporting. I thought it sounded exciting and the money was very good. So I enrolled in the school and got a student loan to start the classes in September.

Some of my friends were going on to colleges or universities in other parts of the country. Sarah Ferguson, my best friend at the time, was not planning on going to school but wanted to work and make some money. Lynn also decided that she did not want to go to school right away and took a job as a waitress.

Looking back I can see that God was already separating me from the friends who were so near and dear to me at the time. He took me away from the environment that I was used to and He was getting ready to do a new thing.

But it was business - or partying - as usual for a while. At the Minnesota School of Business I met a whole new set of friends. These were more goal-oriented people who really wanted to do something with their lives. At the school of business it was not just a school for prospective court reporters, but also for a variety of other careers such as legal and medical secretaries, paralegals, accountants, and other business professions.

I would usually take the bus downtown and then walk the few short blocks to school. Sometimes I would drive my rebel rambler downtown, but then I would have to pay to park in the lot across the street from the school and that got expensive.

I was having the time of my life going to school and then dating a variety of men that I met at school, parties, or other social functions. I felt I was at the head of my game and I couldn't wait to play it out.

Through the Minnesota School of Business they had a job placement program for people going to the school who wanted to work part-time. I took advantage of this program and was sent on interviews to businesses downtown that were looking for a part-time secretary or girl Friday.

I remember getting called to the office and being told that I had an interview at Banker's Life and Casualty Insurance Company. They were looking for a part-time girl to help one of the C.L.U. insurance agents named Dick Smith. The interview was set for 2:30 after school the next day. I looked at the slip non chalantly and thought that it was close to school and not too far from the bus stop to go home so it sounded good to me.

God was starting to put all the pieces together to start reeling me in. Even though I would put up a fight once God caught me, when God has you on the line you will never get away until you are pulled in....and pull God did!

I met with Dick Smith the following day after school and was impressed with him and the whole office staff. It was on the fourth floor of a very nice office building. It wasn't a small company, but it wasn't huge either. There were probably about 10 other agents who worked there with about 15

office staff to support these agents. As I passed the receptionist desk I heard a voice say, "Hi, are you applying for the job?"

I looked up to find a pretty, blonde girl around my age sitting behind the receptionist desk. I found out her name was
Diane and she had only recently got the job herself. She told
me that she had prayed that God would get her the right job
and He answered her very quickly by getting her that job. I
told her to pray that I would get the job as well and we had a
good laugh and she said she would.

The next day the school counselor's office called me in and
let me know that indeed I had gotten the job at Banker's Life
and that I was to start the next day. It would only be about
15 hours a week, but I didn't want any more hours than that
since I had to study for my court reporting courses.

The next day I showed up promptly at 1:30 p.m. to start my
clerical duties for Dick. He was a very nice man, but I found
out from Diane that he was an alcoholic. He had bottles of
booze stashed in many of the drawers in the office. Everyone
knew that he went out for liquid lunches where he would con-
sume quite a few martinis before he would come back for the
rest of the afternoon. He never appeared inebriated to me,
though. Sometimes he would seem a little shaky when he
would need to take another drink, but for the most part he
hid his drinking and was able to function just fine.

I found out from some of the other full time girls in the
office that the receptionist, Diane, was a "Jesus freak." She
was constantly telling everyone in the office what Jesus was
doing in her life. She was not condemning, though, and I still
liked her and stood up for her when others talked about her.
She would constantly be telling me little things such as, "I'm
praying for you Meri," and, "God has His hand on you."

One day as I was getting ready to leave for the day I
remember her asking me a simple question. She said to me,
"Meri, where do you think you are going to go when you die?"

I had never really thought about it much. Once in a while I would think about the subject of death when I was at a funeral, but for the most part it's a subject that many people don't like to entertain. I remember looking up at her and saying, "Probably purgatory. I'll pay somebody to pray me out of there." In the church I had been brought up in if you were not good enough to go to heaven but not bad enough to go to hell there was a place called purgatory (or a middle place) where you would almost wait in limbo until enough prayers were said for you and then God would let you out and then you would go to heaven.

I thought that was a cute answer and was chuckling inside just looking at Diane's face. The answer she told me, though, was the beginning of the change of my life. She told me, "Meri, there is no place in the Bible that talks about purgatory. There is only one of two places that you will go when you die, either heaven or hell." I had never heard that there was no such thing as purgatory. I was shocked and made an excuse to get out of there as quickly as I could. I told her I had to catch the bus and quickly exited down the stairs before she could get another word in.

On the bus ride home that evening many thoughts were going over in my mind. "Did the Bible really say that there was no such place as a purgatory? Why was I told this? If there was no middle ground where was I to spend eternity when I die?!"

I knew that by the life I was living I would not go to heaven. But I could not get into my head that a God of love would send me to hell. I was very confused and decided at that point to find more out about this subject later.

A few years prior my mom and dad had accepted Jesus into their hearts. There was a strong movement going through many mainstream denominations that talked about being born again and receiving the baptism of the Holy Spirit with the evidence of speaking in tongues. My mother would try to invite me to some of her prayer groups and religious meetings. Once I remember attending and laughing when everyone had their hands raised and they all seemed to be speaking in some foreign language.

My mother would also leave Christian literature in various strategic places in our house to try to get me to read it. She would leave some books by my bed, in the bathroom, and on the coffee tables in the living room. This technique worked for her. I started reading different books before I would go to bed. God was really starting to get His word inside of me through these books. The Bible says, "Faith comes by hearing and hearing by the word of God." As I kept reading, the more I started to understand the nature of God and His plan of salvation.

It was amazing during this time how many people that the Lord would send my way. I always say that God has a way and means completely beyond what any human could ever formulate and put together. For instance, I would be waiting at the bus stop to go home from my job and someone would come up to me and tell me about Jesus and how God wanted me to accept Him in my heart. I would always politely listen but then make my escape when the bus came.

I had numerous occasions where God would send someone over to me at a mall, school, and work with Diane constantly telling me about the things of God. I was trying to run from the truth but it was getting harder and harder to do so. My conscience was starting to really kick in and I was worried about the hell issue. Jesus talks about hell more in the Bible than he does about heaven. God was starting to reel me in even though I was trying my best to get away.

One day I was at work and Diane invited me to go to lunch with her. On this particular day I did not have school and was spending the whole day doing some filing that had accumulated and needed to be done. I told Diane that I would go and we went to the top of Dayton's Department Store where they had a restaurant that overlooked downtown Minneapolis. They had a lovely salad bar there and we both got in line and made our salads.

We sat down by the window and I looked down below and saw all the people walking around on the streets below. Diane looked at me and said, "Meri, God really wants to use you. He has a plan for your life and wants you to accept Him in your heart." I looked at her and all of a sudden the reality of what she was saying made sense. It was like a light bulb had been turned on in my brain and now everything was making sense. It was the strangest feeling and I don't know if mere words could express what really took place.

I looked at her and said, "Diane, yes I do want to accept Jesus." She had the most astonished look on her face. I don't believe she thought for one moment that I would give her that answer. She almost screamed for joy and wanted me to accept Jesus right there and then. I told her that I wanted to wait to get back to the office and do it in my boss's office. We quickly finished our lunch and then made our way back to the Insurance Company. I had to try to control Diane's excitement. She was almost doing cartwheels on the way back to the office.

When we got to the office we immediately went to Dick Smith's office. He was still away for lunch and this is where I was working on the filing. We closed the door quietly and prayed first of all that Dick would not come sauntering in from lunch any time soon. Then Diane looked at me and told me she was going to lead me in a prayer of repentance and then ask Jesus to come into my heart. She said she would say the prayer line by line and I should repeat it after her. The words weren't the most important thing, she said, but my heart attitude.

So we both got down on our knees and I invited Jesus to come into my heart. The prayer I prayed went something like this: "Dear Father, I know that I am a sinner. Please forgive me of my sins and wash me with the blood of Jesus. Jesus, please come into my heart and make me a new creation in you. Help me to live the kind of life you have called me to live. Thank you Jesus." It was a simple prayer of faith that I said from my heart to God. I believed what I said had happened and when I got off my knees I knew that if I died I would go to heaven.

Such an amazing feeling of cleanness swept over me. I indeed felt like God had taken all the things from my past and wiped them all away. The Bible says in Isaiah 1:18, *"Though your sins be as scarlet, now they shall become white as snow."* Diane gave me a big hug and welcomed me as her sister into the family of God. She had tears of joy running down her face because she said I was the first person she had ever led to the Lord.

Diane told me now that I should purchase a Bible and read it as much as I could. Just like I needed to eat food to become strong in my natural body, so did I need to eat the food from the Bible to grow spiritually. She also told me that now that I was a Christian I needed to get involved with a church and start associating with Christians. There was a ministry that she was involved in located in downtown Minneapolis called "Christ Center Ministry," which was an outreach to the downtown community. She invited me to go with her sometime and I told her I would.

After work that day I rode the bus home. I felt ecstatic that now I was a new Christian! I couldn't wait to get home and tell my parents what had happened to me. I walked in the door and my mom was making supper for the night. I nonchalantly told my mother that I received Jesus into my heart that day. I will never forget the look on her face as she looked

up from the stove. It was a look of surprise and bewilderment. It's amazing that we can pray for people for years and
then when the answer finally comes we almost don't believe
what we are hearing. I proceeded to tell her what happened
with Diane and she was thrilled at what the Lord had done.

My mother had been praying for so long and had been trying to get me converted through her prayer groups. All the
prayers and the seeds that she had sown by leaving Christian
literature around the house really did plant seeds. When
Diane came along at work all she had to do was basically reel
me in. God already had me on the hook. That's why it is
important that we continue to witness to people even when
we don't think it is doing any good. Only God can look at the
heart and see what condition a person is in. Sometimes the
worse off a person may seem the more they may be open to
the gospel. Or they may seem like the most hardened sinner
you ever met and may blatantly curse at you when you try to
share with them, but sometimes those are the ones that want
the Lord the most and just want to see your reaction as to see
how your Christian attitude is going to react to their behavior.

After that day at work where I received Jesus into my heart,
people started to notice a big change in me. The first thing
that I did was call up most of my friends and tell them what
had happened to me. I thought that everyone else would be
as excited about Jesus as I was and would also jump at the
chance to receive Jesus. Many of my friends thought that I
had flipped out. Some of them thought that I had gotten into
a cult of some kind and actually needed to be reprogrammed
out of it. I was a little disappointed at some of their respons-
es but it did not deter me.

I started going down to Christ Center Ministries with
Diane. There was a man and his wife named Chuck and Sue
Dunning who were the founders of this ministry. They were a
sweet couple in their thirties who didn't have any children.

Chuck had been a successful businessman at one time and a heavy drinker and partier. He met the Lord, quit his partying, and started going to church. He eventually met Sue and married her. Chuck had felt a calling from the Lord on his life for him to go into full-time ministry. He started out having Bible studies, but then eventually the Lord told him to quit his job and start Christ Center Ministries in downtown Minneapolis to reach out to the lost.

Christ Center Ministries was in a prime location right on Nicollet Mall across from Orchestra Hall. Nicollet Mall is a place that has several shops and stores. Many people walk down this street and browse into the windows of these shops. Chuck opened up Christ Center Ministries right in the heart of Nicollet Mall and on the store front windows had scriptures telling people about accepting Jesus into their hearts. They made it into a coffee house where people could just come in and have a cup of free coffee and talk about Jesus.

When I first walked into Christ Center Ministries I wasn't sure what to expect. I was still a baby Christian and everything was new to me. Chuck and Sue immediately welcomed me and made me feel at home. They told me that they were having Bible studies on Tuesday and Thursday nights and invited me to the next one. I thanked them and told them I would be there.

When Tuesday night came I didn't go home from work. I was so excited about going to the Bible study at Christ Center Ministries. It's funny how I used to be excited about going to a new nightclub. When Christ comes into your heart He sure gives you a desire to taste new wine. I walked into the door of Christ Center Ministries and took a seat. They had chairs put all around in a circle. There were about ten people that had already come. Most of the people were in their twenties but a few were in their thirties.

Chuck began the meeting in prayer and then proceeded to teach us about the book of Revelation and what was going to happen in the last days. It was fascinating and I remember being on the edge of my seat listening to every word. After he was through teaching they had a time of prayer over people. Chuck walked up to me and asked me if I was baptized in the Holy Spirit. I knew that my mom had told me about this and she said the evidence that I had it was that I would speak with other tongues as the Holy Spirit gave me utterance. I told Chuck that I hadn't received the gift of tongues yet, but that I had been asking God for the particular gift but to no avail.

Chuck explained to me that when I asked God for something that He would give it to me. God says, "Ask and you shall receive, seek and you shall find, knock and the door will be opened unto you," for everyone that asks receives" Matthew 7:7 . I remember asking God for this gift in my car on the way to work one day and just opened my mouth thinking that God was going to take my tongue and just talk with it. I told this to Chuck and he laughed saying that God wasn't going to just take my tongue and use me like a robot. God gives us a free will and He will work with our tongue and our thoughts to speak.

I still didn't understand everything he was saying to me, but I thought that it couldn't hurt asking God for this gift. Chuck explained to me that the baptism of the Holy Spirit would give me the power in my life to be a witness for Christ. He explained that up until the time the disciples had the baptism they would fall asleep when Jesus told them to pray, they fought over who would sit next to Jesus, denied Jesus, and fought and quarreled. After the baptism of the Holy Spirit on the day of Pentecost they were transformed into men and women of God who literally turned their world upside down for Christ. When Peter stood up on the day of Pentecost and spoke, over 5,000 were added to the church after he spoke.

I listened to everything Chuck said and faith started to well up in my spirit. I told him that I wanted to pray to God and ask Him for the baptism of the Holy Spirit right then and there. As Chuck prayed over me for this gift I remember feeling a strange sensation starting to flood my being. I felt a peace like I have never known before. Out of my inner being I started to speak. I started to get a few words that didn't make sense to me, that must have been the Holy Spirit. As I repeated these words over and over again everyone around me started to rejoice knowing that God had given me the gift of tongues. It comes by faith and I was speaking by faith.

One thing you can be sure of about any of the gifts of the spirit is that if you ask God He is going to give you what you are asking for. If you ask God for the gift of the baptism of the Holy Spirit, God will give it to you. Sometimes the manifestation of tongues doesn't occur immediately. It's not that God doesn't want to give it to you, it's that our natural mind gets in the way and we don't know how to let the spirit flow through us. When I learned to get out of the way and let God move that's when I started to move out in the things of God.

I was saying these two words that I got in the Holy Spirit. I kept repeating them over and over again afraid that I would forget them. It was so exciting knowing that I had a heavenly language and that God was using me. Chuck told me that sometimes people will get a few words of a language just like a baby when she first begins to speak. Sometimes, though, a person will receive the whole language right away. For instance, in the book of Acts after the disciples were in the upper room and the Holy Spirit fell upon them, they immediately went out and started witnessing to people in other languages preaching the gospel even though they did not know the language they were speaking in. They had a complete language immediately after they were filled with the spirit.

I received only a couple of words in the Holy Spirit. As I continued to pray in the Holy Spirit, and use those words that God had given me, I got more. The language started to develop in me. Christ Center Ministries had a prayer room and I remember going into the prayer room and praying my two words that I had received in the Holy Ghost over and over again. The more I prayed the more words that I received from the Lord. Nothing comes to you in the Lord except by faith. The Bible says in Hebrews 11:6 that *"without faith it is impossible to please God"*. As I started to believe that God would give me more words, He did.

This was the first gift of the spirit I received from God. Every Tuesday and Thursday I went down to Christ Center Ministries for Bible studies and prayer. After the scripture reading and studying we would ask God for more gifts. The Bible says that *"you have not because you don't ask Him"* James 4:2. The next gift that I asked God for was the gift of prophecy. I didn't know much about this gift but after reading 1 Corinthians Chapter 12, I started to understand a little about the gift. God would start speaking through an individual as that person started making himself available for God to speak through Him. If you asked God for this gift you must believe that God is going to give it to you. But you must speak by faith. Prophecy is a gift that requires you to believe that God is speaking through you. This particular gift is used to edify an individual or the church. It is to build up the body of Christ.

After I asked God for the gift of prophecy, I believed He had given it to me. When we were at church or prayer meetings and there was a time of silence after we all had been praying in tongues, we would then wait for the Spirit of the Lord to speak. I prayed to the Lord to use me in this gift. Once you ask, you must believe that you'll receive. I did believe and waited for the Holy Spirit to move upon me.

About a week after I prayed for the gift of prophecy, I was at a meeting and felt the Lord give me a few words during a time of silence after worship. It was just a simple phrase of endearment "my children." When I heard the Lord speak this to me I felt that all I needed to do was step out in faith and say these words and God would give me more. That is how the Holy Spirit works in our life. As we step out by faith in whatever we do, He will meet us the rest of the way.

As soon as I spoke the words, "My children," God started to give me that rest of the message. It was a simple but short message to His children; one of exhortation and comfort to the body of Christ. I was so happy that God had used me even though I was a brand new baby Christian. Many people feel that to be used of God you have to be so many days or years old in the Lord. The Lord doesn't look at it this way. If you are willing and obedient and wanting God to use you, God will. God is no respecter of persons and if you want to be used by God, God will use you.

After I gave the word of the Lord to the congregation people came up to me and said they were proud of me that I was obedient to the Lord and allowed God to work through me. But just as there were some that encouraged me there was also a few that tried to discourage me. There was one person that came to me and didn't think that it was God that had used me. They were in a particular denomination that thought you had to tarry for the Holy Spirit. This was an old fashioned term from a few decades ago that thought that you had to really seek the Holy Spirit before God would manifest the gifts in your life. So in essence there were people that literally waited for months to receive the gift of tongues, prophesy, etc. They didn't realize that it was all through faith and that once you ask you received it immediately.

The devil will try to steal from you once you move out in God. When I moved out in the gift of prophesy most were encouraging. But as I said there was one that said she didn't think God would move in a new believer's life that fast. It's so easy to put limits on God! God wants us to use wisdom in what we do and line everything up with the Word of God.

Every week that I attended Bible studies at Christ Center Ministries I asked God for another gift of the Spirit. In I Corinthians 12 7-11 it talks about the nine gifts of the Holy Spirit -

"Now to each one the manifestation of the Spirit is given for the common good. To one there is given through the Spirit the message of wisdom, to another the message of knowledge by means of the same spirit, to another faith by the same spirit, to another gifts of healing by that one spirit, to another miraculous powers, to another prophecy, to another distinguishing between spirits, to another speaking in different kinds of tongues, and to still another the interpretation of tongues. All these are the work of one and the same Spirit, and he gives them to each one, just as he determines."

The gifts of the Spirit are for the perfecting of the body of Christ and also for spiritual warfare. Once we get to heaven we won't need the gifts of the Holy Spirit because the devil will not be in heaven. God doesn't give us a gift of the Spirit to puff us up full of pride. He only gives them to us to that we can edify and exhort other people.

Now Chuck and Sue Dunning were very good teachers. They told us it was more important to have the fruit of the spirit in our lives than the gifts. The Lord says in Matthew 12:33, *"That you will know them by their fruits, not by their gifts"*. The fruit of the Spirit is listed in Galatians 5:22 - *"But the fruit of the Spirit is love, joy, peace, patience, kindness, goodness, faithfulness, gentleness and self-control. "*

The fruit of the Spirit is the most important attribute to have in your life. A gift is given to you instantaneously but fruit takes time to grow. When you receive the Lord, God puts the incorruptible seed of Christ in your heart. As you water the seed with the Word of God and prayer, this seed will start to take root. Eventually it will become a tree and then bear fruit. Remember that Jesus cursed the fig tree which did not have any fruit on it. God is looking for you to bear fruit so that you would glorify Him. In John 15: 2-4 the Word says, *"Remain in me, and I will remain in you. No branch can bear fruit by itself; it must remain in the vine. Neither can you bear fruit unless you remain in me"*. You must spend time in the Word and prayer in order to bear fruit. So when you start seeking to be used in the gifts of the Spirit, also remember that more importantly God wants you to bear fruit as well.

I had such child-like faith when I first became a Christian. God will allow new Christians to experience remarkable answers to prayers and even feelings of abundant peace to show us His love. I remember walking down the street of downtown Minneapolis and literally feeling that God had his hand on my head. It was the strangest sensation. I told Chuck about this and he was a little puzzled about this phenomenon. As I was reading the Bible the Holy Spirit led me to several passages that said, *"And the hand of the Lord was upon him."* I then knew that God had His hand on my life and it was just a manifestation of His divine presence in my life.

Just as I was moving out in the spirit and feeling the anointing of God on my life, the devil also tried to make a play for me. When you dedicate your life to God and renounce the things that you used to do in the world Satan is not very happy. The Bible tells us to *"come out from among them and be ye separate, touch not the unclean thing"* II Corinthians 6:17. Many times new Christians think they can associate with their old crowd and try to witness to them. More times than not it backfires on you and the person ends up being sucked back into the trap that the Lord delivered them out of.

One night my old boyfriend called up and wanted to go over to one of his friend's house. I didn't think that there would be any harm in this. So Dan picked me up and we drove over to Steve's house. Some of his friends were sitting around listening to music. It wasn't very exciting. The things that used to be fun before you became a Christian aren't so attractive or satisfying anymore. I told Dan that I was getting tired and wanted to go home. He got a little irritated with me but eventually agreed to take me home.

On the way home he pulled over to a side street and shut off the car. I was a little perplexed as to what he was doing. He tried to kiss me but I pushed him away and said I wasn't interested. Then he tried to pull out a joint of marijuana and offered that to me. I also refused and told him that I wanted to go home. He started the truck up and drove me home. As we pulled up to my house all of a sudden I felt an evil presence fill the car. I had never experienced anything like this before in my life and it was very frightening. All of a sudden Dan looked at me and started talking in a slightly lower voice. He said, *"I'm the devil. He's sitting right on my shoulder. We are going to do everything we can to stop you from being a Christian."*

I looked at Dan dumbfounded. I remembered that the Bible said to overcome evil with good, so I said back to him, "I don't care what you say, I will pray for you until you know Jesus." Dan then replied back, "If you don't (used a derogatory sexual comment), then just get the **** out of the car." I opened up the truck door and ran as fast as I could into the house. My parents were not home and the house was empty. I remember grabbing the Bible and clutching it to my heart. I just started to sob and sob. I had never experienced anything like that in my entire life. I knew that I had talked directly to a demonic force.

I started crying out to God and prayed for protection. The Holy Spirit immediately gave me a peace that passed all understanding. But God showed me that I could not associate anymore with my old friends in their environment. If I wanted to invite them to church or have them over to my house (on my turf) with other Christians around that was fine. But until I became older in the things of God I needed to stay clear from that. I prayed for Dan that God would save him and deliver him from the powers of darkness.

The next day Dan called and apologized. He said he did not know what had come over him. He mentioned to me that he told his stepbrother, Todd, about the experience. Todd told him that the devil had inadvertently used Dan to talk to me and that he needed to repent. I think Dan was a little freaked out by the experience, but it didn't change his lifestyle at all.

I invited Dan down to Christ Center Ministries and he went a few times. He wasn't too impressed by it and would always try to get me to go to the old bars I used to go to. I remember one day at the ministry he said he had been praying and that He wanted to marry me. I knew that it wasn't God's will for me to marry Dan and I flatly refused. He was very disappointed and I didn't see him until quite a while later.

I write of this story to show you that we need to always be on our guard. The Bible says in I Peter 5:8 *"that our adversary, the devil, is as a roaring lion seeking whom he may devour. The Bible tells us to put on the whole armor of God that we may be able to stand against the wiles of the devil."*

The devil is very cunning and knows our faults and weaknesses. If we let down our guard for even a moment many times Satan will be there with a temptation to try to get the Christian out of God's will.

I am amazed when I hear some young people say that they worship Satan because of the things that the he will give them. There have been certain rock groups that have made pacts with the devil. The devil even made some of these groups famous. But he is not faithful to his followers. If you look at many of the past rock stars, some of them have died of drug overdoses or committed suicide. Once the devil is done using them he will kill them and take them to hell. This is a hard message to hear but one that needs to be told. The devil is not some little red guy with a pitchfork in his hands. God says in Matthew 24:24 *"That Satan will appear as an angel of light to deceive even the very elect"*

God has a perfect will for our lives and as we submit ourselves unto Him, He will give us divine revelation as to what His will is for our lives. Some of you may be asking how do you know what the will of God for your life is? God says in Psalms 37:4 *"That He will give you the desires of your heart."* God puts in your heart the desires that He wants you to do. If you will follow your heart, and pray and believe that God has put those desires there, He will lead you.

I tell people that it is hard to direct a vehicle that is stationary or not moving. It is the same with God. If you feel that God is leading you in a certain direction you need to just step out and start doing that thing that God is leading you to. Remember, when it was time for the children of Israel to enter the promised land, God did not just give it to them. They had to drive out the giants that were in the land first and then go and possess it. There will always be obstacles in our lives that will keep us from our Promised Land. Satan will try to hinder the will of God; circumstances of life will also stand in your way sometimes. You need to take the word of God just like Jesus did when He was in the wilderness being tempted by the devil and say, *"The Word says......"*. Use scripture, God's Word, to attack any negative thoughts, circumstances or situations in your life that are telling you something different than what God would.

It is your time to possess the land and the kingdom that God has given you. You are more than a conqueror, and nothing shall separate the Kingdom of God and your life. Seek and you shall find, knock and the door shall be open, ask and you shall receive. You have not because you have not asked. Ask God and watch Him do great and mighty things over your life. I know you will do it; we serve a great and mighty God.

Chapter 3

A FAMILY PLAN

God has a real plan for your family. An unknown woman gave my mother a scripture at a conference at Notre Dame. The woman gave her the scripture in Acts 16:31 *"Believe on the Lord Jesus Christ, and you shall be saved, and your household"* (KJV). At the time my mother was given this scripture none of her children were serving the Lord. She had to stand upon that word that was given to her even during the times when it looked like everything was pretty bleak.

As she stood upon that Word in faith the Lord made that word come to life in her family. I was the first one of the seven children to come boldly into the Kingdom of God. After I came into the Kingdom of God, I led the rest of the children into salvation by the Spirit of God. The next one to come into the Kingdom was my brother Jack. He was eighteen months older than I; a very handsome guy around 23 years old.

Jack has a very kind heart and loved people very much. Girls really were attracted to Jack not only because of his kind and loving nature, but also because he was so good looking. Jack had dark hair and bright blue eyes that just seemed to radiate an inner peace.

Jack was into the party scene much like I was before I became a Christian. I'm sure my transformation was a shock to Jack. We were not that close at the time and I wasn't sure as to Jack's mindset about my relationship with Jesus. I was his younger sister and other than thinking some of his friends were cute and talking to Jack about parties and little things, we were not that close.

When you become a Christian God puts in you a desire to see other people come into the Kingdom of God. I had a heart's desire to see my family and friends saved. Some of them thought I had jumped off the deep end, but that's the way it sometimes goes when you become a Christian. People will not understand the ways of the Spirit working in your life.

I invited Jack to go to a gathering at a friend of mine, Phil Hansen. He was also a fairly new Christian and he was having some people over to his home for fellowship and prayer. To my surprise, Jack said yes and we went over to Phil's house that night. There were about 20 people there; many of them went to Christ Center Ministries and some of them from a local church called Jesus People Church. Jesus People Church consisted of about 1,000 people mostly under 25 years of age.

At Phil's house we sat around, talked about the Lord, and had some soft drinks and chips. But then we decided we were going to start praying for people who wanted prayer. Jack came forward for prayer that night. We were all a little surprised that a guy who had never been to such a meeting would come forward for prayer that soon, but God saw Jack's heart. As we laid our hands upon Jack and prayed for him, the spirit of God fell upon Jack and he immediately was slain in the spirit. That means Jack fell backward on the ground under the power of the Holy Spirit. There are a few references where this happened in the Bible. One is when Jesus was in the garden before He was to be taken by the soldiers. When they came to get him and asked if he was Jesus, He answered that He was indeed Jesus they all fell backward (John 18:6).

Another reference to this is in the Book of Revelation where John fell backward as if he was dead while he was given the Book of Revelation (John 1:17).

Jack got the gift of speaking in tongues that night. He got up off the ground as a transformed person. I could tell by looking at his face that he wasn't the same person. The Bible says that old things are passed away and that all things are become new.

The same thing happened to Jack that happened to me. Many of his friends thought he had gotten into some cult that had tried to brainwash him. Little did they know that he was brainwashed: his brain was washed by the blood of Jesus and now old things were passed away and all things were become new by the blood of Jesus. Alleluia!!

Jack started going to with me and the rest of my Christian friends to Jesus People Church. It was such a good time because the preacher was so good! His name was Dennis Worre and he had such a phenomenal way of making the Bible come to life. I will never forget the influence that Dennis had on my life, as well as Chuck and Sue Dunning at Christ Centered Ministries.

I was so excited about Jesus and continued to tell everyone about what happened to me. My parents were ecstatic about the change in Jack and myself. They were born again Catholics and continued going to church at the Catholic church, but they would come down to Christ Centered Ministries on a Friday or Saturday night when I was down there helping with the counseling.

Eventually, all of my brothers and sisters received Jesus Christ as Lord and Savior of their life. The next one in my family to receive Jesus was my sister, Terry. She went to church with us one day and went down to receive Him. It is so exciting to know that your family will spend eternity with you in heaven and not just on this earth. Terry has a real gift of laughter and makes everyone around her smile. She also is a hairdresser, to whom God has given the gift of healing. One time when she was in the bathroom at my mom's house she came running out saying that she felt heat radiating from her hands. The Lord gave me the word of knowledge that she had a special gift of healing and that as she was working on people's hair the hands of the Lord would be touching them with His love and power. What a ministry!

I had been going to school at the Minnesota School of Business and finally graduated. It was now time to get a full time job and I interviewed with various employment agencies. At one of the agencies there was a Christian girl named Connie who was helping place me in a new position. I had been on several interviews and all of the companies thought I was very proficient, some of them even giving me offers of employment. I didn't have a peace about any of the jobs that I had interviewed for. I continued to pray and felt the Lord say to just continue on in interviewing and that He would open up the door for the right job.

Connie gave me a job interview for Friday at 1:30 at a telecommunications company called Northern Teleproductions. She said they made commercials and did other forms of broadcasting. I had always liked that type of business because it was so creative, so I was looking forward to going on this interview.

When I arrived at the job, I was nervous but felt that God had his hand on my life. I prayed a silent prayer before I walked through the company door. I interviewed with the president, Tom Collins, who was a very small man with black glasses and a slight frame. He seemed to listen to me and not ask too many questions. Later I found out this was a strategy that many interviewers use to have you talk.

After I left the interview I prayed and asked God to open the door if it was His will that I get the job. Later the next day Connie called me and told me I had the job. I was ecstatic! I was actually going to work with a tele-productions company that did commercials.

The first day of my job I went in and met with the office manager, Cathy Meyers. She was a nice woman who seemed to have a very compassionate spirit. Things went very well the first day and I got to meet everybody at work including the directors, camera people, executives and producers; it was like one big family!

I continued to go to Jesus People Church and work at Christ Center Ministries. I was scheduled to sing at church for a soul winning seminar that a mutual friend of mine, Mark Anderson, was preaching at. After I sang and Mark did the seminar we actually went out on the streets to minister to people, trying to win the lost to Christ.

A good friend of mine, Julie Rakowski, was with me and we went out on Hennepin Avenue to talk to people. Hennepin is a street in downtown Minneapolis that has movie theatres, regular bars, and a variety of unsavory types of businesses such as gay bars, strip joints, and adult movie stores. The whole group of about 40 of us went out on the street to witness.

Julie and I were walking down the street talking when we noticed a brown Baritz Cadillac drive by slowly. Two gentlemen in the car smiled at us. Julie and I just laughed thinking just two more guys cruising Hennepin looking for a little action. The car circled the block and it stopped in front of us in front of a busy movie theatre.

The car window rolled down and one of the gentlemen in the car poked his head out and said, "Hey, Meri! It's me, Rick Harrison, how are you doing?" I looked and barely recognized him because he used to be in a rock and roll band with long hair and a beard. Now he was clean-shaven with a suit on not even looking like the same person.

I couldn't believe it and walked up to the car and started chatting with him. He was with his manager, Rick Crouley, and they were on the way to a bar when they noticed us walking down the street. He recognized me and Rick was interested in me and wanted to talk for a while.

I told them I was a Christian and that we were out on the streets of Hennepin Avenue telling people about Jesus. They both looked at me with an incredulous look on their face not quite believing what they were hearing. They decided to park the car and listen to us tell people about Jesus for a while.

It was quite an interesting night! We witnessed to everyone from pimps and prostitutes, to skeptical businessman and average people just out for a night on the town. After about two hours of this, Rick suggested we go and get something to eat. Julie and I agreed that we were both hungry and decided to meet them at a local restaurant not too far from where we were.

We met them at the restaurant and all ordered a small snack since it was so late. We chatted and Rick Crouley started talking about women and what he was looking for in a wife. I don't know how this topic was brought up, but I thought it was unusual. For the next forty-five minutes we were discussing the attributes of marriage.

Finally, it was getting late and Julie and I had to go home. We said goodbye to the two Ricks and invited them to church the following Wednesday at Jesus People Church downtown Minneapolis. We didn't exchange numbers, but just left with the invitation to church.

As we walked out to our car Julie and I both laughed saying that we thought Rick sure wanted to get married. As I pulled away in my car I thought Rick seemed like a nice guy and I hoped that he would come to church and I would see him again.

The week progressed quickly and Wednesday night was almost here. I had been asked out on a date but the man wasn't a Christian so I invited him to church that night. We were at church and the worship service was in progress. People were raising their hands to the Lord in worship and I happened to glance over to the left. To my surprise I saw the two Rick's there looking around the room at everyone with their hands raised. They seemed to feel uncomfortable.

I immediately thought to myself, "What am I going to do to get rid of the guy that I'm with?" I liked Rick Crouley and wanted to be able to talk to him after the service. I was not at all interested in the guy that I had brought to church, but wanted him to accept the Lord in his heart.

At the end of the service they had an altar call and my date did not go forward to the altar. He did not seem interested in what was going on. I decided he was just there for me, so I wanted to have a plan to get rid of him so I could talk to Rick.

I made up some sort of excuse and told him I would talk to him later (how manipulative of me!). I then went over to the two Ricks and started talking. Rick Harrison told me that he had another engagement and had to leave. Rick Crouley started talking to me and said that he was hungry and asked me if I wanted to get something to eat. I was thrilled he asked me and we went across the street to an Italian restaurant called Cafe D'Nopoli.

We had a great time talking about things; especially about the church service. He seemed very interested in the things of the Lord and wanted to find all about what had taken place that night at the church service. I started telling him about how I accepted the Lord and how I was working at Christ Centered Ministries counseling people. He seemed genuinely interested and we made another date to go to church on Sunday.

That Sunday night George Otis was speaking. He had been a successful businessman with Lear Craft Company and had literally made millions of dollars in his business ventures. He had accepted the Lord through a string of life catastrophes and he was giving his testimony at Church. Why does it sometimes take problems in our life to get our attention? Sometimes when things are going great we forget about God, and so God lets the bottom drop from underneath us and we call out to him for help. The scripture says in Psalms 50:15 *"That I called out to the Lord in times of trouble and He heard my cry."*

If you are in trouble today know that no matter what the situation is you can call out to the Lord in times of trouble and He will deliver you from what you are going through. God knows what it is going to take to break you from your situations in life. When things are going well we don't always call upon Him. If you are in a mess today call out upon the Lord your God. He is waiting for you to ask for His assistance.

At the end of the service, after George Otis was done speaking, he invited people to come down to accept Jesus into their heart. He also talked about receiving the baptism of the Holy Spirit and how it was important for a Christian to ask for this gift. He explained that before the disciples received the baptism of the Holy Spirit they were fighting amongst themselves as to who would be the greatest. Peter denied Jesus three times and many other incidents happened where they all seemed weak. But after the Holy Spirit came down upon them on the day of Pentecost they all boldly proclaimed the gospel. All of the disciples, except for one, lost their lives by martyrdom for the cause of Christ.

When the altar call was given, Rick went down to the front to be prayed for. I was really excited and knew this would make a definite change in Rick's life. Rick was down there for about a half hour and then he went back to his seat. He had a glow on his face and seemed genuinely happy that he had gone forward.

After Rick accepted the Lord in his life and received the baptism of the Holy Spirit it seemed like things really took off with us. When he came over to meet my family everyone immediately fell in love with him. We would be sitting around the kitchen table with all my brothers and sisters (except for Jack who was in Bible school in San Diego) laughing and talking about God.

Rick and I would go to church every Sunday and Wednesday. We also used to go down to Christ Center Ministries for services as well. It was really an exciting time. It was the late seventies and God was moving with the Charismatic movement and the Jesus People movement was exploding at the same time. There were so many young people accepting the Lord all over the world. God was doing a new thing and raising up a whole new generation of baby boomers to go and spread the gospel around the world.

Rick and I had only been dating a few months when I got the call that my brother Jack was going to be returning home from Morris Cerullo's School of Evangelism. He had gone there for two years and had graduated. I was really excited to see Jack again and planned a surprise party for him with all of his old friends from Jesus People Church. The plan was that I would pick up Jack from the airport with Rick and drive over to my parent's house where we would have about thirty people waiting for him there. I had the house decorated with balloons and crepe paper. I also had a welcome home cake, some tasty appetizers, and other munchies for the people to snack on.

Rick and I went to the airport and I remember seeing Jack's face as he got off the plane. He had a beautiful smile that just lights up his whole face. I was so excited that he would get to see all of his old friends and have a welcome home. Jack and I had gotten so close to each other since we both had accepted the Lord. It is amazing what the Spirit of the Lord can do to make even family members who were close before even that much closer afterwards.

I ran up to Jack and gave him a big hug and kiss. It was so good to see him after all that time. Then I introduced him to Rick and they both seemed to hit it off great. Jack and Rick even had certain similarities in appearance where they looked almost like brothers. We drove Jack back to my parent's house laughing and having a good time with catching up on the news about what was happening around town with everyone we knew.

As we pulled up to the house all looked quiet on the home front. Little did Jack realize that about thirty people were hiding behind couches and wherever else they could find to hide. I was so excited, wanting to see the look on Jack's face as he walked in and had everyone jump out and yell "Surprise."

Jack looked a little puzzled and asked us where everyone was. We have a large family and usually everyone is around to welcome someone when they come home. I made up some excuse and as we turned the key and walked in everyone jumped up and yelled "Welcome home Jack." You should have seen the look of surprise on his face. But it soon went from a look of surprise to a look of elation. He was so happy to be home.

I know that is how we are going to feel when we get to heaven. Sure, this earthly home seems nice at times, but deep down inside the Bible says that we long to be in heaven. It sure will be a blessing to see Jesus and all the saints that we have known all of our lives in heaven just praising the Lord. There will be no more sorrows or problems. All we will have to think about is Jesus and how happy we are to be with Him forever.

We had a wonderful party for Jack! Jack talked to all of his old friends and recanted all of his adventures in San Diego. Jack had grown a lot spiritually and everyone was anxious to hear about his adventures. My mom and dad were especially happy to have Jack home and so were my brothers and sisters. The interesting thing was that Rick and Jack really took a liking to each other. They talked a lot that night about a number of things. Rick told me later that he felt that he had known my brother Jack for a long time. Rick told me that he never felt very close to his own brother growing up. He said that he felt that Jack and him were brothers in many ways. It touched me to hear Rick talk about my brother in that way.

Once Jack got home things seemed to go back to the old business as usual. We all started going to church again together and going to many Christian events. It was just like old times. We would all sit around and talk for hours about the Bible. God put a fire in our spirits and we hungered for more of God every day.

Rick had been working as a national sales manager for a contracting company for a few years and started to branch out on his own. It was during this time that Rick asked Jack if he wanted to work for him in sales. Jack agreed and they went off on their adventures in the contracting business.

I'll never forget one story that they both told me after an especially eventful day. One woman had called Rick's company and wanted some more insulation put in her attic to keep her home better insulated against the cold during the winter months in Minnesota.

Rick was not used to doing insulation. They normally were contractors for siding on the homes, windows, roofs, and other things, but not insulation. One of the men at the church had a big truck which he let them use to carry the insulation to the job. You had to rent a big hose to blow the insulation into the attic. They got to the woman's house and

Rick introduced himself to the woman and said they were going to go up to the attic to do an inspection before they started blowing the insulation.

Jack was down below in the hallway and Rick went up into the attic. Rick had never done this type of job before so they were very cautious as to what they were doing. Rick was walking along in the attic when he accidentally stepped in the wrong area of the attic and his foot went through the ceiling.

Jack then went up in the attic to try to help Rick. Jack was walking across the attic when his foot went through the ceiling as well. Jack and Rick had their feet sticking out of the ceiling with the old woman in the hallway looking up and shaking her fists saying, "You boys come down from there right now."

Somehow they managed to get out of the house in one piece apologizing profusely as they went. They got into the big insulation truck and hightailed it down the street. The funny part is that the doors of the insulation truck had the words "Jesus loves you" painted on the outside of the doors. Imagine the sight of Rick and Jack peeling out from that old woman's house with the doors of the truck swinging open and shut with "Jesus love you" on the back. Rick and Jack had a good laugh later on.

How many times in our life can we look back and see humor in circumstances later that at the time the incident occurred we thought was so traumatic? That's why God wants us to trust in Him and not sweat the small stuff. God has your life under control if you put your life in His hands. God will rearrange the circumstances and order of your life once you put God first. The Bible says in Psalms 37:23 *"That a righteous man's (or woman's) footsteps are ordered by the Lord."* God will order your steps and direct you as you trust in Him.

There are some of you reading this book and you are saying to yourself, "Yeah, but you don't know my situation or what I have been through!" No, I don't know everything that you all have been through, but God does and the Bible says that *"He is able to make all things work together for your good to those who love God and are called according to His purpose"* (Romans 8:28)

One thing you all have to get into your head is that God is on your side. The Bible says that if God is for you who can be against you. God wants you to succeed and be successful. God wants you out of debt and to be able to pay your bills. The scriptures say that the thief (or the devil) comes to steal, kill, and destroy, but that God has come to give you life and give it to you in abundance. Don't let the devil keep you down! Give him a black eye by trusting in the Lord with all of your heart and not leaning to your own understanding. The Bible says in all your ways acknowledge Him and God will direct your paths. He loves you so much and is able and willing to move on your behalf.

Chapter 4

BEARING FRUIT

Rick and I had been dating for almost a year and everything was going along just wonderful. We were going to church two to three times a week. Rick had his home improvement business and I was working at Northern Teleproductions. One day at my parent's home when everyone else was gone, Rick surprised me and asked me to marry him. He told me that he wanted to ask me that night at dinner but he was so anxious that he broke the silence earlier.

We had talked about marriage before, but I always thought that I would be around thirty when I got married. I was still only 22 at the time and it seemed quite young to me. I was excited that he asked me, though, and told him that I would have to think about it. Rick was a little bit dismayed that I didn't immediately jump up and down and yell "Hurrah, yes!," but that wasn't my style.

At this point in my life I wanted to seek God's direction for such a big decision. Many people rush into marriage too quickly without waiting upon the Lord and make a decision that can affect their whole lives in a single minute.

A word to the unmarried who are asking for a mate: make sure that the person you are dating is a Christian. God says in the Bible not to be unequally yoked with unbelievers. If you are dating someone who is not a Christian and you are asking God if this is the one the answer is "No"! God is not going to go against His word.

Another thing I always say to those I am talking to about making a lifetime decision regarding marriage is to marry someone who is a lot like you. You know the old adage that says opposites attract. Well, they detract big time once you get married. The same things that brought you together before you were married will cause you to be repelled after you are married.

For instance, I knew a girl named Sue who was very quiet. She met a guy named Fred at a youth concert one night. He was outgoing and the life of the party. Everyone knew who Fred was and they thought he was the greatest guy. One of the things that Sue was immediately attracted to in Fred was the fact that he was not afraid of anyone or any situation. Unlike herself, Fred could go into a room where he did not know anyone and by the end of the night know everyone by first name.

Fred was attracted to Sue because he thought she was very composed and wasn't always opening her mouth trying to talk to everyone like some girls he knew. Deep down Fred admired this trait where she could listen to people and not always have to be the center of attention.

Fred and Sue got married and everyone thought they were going to be the perfect couple. At first everything went along smoothly, but soon the very thing that had attracted them to each other started to wear on each other.

Fred started wondering why Sue wasn't more talkative and how come she was such a bump on the log. "Loosen up and enjoy yourself," he used to say to her at a party. Sue on the other hand was starting to get annoyed about how Fred could never keep his mouth shut and how he kept going on and on about something. Sue wanted to spend some quiet evenings at home with Fred and not always have to be on a social whirlwind. Eventually, through communication, they learned to compromise and not expect so much of the other and work within each other's strengths and weaknesses.

So when I say marry someone that is a lot like you, I mean marry someone that likes to do a lot of the same things as you do. If you are an athlete and it is important to workout in your daily routine, find a girl who likes to do this as well. Do you like reading, going to movies, taking short walks together, surfing, or bicycling? Find someone who is going to compliment you in these areas and who enjoys many of the same things as you. If all you go on before you're married is a romantic feeling, many times after the honeymoon is over you have two people looking at one another feeling like strangers.

Another thing that is important is getting wise counsel. After Rick asked me to marry him the first thing that I did was pray and ask the Lord for direction. The next thing that we did was make an appointment with our pastor and talk to him about this decision. We had been going to this church during our entire dating period and our pastor knew our strengths and weaknesses. Not that we were expecting the Pastor to make a decision for us. Pastors and other people who know us sometimes have great wisdom and insight that we often don't see.

One of my biggest concerns about marrying Rick was making sure that his commitment to Christ was as committed as mine. I had been a Christian longer than Rick and had always prayed for a Christian husband. I knew that if my husband put God first in his life that he would be a good husband.

After a few months of praying and counseling I felt the Lord say that we were ready for marriage. I didn't take this decision lightly because I knew that when I made those vows at the altar they were for a lifetime, in sickness in health, good times and bad, until death do us part. Many people make those vows hastily thinking that if it doesn't work out they can just get a divorce and start all over again.

My parents liked Rick very much and were excited about us getting married. I was the oldest girl and it would be the first wedding in the family of seven children. It was an exciting time of planning the wedding, finding the dresses, picking out flowers and bridesmaids, and on and on.

The wedding was on April 17th and it was a beautiful day. We had an evening wedding at 7:00 p.m. It was a very busy day with the pictures and all the various things that go on before a wedding. I felt the peace of God on me and I was excited about becoming Rick's wife.

The church was filled with about three hundred people and the music began with the bridesmaids walking down the aisle first. Then it was my turn and my dad very lovingly took my arm and smiled at me and away we went.

I'll never forget Rick's face as I was walking down the aisle. He looked white as a sheet. I had never seen Rick look that nervous in my life. I wondered if he was getting second thoughts! By the time I got to the altar and we joined hands I remember the minister bending over to Rick to ask him if he was all right. I think Rick was almost on the verge of passing out. He took a deep breath and we went on with the ceremony and our wedding vows.

It was a very special moment and when we lit the unity candle symbolizing our becoming one, I felt the spirit of the Lord very strongly on our lives and that indeed the two had become one flesh. The Bible says that this is a mystery. It is also symbolic of the relationship between Jesus and His Bride, the church. Jesus is going to come back for a bride without spot or wrinkle. The church is His bride and the Lord is ironing out all of the wrinkles in our garments. Some of you reading this today may seem like a mess. But God is going to iron out those problems and make you without spot or wrinkle.

After the wedding we went to a beautiful reception at the University Club in St. Paul. It was a wonderful evening filled with food, music, dancing, and good friends. At the end of the evening when I threw my bouquet from the top of the spiral stairs I looked down wistfully not wanting that night to end.

Rick and I took a short honeymoon at a nice resort in Chicago. We only had a few days since Rick and I were young and needed to make a living. I remember on the honeymoon how it was just great to see many of the sights and restaurants in downtown Chicago. I would have liked to go to a more tropical environment but we didn't have the time or the money.

On Sunday morning we woke up and wanted to go to church and celebrate Jesus together as man and wife. We looked in the yellow pages for churches and found one that was located not too far from where we were staying at the Marriott in downtown Chicago.

We walked from our hotel to the church. It was located in a high-rise on the 20th floor of a nice office building. We took the elevator up to the floor and noticed there was a very pleasant looking man with wire rim glasses standing by the door as you got off the elevator. He welcomed us and we told him that we had come for the church service that morning. He directed us into a nice room with about fifty chairs set up. The chairs were nicely padded and bright blue. The room had a nice view of the city.

We thought to ourselves, "What a lovely church with a view!" We had gotten to the service about twenty minutes early and there were not that many people there. The pastor of the church came over and introduced himself to us. He was a man in his sixties with white hair and a twinkle in his eye as he talked. We told him that we had just gotten married a few days ago and that we wanted to celebrate together for the first time being married. He was astonished that we would go to church on our honeymoon, especially since we had just gotten married two days ago!

The people of the congregation started strolling in. The average age of the people in the congregation was about 65. It was an older crowd, definitely, but we knew that there are no age, race, or color barriers with God. The pastor of the church changed his whole sermon for the day around us. It truly amazed him that we went through all the effort of finding a church in the midst of a busy metropolitan city, walk to the church, and not know a soul. We thought it was no big deal. When you love God you want to be worshipping Him and fellowshipping with him not only on Sunday but every day.

After the church service everyone in the congregation came up to us and congratulated us on our wedding. They all started giving us little bits and pieces of advice on what they felt would make a happy marriage. It was hilarious! We both walked away with a smile on our faces knowing that God had touched our lives and that we had touched their lives.

We came back from our honeymoon refreshed and ready to take on whatever God was going to put in our path. It wasn't too long after we married that I found out I was pregnant. I was ecstatic, wondering if the baby inside of me was a boy or a girl. It's amazing when you first hear that you're pregnant the thoughts that go through your mind.

We first found out when we bought one of those home pregnancy tests and followed the directions explicitly. It said to wait about an hour and that if there was a ring in the tube that meant that you were pregnant. Those tests have since gotten a lot more accurate than they back then. But Rick and I decided to take a nap and when we woke up we would have the results.

I remember looking at the clock and it said 3:00 p.m. We had done the test at 1:00 p.m. that afternoon after church. I nudged Rick and we both looked at each other and said, "Let's go see what the results are." We walked around the corner to the bathroom and when we both peaked around the corner we saw to our delight that there was a ring in the test tube. That meant that I was pregnant! We both hugged each other thrilled that God had blessed us with a child!

I remember calling my mother up and informing her that she was going to be a grandmother. I thought I heard the phone drop because there was no sound on the other end of the receiver. But then she said she was just speechless, too happy for words to even say. My dad also got on the phone and congratulated us.

Since I was the first one in the family of the children to become pregnant it was a big deal with everyone. I was always being asked, "How does I feel?" and "When is the due date?"

Rick and I were living in a three bedroom apartment which I had decorated really cute. I was working temporarily as a secretary at a company called Toshiba, which made ultrasound equipment. It was really fun working there because the other girl who worked in the office was pregnant also.

On our breaks, the other secretary Maria and I would go in the back where the ultrasound equipment was and put the wand to our bellies and get to look at how big our babies were growing. Sometimes we would watch them kick and squirm around. It was such fun and we got an equally big kick out of it!

Rick was still working in the home improvement industry where he was doing construction and selling improvements for the home such as windows, doors, and roofs. Rick was such a good salesman I think he could have sold ice to the Eskimos! God was good and He always provided our needs.

Whenever it seemed like the money was a little low God would allow Rick to have another big siding job come through.

Time passed quickly and we were busy getting prepared for the baby's birth. We had done a nursery in one of the bedrooms of the apartment and I fixed it up so it could accommodate either a boy or a girl.

I felt the Lord tell me that I was going to have a boy. I had already picked out the name, Jeremy Joseph Crouley. Back in those days the ultrasound equipment was not as sophisticated as it is today and the sex of the baby was not always known. I really didn't want to know the sex of my child anyway; I wanted it to be a surprise.

One day I was laying in bed around 7:00 a.m. and thinking that I had better be getting up to go to work when I noticed that there was water starting to seep through my nightgown. I remember from my Lamaze classes that Rick and I had taken at the hospital to prepare for the birth of the baby that they said there could be an occurrence called "my water breaking" before labor started to occur. I yelled to Rick who was in the other room. He ran in and saw all this water on the bed and immediately helped me to the bathroom.

Rick ran in the other room and called the doctor and asked him what to do. It was so cute to see how Rick was during this time. He was the typical nervous husband rushing around in a state of panic. The doctor told him to remain calm and to come to the hospital around 11:00 that morning. That was another four hours away and I was sure that the doctor did not know what he was doing. "My water has broken and I should come in right now!" I thought.

I already had a little bag packed and added some more things to it and got the house already for the baby when we came home from the hospital. I called my mom and told her I was in labor and she said that she would meet me down there a little bit after noon. I was so excited! My own child that God had given me I was going to bring home with me!

At 10:30 sharp we got into the car to head for the hospital. Once we got there we went to admitting and checked into the hospital and they put me in a wheelchair and wheeled me down to get me ready for my room.

Once in my room I was given a hospital gown and changed from my street clothes into the gown. The nurse put my things in a nearby closet and told me about what was going to be happening to me as labor progressed.

By this time I was getting fairly sharp contractions several minutes apart. She told me that if things got rough in regard to the pain that I could be given some sedatives to help take the edge off the pain.

I was trying to have the baby natural so I told her only if worse came to worse.

I got out my Bible and started reading in between contractions. Rick was right along side of me helping me all through the labor. As the contractions got closer together the intensity of the contractions got stronger as well. I never knew that labor was going to hurt this much! My mom had come down to the hospital by this time and was with me as well. I was breathing the way they taught me to in the classes. That helped a little bit but it still was very uncomfortable.

God has since shown me that life during trials is like contractions. During the worst trials in your life if you will breathe with the Holy Spirit and relax in Jesus, the pain of the trial will not be as severe. But if you fight against the trial the pain will only intensify and seem worse. If you do that the trial only seems longer than it is.

At around 3:30 that afternoon things really started to speed up. I was dilated to around 9 centimeters. They got me ready to be wheeled into the delivery room. My Mom was still in

the room and she said that she was praying and that everything would be okay.

Rick looked very nervous but had a peace in his face and
knew God was in control. As they wheeled me down the hall
to the delivery room, the pain was growing unbearable. I had
an overwhelming desire to push and the nurse said to wait
until she told me to push.

In the delivery room after everything was situated for the
delivery of the baby, the nurse came to my side and gently
took my hand. The doctor had come in and was telling me
that he wanted me to push when he said. With Rick holding
one hand and the nurse holding the other the doctor said,
"Push, Meri, push!"

I pushed with all my might! The doctor said that was good
but he needed another few pushes and the baby would be
there. I kept pushing and pushing whenever he said. Finally,
when it seemed that there was not another ounce of strength
left in me I could feel a release of the pressure. The baby had
come out and the doctor was holding the baby in his hands.
He quickly severed the umbilical cord and placed the child on
my stomach. They do this for the baby to immediately bond
to the mother. The doctor said, "Mrs. Crouley, you have a
beautiful baby girl!"

I looked at my child lying on my stomach and just started
crying. Rick had walked around to take a better look at her in
amazement. She looked perfect in every way. She started to
move her head around and I couldn't believe that God was so
good to give me such a perfect child.

I was surprised, though. I had thought that I was going to
have a baby boy and we were going to name him Jeremy. I
had not even thought of a girl name because I was sure that it
was going to be a boy.

The nurse came over and took my baby away saying that
she had to be cleaned up and that she would bring her back to

my room in a little while. I didn't want her to take my little precious baby away after only getting acquainted with her for a few minutes, but I knew that she would be back soon and I couldn't wait to cuddle her in my arms and just nurse her and cherish her.

Later on I was in my hospital room and was waiting for them to bring me my daughter. I was still not sure of a name yet. I wondered why they had not brought her in yet. It was already over four hours. Rick went and inquired at the nurse's station and they informed Rick that the baby looked a little jaundiced and that they had her in an incubator for a while. I was shocked and wondered why they had not told me this fact earlier.

Rick and I prayed together that our baby would be fine and that nothing would be the matter with her. We also prayed as to what to name her and right after our prayer I felt the name "Christina" come into my mind. I said to Rick, "What about naming the baby, Christina?" Rick said, "Christina Crouley, that has a nice ring to it." I also liked the fact that Christina had the word "Christ" in her name. I thought to myself, Christina or Christ in a baby.

So it was decided! The baby would be called Christina Marie Crouley. I was glad that we finally had her named. Right after we named her, the nurse brought Christina to us. She was all bundled up in a blanket and looked so pretty with only her little face sticking through the blanket.

As I held her in my arms I was thanking the Lord that she was so healthy and looked so beautiful. Life is such a wonderful gift from the Lord! I nursed her for the first time, which didn't work out that well but we tried anyway. The nurse said that sometimes it takes a while for the baby to get the hang of things.

After about two hours of having Christina with us the nurse came to take her back to the nursery to check her vital signs. I didn't want to give her up but I knew that this was a normal thing and gave Christina back to the nurse. The nurse told me she would be bringing Christina back for her 3:00 a.m. feeding and that I better get some rest. The days of sleeping eight hours straight were going to be gone for a while so I had better take advantage of the free time and sleep.

At three in the morning the nurse woke me and told me that Christina's vital signs were a little unusual and they wanted to keep her in the special care for infants section where she would be in isolation for a while. They wanted to monitor her vital signs and make sure that everything was okay.

I was very scared! She seemed so perfect just a few hours ago! What could be the matter with her? When things like that happen in your life that is when you have to run to the word of God and take refuge in the almighty God. God says in Psalms 50:15 *"To call upon me in times of trouble and I will answer you and bring you out of your distress."*

Well, I called out to the Lord that night. Rick had gone home to spend the night back at our apartment and get some new clothes and freshen up. I called him on the phone and explained to him what was happening. Rick said he would be over right away and not to worry.

I thought to myself, "How do I not worry?" I felt like I had no control over the situation. I got the Bible out and started reading the Psalms. Whenever I am troubled many times I will read Psalms and God will give me peace. David went through many trials and God always delivered him. The Bible says in Psalms 34:19 *"That many are the afflictions of the righteous, but God will deliver him out of them all."*

As I was reading and praying I felt the Lord assure me that everything was going to be fine. I didn't hear Him speak to me in my spirit, but just had an assurance that God had Christina in the palm of His hand and that He had not brought me this far to leave me now.

Rick walked in the room at that moment and we both held hands with each other and started praying. The Word of God says in Deuteronomy 32:30 *"That one will put a thousand to flight but that two will put ten thousand to flight."* Basically this scripture means that two people praying together are ten times more powerful than one. There is also something very special about a husband and wife agreeing together in prayer for something concerning their family.

I know that is why the enemy opposes and fights families so much. It is God's divine purpose for families to be together in unity and pray and seek God's will for our lives. If the enemy can get us arguing and fighting each other that is his goal. Once we are divided he will then conquer. In Matthew 12:25 it says *"A house divided against each other will not stand."* So when a trial or circumstance hits your family and you have the temptation to start blaming each other, start praying together. God will do more through prayer than any other one thing that you can do as a couple together.

After we prayed we both had the assurance that Christina was in God's hands. It was almost morning now and Rick curled up on the couch to catch some sleep before visitors would start coming again. Since it was my first baby I was having a steady stream of visitors continually coming to the hospital with flowers and gifts for Christina. It was so much fun to be able to visit with friends and family and talk about the birth of a miracle.

At 9:00 a.m. the nurse came in and asked if we wanted to go down and look at Christina in the special care unit. We followed her down the corridor and through a set of double doors. As we walked into the room it seemed like everything looked so sterile and clean. Across the room I spied an incubator with Christina lying in it looking at us with tubes coming out of her arm. She looked so helpless in there I just wanted to run to her and grab her up and take her to a safe place.

The nurse told us that in the middle of the night her vital signs started to do better and everything was stable now. They were keeping an eye on her for another few hours and then she could go back to the regular nursery with the other newborn babies. Rick and I were so relieved and we started thanking the Lord silently for what he had done.

Later that morning Christina was brought to me again for her feeding and she looked a lot more alert than she had the day before. I was ecstatic that everything had turned out so well and she was going to be fine.

For the rest of my hospital stay everything went along as well as could be expected. Between phone calls from friends, visitors, and scheduled feedings of Christina, my life was pretty hectic.

After I was there three days the nurse came in and started getting me prepared for my return home. The hospital was a nice place to be for a while, but I was anxious to return home and put Christina in her own crib for the first time.

I had a little outfit all picked out for Christina to wear home from the hospital. It was a pretty pink sleeper with a matching little bonnet. She looked adorable as I dressed her in this outfit and prepared her for the ride home. I also got out of the nightgown that I had been in for the last three days and into some clothes that I had brought.

They wheeled me down the hall of the hospital with Christina in my arms and Rick on the side of me with some products that the hospital had given us. Rick ran and got the car and pulled it up to the curb where he gently helped me into the car and we strapped Christina into her car seat.

The ride home wasn't long and before we knew it we were pulling up to our apartment. Our apartment was on the third floor and we took the elevator up to it. On the way up we saw a few neighbors who congratulated us and cooed at Christina. Everyone loves a baby! It's so hilarious to watch how people will try to make a baby smile with all their faces. It only made Christina start to cry and we immediately told them we had better get her upstairs and put to bed. We chuckled to ourselves walking down the hallway wondering what thoughts were going through little Christina's mind as she saw Al making those faces at her. Maybe she thought she saw a monster.

Once inside our humble abode we walked to the nursery and just sat there staring at it. After all those months of preparing it for the baby, we were finally home. The crib had sheets and blankets all ready for Christina to take a nap. We laid her on her back and said a little prayer over her. We asked God to watch over her and not let anything happen to her when she was asleep.

I was nervous about Sudden Infant Death Syndrome. I had a few girlfriends whose children had died in their sleep and there was no known cause. They now have found out that many babies who are laid on their stomach could die by not getting enough oxygen.

I remember I used to just go in her room and watch her sleep. The first thing I would do was make sure she was breathing. When I would see her little chest rise and fall I would breathe a sigh of relief that all was well.

Everything went smoothly the first few months after Christina was born. I had gotten her on a schedule and she was adhering to it perfectly. She was already sleeping through the night after only a few weeks and I thought life couldn't get any better than this.

You never know when a situation will occur in your life that can change your world though. One day Christina had been napping for a couple of hours on Sunday afternoon. She had wakened up and started to cry. Rick said to me that he would go and get her. All of a sudden I heard Rick yell for me to quickly come into her room. I raced into Christina's room not knowing what had happened. There Christina lay in Rick's arms. She had turned blue and Rick was trying to revive her by gently saying her name and rubbing her back.

I thought that my worst fear had come true, that this was an aborted Sudden Infant Death Syndrome. I was completely in a panic not knowing what to do. I ran to the phone and called our pediatrician who immediately told me that he would meet us down at Children's Hospital within the half hour.

We raced her down to the hospital and got Christina admitted. They said they wanted to keep an eye on her and do extensive testing as to what the problem could be. Rick and I were both planning on spending the night with Christina in her room by her little hospital bed.

They had a chapel in the hospital and I went down there to pray for a while. I was crying to the Lord saying, "God, how can you give me such a beautiful little girl and then take her away from me?" I was so scared of losing her that I was almost besides myself.

At that moment I heard the Lord say to me, *"Be still and know that I am God."* God was comforting me and assuring me that everything would be all right. I felt the Lord remind me that Christina was His to begin with. God had only given Christina to me for a short time on this earth. Whether she were to live eight months or eighty years she was still God's child. I was to trust in God and not to worry what the outcome was. I was to pray and believe for God to heal Christina but then leave it in God's hands for the outcome.

God also reminded me in the chapel about the story of Abraham and Sarah. They had wanted a child for so long and finally after Sarah was 90 years old she conceived a child whom they called Isaac. Isaac means "laughter" in Hebrew, and I'm sure that many people laughed when they heard Sarah was pregnant with a child long after her childbearing years.

They loved Isaac and I'm sure spent many wonderful times as a family together. But there came a point when God told Abraham to go into the wilderness where he was asked to sacrifice Isaac to the Lord. I'm sure that Abraham was aghast when he heard what God was requiring him to do. But he didn't question God. He knew that if God could give him a miracle child in their old age then God could also work out the situation with Isaac. As he was raising his knife to kill his son an angel of the Lord came and stopped him.

God gave him back his son. God was testing Abraham to see what meant more in his life, his relationship with the Lord or his son. The Lord says in Matthew 6:33 *"That if we seek first the Kingdom of God and His righteousness then all of these things will be added unto us."* God wants us to put Him first even before our children, spouses, jobs, and so on. He will make a way where there seems to be no way, and as we trust in Him He will work it out. It isn't always the way we think it should work out. Just trust in Him!

As I got up from my knees in the chapel I felt like the weight of the world had been taken off my shoulders. That's why the Bible says in Psalms 55:22 *"To cast your cares upon the Lord and he will sustain you."* As I prayed and cried out to God He took the weight off my shoulders. I felt a peace that I hadn't felt since I first saw Christina limp in Rick's arms.

After two days of a myriad of tests they still had not found anything wrong with Christina. The doctors wanted to keep Christina a few more days. I wanted to just bring her home so she could get back into her normal routine, but I also wanted to know what was the cause of her blacking out the way she did.

One of the doctors was holding Christina in his arms as we were talking about her situation. All of a sudden Christina started to fuss and cry. She had only been crying a minute or so when she just went limp in his arms and turned blue. We all looked at Christina in disbelief. She had done it right in front of our eyes.

The doctor started to laugh. I almost got mad at him wondering why he would be laughing when my daughter had just passed out in his arms. All of a sudden Christina came to and looked around dazed and confused. The doctor said to us, "Don't you just understand what happened? When she cries she wants her way so bad that she literally forgets to breath and passes out. That is what must have happened to Christina when Rick found her that way in the crib. She had been crying for a few minutes before he walked in and she passed out from not taking a breath."

We all breathed a huge sigh of relief. It wasn't anything serious after all. It wasn't an aborted Sudden Infant Death Syndrome. It wasn't some horrible problem that would keep Christina in the hospital for months. It was just as simple that we have a strong willed daughter who holds her breath when she wants her way.

I thought to myself, "If she's holding her breath at eight months old trying to get her way what is she going to be like as a teenager?" I was just relieved that she was fine.

Isn't that just like how our lives go? It seems like there is a huge dilemma or tragedy that comes along. One day we are rolling through life with no problems and then one day there is a huge pothole in the road that causes some serious problems in our life. We get all freaked out and start thinking the worst possible scenarios.

That is why God tells us to trust in Him and not to lean to our own understanding. Ninety percent of the fears we have in our minds will never come to pass. We waste all of this energy on worrying when we could be doing and thinking things so much more productive. The Bible says many times not to fear. It actually commands us to "Fear Not."

Fear can actually be sin in our lives. It is not trusting in the Lord and looking at the circumstances more than looking and trusting in God. If you are going through a trial or a problem that seems too great for you to bear, I want you to stop right now and pray. Ask God first of all to forgive you for not trusting in Him, then release your problem or circumstance to Him and believe that He will make it work for your good. Then you need to rest in Him and stop your fretting and worrying. It only leads to more problems. God will make a way where there seems to be no way.

Out of your greatest trials will come your greatest triumphs. Unless David fought Goliath how would he ever have known the power of the almighty God to bring deliverance? You may be facing your Goliath right now. Take five smooth stones - faith - and run at the enemy with all your might. There is a saying that if you face your fear it will disappear. Run at your problem with faith trusting in the Lord that God will defeat it. Then watch what God will do. You will have a testimony as mighty as David's if you believe and trust.

Our problem with Christina at the time seemed life threatening. God knew all along that it was not serious. God knows the answers to all of our problems and trials. Put them in His hands and watch the hand of the Lord move to deliver you.

Chapter 5

THE MOVE

"You're pregnant," the doctor stated calmly. I could not believe it! Christina was only nine months old and I was not feeling very well lately. I went to the doctor for a checkup and got the news that I was pregnant. Praise the Lord! I had always wanted a big family, but was not expecting it so soon.

Everyone in my family was happy that a second addition to the Crouley family was on the way. I was busy taking care of Christina and very involved with doing things with the church that we attended. So life was going along pretty smoothly at this time.

We were still living in the three bedroom apartment. We knew that with another child on the way that we were going to need more living room, so we started looking for houses that we could buy. There was a couple who attended our church and were selling their house because they had a home that they were having built for them. We looked at the home and fell in love with it. It was down the street from a beautiful lake which we had a side view from the living room. It was on a large lot and had many wonderful trees and shrubs.

After looking at this home and then comparing it to other homes that were for sale in the surrounding areas, we finally decided that we wanted to buy the house by the lake. We put an offer in on the home and everything went through smooth-ly.

I was about four months pregnant at the time when we moved into the home by the lake. We had a moving truck and many of our family members helping us out. It was a long day and that night as I was lying in bed Rick and I thanked the Lord for giving us our first home. Little did we know that our journey in that home would not be that long.

We enjoyed living in our first home. I decorated the house with different kinds of wallpapers in the various rooms of the house. It was fun going out and buying things that would make our first home look cute and cozy. It was a wonderful time in my life and I still look back to adventures in our first home.

I was getting ready for our first Thanksgiving. I was so thankful to God for all of the things that He had blessed us with the last few years. Not only did I have a beautiful daughter, but now I was pregnant with my second child. God had also given us a beautiful home to live in with my family. Life was good!

The weekend of Thanksgiving I had my brother Jack spend the night with us in the spare bedroom. I enjoyed spending time with my brother because we had a lot of things in common since we both had accepted the Lord. He loved playing with Christina and tickling her and telling her stories.

I went to bed early that night since I was getting indigestion and didn't feel very well. I excused myself while Rick and Jack continued to talk into the night about business and other things. It was around 2:00 in the morning and all of a sudden I woke up with a start. I was getting fairly significant contractions. I woke up Rick and said that I thought he should drive me to the hospital.

Thank goodness Jack was there because he was able to stay with Christina. We raced down to the hospital and they admitted me in the middle of the night. I remember going through labor around 4:00 a.m. in the morning only to have my beloved husband snoozing on a chair next to my bed. I thought to myself, "the honeymoon is over! What happened to helping me with the breathing?"

Rick was not a very good late night person and could not keep himself awake during the labor pains. It was so different from my first delivery, which took place in the middle of the afternoon with all of the activity at the hospital. My mother had been there and I was on the phone talking to various friends letting them know I was in labor and to pray.

With the second labor I was basically all alone except for a nurse that would peak her head into the room periodically to check on me and see if I needed anything. As the labor started progressing she would come in to see if I had dilated.

But then the contractions started coming closer together and feeling much more intense than the others. I buzzed the nurse and she came running in. I told her that I thought it was time and she checked me and said that I was dilated to 10 and that she would immediately call the doctor.

By this time Rick had awoken from his slumbering state (thank God for miracles). He raced with the nurse and me down the hall on the gurney going to the delivery room. This last set of events happened at breakneck speed. I hoped that my doctor would be there in time!

As they were getting me ready for delivery again I flashed back to my first delivery with my daughter Christina and how special it was. Rick was holding my hand and I was getting apprehensive waiting for the doctor to get there. The nurse kept telling me not to push! I wanted to push so badly but the doctor was not there and they didn't want the baby being delivered without him. They did have a standby doctor ready in case my doctor didn't show up.

All at once there was a flurry of activity in the room. The doctor had raced in and was washing his hands and getting ready to deliver my baby! I was so relieved that he had finally come. How many times does God do that to us in our everyday lives? It seems like we have been waiting for Him forever to show up on the scene. It almost seems too late but then God shows up and all is well. He has our live in His hands.

Now the doctor was ready to deliver my baby. He was positioned at the end of the gurney and he told me that I needed to push with all my might. I had been pushing for about fifteen minutes and was getting very tired.

All of a sudden I heard the doctor say to Rick, "I see the head and it looks very big, I think I will have to use forceps on it." I had visions in my mind of my baby having a huge water head. And the forceps part I was not sure of what he meant. All of a sudden I saw the doctor take this big instrument that looks like salad tongs and started getting the baby out. I thought to myself, "Great, I'm in the middle of labor and all this doctor can think about is tossing a salad!"

The forceps did the trick and my son was born at 7:18 in the morning. I knew that God had told me that I was going to have a son and that his name would be Jeremy Joseph. I was so confused when I originally had a girl for my first one. But I knew that God knew what He was doing. He gave me a beautiful 7 pound 8 ounce baby boy.

I was so tired but extremely happy. I now had a boy and a girl. What could any parent ask for? I had one of each. They put Jeremy on my stomach and I just held him in my arms and cried tears of joy. I don't care how many births you go through; every one of your children is a miracle in itself. Each one is so unique and so special. They truly are a gift from God.

We brought Jeremy to our home by the lake and I thought I was ready to settle in with my two little children. Little did I know that I was going to be taken on a huge adventure to another state. The economy was not very good at that time in Minnesota and most of the Northern States. Many people were packing up and moving down to the Southern States such as Texas, Georgia, and Florida.

The same week that I brought Jeremy home from the hospital, Rick came walking in one day saying that he had gotten a call from his old friend, Steve Kramer. Rick said that Steve was now living in Dallas, Texas, and that he was working for a home improvement company that needed salespeople. Steve said the economy was booming and that we should pack our bags and come down for a while.

Rick had been working at getting several new businesses off the ground at this point and nothing had really blossomed into anything fruitful. Rick was looking at me trying to figure out what I was thinking. My mind went blank! I didn't really want to leave my home state of Minnesota and my family. But I also wanted Rick to have opportunities in his career that would benefit our family. I told Rick that we should pray and see what the Lord said.

We went to bed that night and prayed that God would direct our footsteps. As I turned off the light to go to sleep, I felt an assurance from God that He had everything under control and not to worry. So many times if we look at the circumstances in our lives we can get beside ourselves with worry and fear. I just put my trust in the Lord and did not lean to my own understanding.

The next morning Rick woke up and said that He felt that God had given us the green light to move. I asked him what we would do with the house. He told me that he didn't want to sell it just yet in case we didn't like Texas. In that case we could just move back. I still wasn't sure about moving and his plan but I consented and we started making the arrangements to go.

When I told my mom and dad that we were going to move you should have seen their faces drop. Here we were going to be taking their only two grandchildren out of the state one thousand miles away. My parents, though, do not meddle and they encouraged us to do whatever we felt was best for our family.

We found some people to lease our home and started making preparations for the trip down to Texas. Steve said that we could stay at his home for a few days until we found a home to lease. I remember the cold, snowy day in January that we embarked on our trip down to Texas. We were at my mother's house saying goodbye. We left most of the furniture in the house, but we had our car loaded up with clothes and a crib tied to the top. We were young and we didn't care what it looked like. What an exciting journey was going to lie ahead of us. We had a little money and a lot of faith for our trip down south.

The trip down was not an easy one. With Christina being only eighteen months old and Jeremy being only one month old, it was challenging to say the least. We tried to make good time driving when they were taking their naps. They both took a morning and an afternoon nap, which I was very grateful for. We stopped one night in a hotel on the drive down. It was our plan to drive to Texas in about two days.

I remember as we pulled into the city of Dallas driving on their freeways. Everything looked so big and clean. It was winter in Dallas but they did not get snow, and the cars and buildings looked clean and shiny. I did not know one soul in the whole town except for Steve, but that didn't seem to bother me. We finally found Steve's house and he welcomed us warmly. We had a beautiful dinner together and then we hit the sack for the night in his home.

The next day we went out looking for houses or apartments. There was not a lot available at this point since there was so many people coming down from the north that there was a shortage of rental properties. We started getting discouraged toward the end of the day. Christina and Jeremy were tired of being dragged all over town looking at places. Finally we found an apartment that we thought looked nice and they had a vacancy. I really didn't want to live in an apartment, especially since we had a beautiful home in Minnesota. But I thought that this wouldn't be bad since we could rent it month to month. If things didn't work out we would not have to break our lease.

We ended up renting furniture for our apartment since we had left our furniture in our house. We got everything moved into the apartment and laid on the couches exhausted. We finally were in Texas and had a place to live.

Rick was working for Steve's company selling home improvements for the home. He enjoyed it and seemed to be doing well. I didn't know anybody yet, but made it a habit of taking walks in the stroller with the kids every afternoon. I was a little homesick but I tried not to dwell on it.

One day Rick told me that he saw a sign painted on a water tower that said, "Jesus loves you" and underneath that inscription were the words, "Word of Faith Family Fellowship." Rick said that this was a church and that he had heard from another person that it was a great place to fellowship with other Christians.

We called the church and found out that they had services on Wednesday nights and Sunday morning and evening. There was a service that night and they said they had childcare available for the services. I thought, "Great, let's go." We went to the Wednesday night service and fell in love with Word of Faith. A young couple was the pastors, Bob and Marte Tilton. Bob was very dynamic in his preaching style. They had wonderful praise and worship and the people that were in the congregation seemed great. I truly felt that we had found a good home church.

After the service that evening we started talking to another couple who were sitting by us named Carey and Michelle Ruybalid. We ended up getting a bite to eat with them and we felt that we had met our first two friends in Texas. It's amazing when you go to a new town how lonely you can feel even though you have thousands of people living around you.

They told us a number of things about Texas and said that they would introduce us to many couples and events in the area. I was very excited and thanked God that He was directing our paths. Michelle informed me that they were starting up a new choir under the direction of a new choir director and wanted to know if I would audition with her. I told her I was a singer and I would love to do this. The audition was next Thursday evening and they were going to have a nursery provided for the children.

The week seemed to fly by! I was so excited to be a part of a new choir. I never really had been in a choir before. I had always done solos at our church or at other churches in the area. I had also done several television programs where I was able to do various Christian songs. I thought the choir would be a good way of meeting people and being able to sing praises to the Lord at the same time.

Finally, Thursday came and Michelle picked me up for choir practice. We had sold my car when we moved from Minnesota and only took Rick's car down to Texas. It was our plan to buy a car after a few months, but we had not done that yet. I was without a vehicle and many times Rick was working at nights on appointments. It was a real blessing when Michelle offered to pick me up.

There were about fifty people in the choir rooms who were all getting seated. There was a gentleman at the front of the room instructing people to take various sheets of music according to their range and ability. I walked up to the gentlemen and found out that this was the choir director, Dan Petty. I introduced myself and told him that I was a soprano and he handed me some sheet music and told me to find a seat anywhere that was available. There was a lot of excitement in the room and everyone was looking around and introducing themselves. It was a very festive atmosphere and I was excited to be a part of it.

That first night at choir was so much fun for me. Michelle introduced me to her sister-in-law, Jill, as well as several other girls. This was like a breath of fresh air to me to finally be meeting some girlfriends. I had many girlfriends in Minnesota that I had known for a number of years. But when you move to a new city or state you realize how valuable those friendships are.

After choir, Michelle drove me home and we talked all the way about how great the choir was going to be. They had a good selection of voices and we were excited about the piece that Dan Petty was going to have us be performing. Easter was coming up in a few short months and they were going to be renting out the Dallas Convention Center for a big Easter musical.

Between taking care of Jeremy and Christina during the day and choir rehearsals two times a week in the evenings, I was quite busy. It was during this time that Rick started realizing that he was not happy working with Steve selling home improvements for his company. We were not making the money we needed so Rick started looking for other avenues of employment.

Rick went to an employment agency that handled top sales performers and was immediately sent out on an interview with the Winner's Circle. The Winner's Circle was an exclusive company that hired and trained top professionals for various businesses. When Rick walked up to the receptionist to say that he was there for the interview, the girl told him they had already hired someone. The man Rick was to meet happened to be walking out of his office at the same time and overheard the receptionist say this to Rick. He looked at Rick and said, "I guess I have time for one more interview."

Rick and the man were together for over three hours. The man had told Rick that they had been interviewing for over three weeks and went through seventy applicants. The man was so impressed with Rick and his skills that he hired him immediately on the spot. Rick asked him about the other gentleman they hired and the man said he had another position that they could put him in.

Rick was going to work for a large homebuilder in Dallas. He had a lot of homes in his inventory that had not been able to sell. The interest rates were very high at this time. They were around 18 percent and many people were not buying new homes. It was going to be Rick's job to sell these 20 homes that had been sitting empty for over one year. It was a difficult job, but Rick was offered a very nice salary and bonus with the sale of each home.

When Rick came home and told me that he had been hired out of seventy applicants, I was thrilled and knew that God had answered our prayers. Even though our home was being leased out in Minnesota we still had to make up the difference on the payments to the bank. We were paying for our apartment and for our house and it was becoming very challenging to make ends meet.

Rick started working for the homebuilder and the Lord started to immediately bless us. One of the things that we learned from going to Word of Faith was the principle of tithing. The Bible says in Malachi that we are to give one tenth of our income back to the Lord. It says that if you don't that you rob God and that you are cursed with a curse. We had not always practiced the principals of tithing in our life up to that point.

We started giving faithfully one tenth right off the top once we received our check. It was exciting to see how God was honoring our giving back to Him. It was miraculous watching how Rick started selling these new homes that had been sitting vacant for over a year. The first week Rick started working for the homebuilder he sold three homes. The next week he sold another four. By the end of end of two months Rick had almost completely sold all the homes that had been on the market for such a long time. The homebuilder was ecstatic with Rick and gave him a very large bonus.

One of the other perks that we received working for this company was that they let us move into one of their new homes. We had been living in that apartment for a few months and I really was not very happy. It was not a new apartment and there were things that needed to be fixed inside that never seemed to get done by the landlord.

One day Rick had mentioned this to the owner of the homebuilding company and he told Rick that we could move into the house on Concord. He originally had been saving it for his mother-in-law to move into but plans fell through for her move to Texas from the East coast. The owner told Rick that we could move in as soon as we wanted to because it was vacant.

I remember when we first went over and looked at it. It was a cute one-story brick custom home. It was around 1700 square feet with three bedrooms and two bathrooms. It had a nice back yard with a fence around it as well as a nice sized front yard. Everything was brand new since it had never been lived in after being built. I was so happy and went from room to room with thanksgiving that God had given us a nice home to live in.

As you trust in the Lord with all of your heart and not lean to your own understanding, God will make a way for you. When it seems like you can't make ends meet and the bills aren't getting paid, as long as you tithe, trust in the Lord, and work as hard and as diligently as you can, God will make a way. I know some of you may be saying that you have been doing that and it isn't working. God's ways are not our ways. His timetable is not the same as ours. The main thing God wants us to do is to trust in Him. If he opened the Red Sea for the children of Israel when they had the armies of Pharaoh following them, He will do it for you.

Many times it seems that God waits until the last minute before He answers us. God does that because He wants us to believe and trust in Him. When the answer comes we know that only God could have pulled it off. Why do you think He waited until the last minute to open the Red Sea for Moses and the children of Israel to go through? He could have opened it up a mile up the road so they could have seen the provision He made for them. Many of them were fearful, I'm sure, and unbelieving thinking, "Moses, why did you bring us all the way out here to die in this wilderness?"

But Moses had faith and knew that God wouldn't have let them come this far only to leave them now. As Moses raised the staff in the air, the Red Sea immediately started to part. As they walked through on the dry land I'm sure they must have been rejoicing and praising God. It was a divine miracle that they all had witnessed and been a part of. They would be able to tell this story to their children and their children's children for years to come.

But then someone turned around and shouted, "Pharaoh's army is right behind us! They are following us and are going to kill us." Many times after God does one miracle the enemy will immediately try to use another measure to destroy us and our faith. Moses turned around and was not at all affected by what he saw. He had faith that if God opened the Red Sea that he could deal with Pharaoh's army that was following.

As soon as they had all crossed over on the other side of the sea, immediately the Red Sea closed up on the armies that were close behind the children of Israel. They all rejoiced and started singing praises to the Lord. One of the songs they may have been singing is this, "I will sing unto the Lord for He has triumphed gloriously - the horse and rider thrown into the sea. The Lord, my God, my strength my song, has now become my victory."

The Lord had proved Himself strong toward the children of Israel. He had miraculously opened the Red Sea and shut it on the pursuing armies. God will do the same thing for you as well. He is no respecter of persons. If He did it for them, He will do it for you.

Chapter 6

ON SATELLITE

One night at choir practice Dan Petty, the choir director, mentioned that he was forming a new group; he was auditioning every member from the choir. He said the name of the group would be called "The Word of Faith Singers" and that they would perform special songs before the congregation. The auditioning would take place the following week during the normal choir practice.

I was thrilled to be a part of this audition. I knew God was with me and had faith to believe I would be chosen. The day of the audition quickly came and I remember waiting on a metal chair for my turn to go in and see Dan. When my turn came, I walked into the room and Dan gave me some sheet music. He had me run through singing some scales first so he could see the vocal quality of my voice as well as my range. Then he had me sing some of the sheet music. It was over in five minutes; and I walked out of the room feeling good, but not knowing exactly if I would make the group or not.

After everyone was through auditioning, Dan gathered us all together and told us that he would have the fifteen names of the singers posted at the next choir rehearsal on Thursday. He said it was going to be a hard decision since there were sixty in the choir and he could only choose fifteen for the new group. He said he did not want anyone's feelings to be hurt if they did not make it, and that we needed to be mature and happy for the ones who were chosen.

As I walked to my car after the audition I prayed to the Lord that I would be on the new Word of Faith singers group. But regardless, I said "Not my will but thine be done." I prayed the prayer of relinquishment. After we have done all that we can do, we then give it up to God and wait for the Lord to answer our prayer. This is only done after you have exhausted all of your own resources in the natural. Many people don't try hard enough because they are lazy and are waiting for God to do everything for them. God gives us the energy and the abilities to push ahead in life. Sometimes we hit walls or roadblocks where only God can move. That is when you pray the prayer of relinquishment.

The following Thursday I raced down to the choir rehearsal and bolted in the door. On the wall was posted a sheet of paper with all the names of the new members of the group. There was a group of people clustered around the announcement. I could hear some exclamations of joy and others just turned and walked away without saying a word. I could tell these were the ones whose names were not on the announcement.

It made me think of how we will feel when God opens the Lamb's book of life. Some whose names are printed in it will be able to enter into God's Kingdom, while others will turn away dejected but only because they did not receive Jesus into their heart. We all are given the same chance to have our name in the lamb's book of life. In this case it will not depend on our abilities or talents, but only on our faith and trust in the Son of God who died on the cross for our sins, Jesus.

As I walked up to the sheet I looked at the paper with trepidation. Would my name be on the list? As I scanned the names to my heart's delight I saw the words, "MERI

CROULEY" halfway down the list. One of my other friends, Janie Fields, was also on the list and she congratulated me. Dan had picked a good group of voices who would blend very well together. The ones who were chosen all formed a little group congratulating each other.

Dan Petty then came out and congratulated us and told us we would be meeting for practice with the new group the following night. He said he had some important news he wanted to share with us that was very exciting and would be a real opportunity as a group.

The next night came very quickly as I was anticipating what Dan was going to share with us. As we all sat gathered on chairs in a semi-circle surrounding Dan he started to share with us what the news was. Dan told us that Word of Faith was going to be launching a new ministry and that it would be televised by satellite all around the country into various churches. Special speakers were going to be coming in such as Kenneth Hagin, Kenneth Copeland, Oral Roberts, Charles Capps, and other notable faith preachers. The ministry was to be named the Word of Faith Satellite Network.

The program had just started and already 100 churches were signed up to receive broadcasting into their church. The purpose of the network was to have these churches on the network so that their congregation could have access to these great men of God and their teachings. Many of these churches were small and some of these speakers (because of their schedules) would never have an opportunity of ministering at their church because of time. The reason Dan was so excited about the Word of Faith Singers was that we were going to be doing special music on the monthly meetings. This would expose not only the group, but the individual singers as well as they gave solo performances along with the singers.

We all sat there and looked at Dan dumbfounded. Literally overnight we were going to be singing before thousands of people. We all thought that it was a great opportunity for ministry; and as a group to be showcased before many people that would not ordinarily get the chance to come to Dallas, Texas, and hear us sing and perform.

The group was practicing three times a week getting ready for our first performance. We were going to be opening up the Satellite Network with one song that Dan had written himself. We practiced this song until we almost couldn't sing it anymore.

We also went out and purchased dresses for the women, and the men were told to wear blue suits so we would look like we were a singing group. The dresses were a beautiful light blue that were made of satin. We all went down and got fitted for our size. The dresses were ordered and came in two days before the performance.

The night of our performance I was really nervous. I thought to myself, "Just four months ago I moved to Dallas and the Lord is really opening up doors." I was excited and knew the performance would be anointed and that the Holy Spirit was going to touch people all over the country.

I drove to the church and everyone was starting to arrive at the same time. The service started at 7:30 and we were told to arrive at 6:30 for a sound check and to rehearse. The rehearsal went smoothly and everyone sounded great. I could tell Dan was nervous by the way he had to keep wiping perspiration off his forehead with a handkerchief. Finally, the cameras were ready, the lights were in place and the cameraman gave us a cue with a countdown before we were to start. Three, two, one and then the music came on and we were ready to sing. We all smiled and sang our hearts out. We had prayed before the service in the choir room in back of the stage. We all knew that God was going to move in and through us as we sang. I felt the Holy Spirit so strong during the song that I almost couldn't stand. By the time the song ended there were bursts of applause and a standing ovation.

They weren't standing for us, but for the Lord Jesus. The song gave such a tribute to the Lord that there was hardly a dry eye in the place. We walked off the stage knowing God had used us and that many people around the country had felt and seen the hand of God working in our lives.

I got a call from a friend of mine the next day in Minneapolis. She was going to a church where they had the Satellite Service broadcasted. I did not know everywhere the program would be on so I was surprised when I got the call. She told me she saw me on the screen and was shocked. She didn't even know I had moved. As she watched the Word of Faith singers she was not only impressed with the quality of the sound, but also with the presence of the Lord she felt. I knew that if it touched her and the people in the congregation that it had touched many others as well.

The reason I am going into such detail about this incident is that many times in life we work and pray and believe that God is going to work in our lives. We struggle and press on and sometimes it seems that nothing ever changes. If you continue to press on and don't give up, eventually things will change and you will have some real victories for you to savor after they are over. This was one of many times in my life that I can look back and savor what God did through and in this situation. The key is to always believe in God and don't give into feelings of depressing and self-pity. The devil will always try to steal your joy which is your strength. God is able to do exceedingly abundantly above all that we could ask or think. We just need to ask Him and then believe He is going to move. Just wait and see what God can do with a person or a group of people who will submit to Him and then move out in faith. It takes not only submitting but action. Many people pray their whole life waiting for God to move and change circumstances. It's good that they pray, but there is something missing. The Bible says Faith without works is dead. You need to also move in the direction you feel you are called with the appropriate actions of faith.

If you don't aim for a target, the arrow you release will just fly through the air and fall on the ground, never having accomplished any goal. But if you set up the target and aim the arrow and then release it, you will see progress. Maybe you missed the target the first time completely. But at least you knew you missed and redirected your bow in a different direction for more accuracy. Just because you have tried sometime and didn't succeed, doesn't mean you should give up. Failure will be your biggest teacher because you will learn what not to do next time. Pick up the arrow again and keep practicing until you get a bull's-eye. It's up to you! You're destiny is in your hands. Maximize your victories and minimize your failures. You're on a winning course but don't get sidetracked by the detours. Go around them, persevere, and see how God will move in your life.

Chapter 7

THE EXALTER

I was in a water park pool in Carrollton, Texas, when I got a page over the loudspeaker saying, "Meri Crouley, please come to the main office for an urgent message." I thought to myself, "What happened, did somebody die, how did anybody know that I was here?" I had gone to the water park with my two children and was having a great time relaxing and soaking in some rays. I had gone with a friend who also had her children there and told her to watch my kids while I went to find out what the message was.

As I walked toward the main office I had a weird feeling in the pit of my stomach not knowing what was going to be at the other end. As I walked up to the counter where the phone was I anxiously told the girl at the desk that I was Meri Crouley and I had just been paged. She looked at me and said that there was a caller on line three and she would get me a phone. I grabbed the phone expecting the worst when I heard the voice of my choir director, Dan Petty, saying, "Are you having a good time at the pool?" My mind was not comprehending what was going on. How did he know that I was going to be at the pool that day and even if he did know why was he calling me?

Dan told me, "I have an exciting opportunity that has just opened up! Word of Faith has just asked me to take over the position of Praise and Worship leader and I am picking three people from the Word of Faith Singers to form another group called "the Exalters" which will help me lead the congregation. I want you to be one of "the Exalters." I just sat there stunned for a minute. I had only been living in Texas for a few short months and the Lord was already opening major doors for me. I told him I would have to talk to my husband first, but it sounded great to me! I hung up the phone and went back to the pool enthusiastically letting my friend know what had transpired on the phone.

After drying the kids off we made our way home and as I walked in the door I heard my husband yell out, "Did Dan Petty call you at the pool?" I had wondered how Dan had discovered that I was at the pool! I explained to Rick what had transpired on the phone and we prayed about the decision. Later that night we both agreed that God was opening up the door for me and I should take the position on the worship team.

I called Dan Petty back and told him that I wanted to be on the Exalters. We met the following week for our first practice. One of my other friends in the choir, Janie Fields, was also chosen as well as one male named Tony Johnson. We met in the small room adjacent to the choir and started working on melodies and choruses.

God is so faithful to us! If we stand faithful in the areas that He has called us to and don't get stuck in depression or self-pity, the sky is the limit. God wants to promote us more than we want ourselves to be. Many times, though, we limit God by not trusting in His word and believing His promises during trials and tough times. It is easy to walk in the flesh and get negative and sink in the mire of despair. You need to fight this feeling! Push yourself ahead and set goals for your life. Work toward that call everyday and you'll be amazed at the end of the year how far you have come. Remember the story of the tortoise and the hare? The hare was much faster than the tortoise. The hare would run ahead and look back at the tortoise and laugh. The hare would spend much of his time resting along the side of the road taunting the tortoise. He knew he was capable and was able to beat the tortoise easily, but the tortoise never gave up. The tortoise plodded along inch by inch, minute by minute, day by day. Before you knew it the tortoise was crossing the finish line while the hare was taking a nap totally unaware that he had lost the race.

How many times are we like that in life? God has gifted us with many gifts, but we don't utilize those gifts. We might look at others around and think smugly to ourselves that we are more competent than they. We criticize and judge those around us because it makes us seem more important. But the ones in the body of Christ who continually press in and don't look to the right or to the left but to the finish line are going to be the victors. They are the ones who move a little every day and don't give up. Sure they might get tired. Sure they might get discouraged. But they don't let it stop them! Keep on going and you'll be the victor.

Many times when you become the winner there will be others around you who will be jealous of your accomplishments. There will be those who will try to discourage you from trying or plodding along in faith. You need to walk right on by those people. They are not your friends. They don't want you to get ahead because it will pass them up. You need to surround yourself with friends who will encourage you in the Lord and in your faith.

This very thing happened to me after I was promoted from the choir to the Word of Faith Singers. Dan had chosen me along with Tony and Janie for the worship team as well as the choir. People in the choir were initially upset about not being on the Word of Faith singers. But there were a few that got downright angry when they weren't chosen for this other group called "The Exalters."

God is the one who will promote you if you are faithful. God can also demote you if you have the wrong attitude. It is important to realize that if there are those around us who God is blessing, we need to be happy for them as if it were happening to us. This is called character building. One of the works of the flesh is envy and jealousy. We need to put that feeling to death in our hearts by acknowledging it as sin to the Lord and repent. Just because we don't feel like walking in love toward others doesn't mean that we have sinned. The main way we sin in this area is with our tongues. We'll get caught up in gossip and talk about it to someone else to alleviate our own feelings of insecurity. We all have feelings like this and we need to keep those feelings nailed to the cross. That is why the Lord says to crucify your flesh daily. The natural man is always going to have these types of feelings. But we don't walk in the flesh; we walk in the spirit. The Bible says that if we walk in the spirit, we won't fulfill the lusts of the flesh (Galatians 5:16).

Children tend to be very self-centered and temperamental when they want their own way. What a two year old does that looks cute may look totally ridiculous when a fifty-year-old man or women does it.

It's time to grow up and start acting like mature Christians instead of babies.

As I started singing with "The Exalters" and leading the worship during the service, I felt that God had really answered my prayers. I not only was in "The Exalters," but I also was still singing in the "Word of Faith Singers." It was a very exciting time in my life. My life consisted of taking care of Christina and Jeremy in the day and then two times a week practicing with both of the groups. I was also at church every

Wednesday night, and singing as well at both services on Sunday. I was truly enjoying myself!

Thank the Lord for those times in your life when you can look back and really feel God has opened up doors for you. There are many times that we are going through trials and persecutions, which also are a blessing but in a different way. But thank God for those times in your life when everything is going smoothly and you are walking in God's divine purpose for your life. This is when you have the strength during the trials to look back and remember His divine appointments and know this current trial shall pass and God will open up those new doors for you.

Everything was going so smoothly and wonderful that I felt that things couldn't get better. One day I was at home and started to feel a little bit nauseous. I thought I was coming down with the flu. I went to the doctor to have it checked out after it still did not go away after a week's time. When I was at the doctor's office my sweet Doctor Patterson walked in and said, "Congratulations, you're pregnant!"

I about dropped off of the chair. I said, "I'm pregnant! It can't be."

Christina was only two years old and Jeremy was nine months. I was going to have three children within four years. I thought I was just starting to have a little freedom in my life, but now it all seemed to shatter. It wasn't that I was not excited about having another child; it just seemed like they were all so close together.

As I drove home from the doctor's office I wondered to myself what God was doing. I started to ask God why He allowed me to conceive again so soon. As I was driving I heard the Lord answer me in a still, small voice: "Meri, I have your life in my hands. It is my desire that you have another child because all of your children will be used in a tremendous way in the Kingdom of God. Just trust in Me now and don't lean to your own understanding. I will work it out."

God spoke to me very clearly but it wasn't audible. It was in a still, small voice in my mind. The Bible says in John 10:27 *"That His sheep know His voice."* There are three voices that a person will hear. One will be your own voice. The second will be the voice of God. And the third will be the voice of Satan. We have to learn to be discerning to know which voice is which.

I walked in the house and started fixing dinner for the family when Rick walked in the door from work. I put down a salad bowl and told him that I had something important to share with him. While Christina and Jeremy were in the other room playing peacefully, I told him about my visit to the doctor and that I was pregnant again with another child. Rick's face went white for a moment, but then he smiled really big and said he was thrilled. He came over and gave me a big hug and kiss. I had been nervous up to that point as to what Rick was going to say. But all of my fears lifted from me at that moment. I knew that God would provide and take care of us.

Sometimes in our lives it seems like God throws us a curve ball. We are expecting the pitch to go straight but then it takes an unexpected curve. That is what happened in my life at this point. I had my path all carved out with my two children and Rick. I as singing at the church and it was being broadcast on a national satellite television. It was all so new and exciting to me that I actually started getting caught up in the ministry. It is important to have dreams and work toward your goals, but when we start putting the ministry ahead of family many times God will put an unexpected detour in our path.

If you seek first the Kingdom of God and His righteousness then all of these things will be added unto you. As you seek

God and His will, all the other doors in your life will open if your priorities are in order. My priorities had gotten out of order and God was showing me that my children were to take a first place position in my life. I was always a good mother and took excellent care of my children, but I started dreaming about traveling and doing all of these wonderful things for the Lord. God had big dreams for my family and me. It was just important I put my priorities in order and He sure saw to it by what had happened. *"Trust in the Lord with all of your heart and lean not to your own understanding, in all your ways acknowledge Him and He will direct your paths"* (Proverbs 3:5). This scripture took on new meaning during this time. I started to seek God in a new and dynamic way. God had another exciting journey coming up along the way. We were soon to discover the divine provision of God.

Chapter 8

THE MARCH

I was only a few weeks pregnant with my third child and Michelle Ruyballid had come up to me one day at church and said there was an evangelist named David Allbritton who was looking for someone a few days a week part-time to help out with the ministry. Rick was doing well at his position selling homes, but there were some expenses that we still needed to get caught up on. I mentioned this to Rick and he said it wouldn't bother him to have me work part-time for a few months. There was a woman named Jan who lived down the block from us who took a few children in her home part-time. She was a very good mother and took excellent care of the children so I didn't feel guilty about even thinking of applying for the job.

I met with David and his wife Linda at their office the following day. They were very sweet and really needed help with having an office manager come in and help them with booking his crusades and writing his new book called "Get Your Hopes Up." We instantly took a liking to each other and they gave me a very good hourly wage (considering that I hadn't worked in a few years). We determined I would start the following week. They knew I was pregnant and that it was only going to last for a few months until they had the funds to hire someone full-time.

I got the babysitter situated with the children and it was arranged the kids would go there from 9:00 a.m. until 3:00 p.m. two days a week. I did not look forward to leaving them, but I knew another child would be here in eight months and we wanted to pay a few of those bills off before the third child arrived.

Work was really fun at David Allbritton's office and the Lord really used it to help build my spiritual walk. The first few weeks I was typing from his manuscript and it was spiritually stimulating to read everything He was writing about, encouraging people not to lose hope in God. David was an evangelist who did crusades all over the world. His main thrust was to the lost and many times in his crusades he would have large Jesus marches in the cities to make a statement and win souls for the Kingdom of God.

When he was in prayer one day the Lord told him he was to do a large Jesus march in downtown Dallas. David had a radio show and was on everyday on a local radio station. He started advertising this Jesus march on radio and through local churches. It was my responsibility to call the local pastors and tell them about the march and have them tell their people from the pulpit. It was a big job and I got a few volunteers to help me.

The day of the Jesus march rolled around very quickly. I had been working for David a few months now. It was the end of March and we prayed that the weather would be good. In Dallas you never know what can happen. Sometimes the weather can be 80 degrees one day and the next day get down to 30 degrees.

Many people were praying for the crusade and we knew that God was going to move in a powerful way. I remember waking up that morning and looking out the window to see the sun shining down. I was so happy it was not raining and the weather was good that I just started singing praises to the

Lord.

Rick was working that day since he was selling real estate for the Homebuilder and Saturday's were one of their biggest days. I invited a few friends and we all took our children. By the time we made it to downtown Dallas and parked I started noticing people coming from everywhere. It was really exciting knowing that I had a major part in getting this organized. There is always a question in the back of your mind what the attendance will be when you put on an event. We had no idea of how many people would come. Hopefully, a thousand people or more would be attending!

But that morning we saw busloads of people showing up. They just kept coming and coming. David and I were amazed! We just started glorifying God and rejoicing. We had over 5,000 people that showed up for the march for Jesus. It was really great to see everyone all in unison and rallying around the gospel of Jesus Christ and taking it to the streets.

We had everyone meet in the large park in the midst of downtown Dallas where Kennedy had been assassinated. We had a prayer meeting for about fifteen minutes and asked God to bless the march and that people who were bystanders on the streets and in their cars would dedicate their life to the Lord.

There was a big truck pulling a flatbed trailer where an eight piece praise band was worshipping God. David was in the lead and I was not far behind. The truck was also behind us with the rest of the five thousand people marching through the streets of downtown Dallas. We had police escorts following us in front and in back of us. Many people just stopped and watched with their mouths agape. Some people would drive by and honk their horns in support. Others would look and mock, laughing at us like we were a bunch of idiots.

The Bible says that all those who live Godly in Christ Jesus will suffer persecution. When you stand up for the gospel and tell others about it the devil doesn't like it. If they laughed and scoffed at Jesus, know they will do the same to you. You don't need to worry about this though because the spirit of God is on you in such a strong way that it is an incredible feeling.

As we marched along the streets of Dallas we were singing praise songs in unity. It was such a beautiful sight to see thousands of Christians not fighting over doctrine or who had the biggest church, but walking side by side, praising the Lord regardless of church affiliation.

We walked about three miles along a planned route we had mapped out. On the way many people in the crowd were telling other bystanders about Jesus. Quite a few people that day ended up accepting the Lord into their hearts because of the boldness of those marching. It is important to note we are strengthened when we are together with others in the body of Christ. The devil will try to get us by ourselves and then prey on you. Just like the story of the sheep and the shepherd. As long as the sheep are together in the flock being watched by the shepherd they are fine. But the devil will try to lure the sheep away so the wolf can devour the sheep when they are least suspecting.

If you are not involved with a local church you need to be. The Bible says in Hebrews 10:25 *"Not to forsake the assembling of ourselves together."* If you are not going to a church, find one. God will strengthen us and mature us through the five-fold ministry of the church. Remember, though, there are no perfect people so do not expect to find the perfect church. A lot of people keep hopping from church to church thinking they are going to find the perfect church. It is better to find a good church and stay there. Once you're planted allow time for yourself to establish roots and grow. If a farmer were to dig up the seed a few days after he planted it and try to bring it to another field to plant, the plant would never grow. But if after the farmer plants the seeds, waters it, nurtures it, and cultivates the plants, he will reap a great harvest.

I have seen many ministers in the body of Christ who had great gifts. The Bible says when He gives us a gift He doesn't take it back. So in essence if God gives a minister a gift and they fall in sin they still have the gift. That is why you can see a man or women of God who later was found out to be in sin and the Lord used them tremendously even though they were sinning against Him. But these same ministers who had such tremendous gifts had no fruit in their lives whatsoever. Many times their families were a mess and their marriages were on the rocks, however they were out ministering for God under "the anointing."

We need to get back to our roots. Get established and planted in a local church and then stay faithful. Let God develop you and have your roots grow deep and strong as He matures you through the Word of God. You will one day wake up to find you have much fruit starting to grow in your life. God is faithful. We just need to be patient and stay grounded in the things of God until we start growing up in the faith. On this journey in the Lord it is not always easy, but I can tell you that it is never dull or boring either. Stand strong in the Lord and in the power of His might.

Chapter 9

BUILDING HOMES

"I want to start my own homebuilding business," my husband said to me on the phone when I was at work at David Allbritton's office. I said, "What!? You have never built a house before and don't know what you are doing. You don't even know how to pound a nail straight."

Rick told me that he had been researching the homebuilding business and that he was only making a mere one percent commission compared to what the builder was making around 20 percent. My husband is a very industrious person and never lets grass grow under his feet. When he found out that he could be making twenty times as much, he started researching the building business without me knowing about it. He basically found a piece of paper in one of the file cabinets at work that laid out all of the steps needed to be taken in order to build a house. From this he developed enough faith to start stepping out and mentioning it to a few people that he was going to be starting his own company in the near future.

Most of the homes by the builder he was working for were already sold and he was almost out of a job anyway. Rick had started asking around at church and other places (unbeknownst to me) that he was starting a homebuilding company and he was looking for people to build homes for. One day there was a man named Johnny Guiterrez that said when Rick started the company he would allow Rick to build a house for him. But only if Rick gave him an incredible price since it was his first home. Rick told Johnny that he would get back to him in a few days.

This is the point when Rick called me. He told me the whole story about what had transpired and asked me to pray. Rick knew I heard from God and wanted a confirmation that it was the timing of God to move out. Rick was also going to pray and seek God's face as well. We hung up the phone and I just stared into space thinking, "What is he going to do now?"

I noticed the Bible sitting on the end table and immediately went over and picked it up. David and his wife Linda were out of town so I knew no one would be coming in that day to disturb me. I fell on my knees with the Bible in front of me and started to pray to the Lord. I said, "Dear God, I don't know what Rick is doing now but please give me a scripture to show me that he is on the right track." No sooner did I pray the prayer that I opened the Bible to Jeremiah 29:5 and saw the scripture that read, *"Build ye houses and eat the fruit of them."* It literally leapt off the page at me. I could not believe it! I was so excited that I literally started doing a praise dance down the halls of the office building. I knew God had ordained that we were to build houses and He was going to bless it. Then I heard the spirit of the Lord speak to me and say, "I want you to name the building business "Kingsway Custom Homes" because you will follow the Kings way into the Kingdom of God and the blessings of God will follow you.

I immediately called my husband Rick and told him what the Lord had shown me in the Bible and how God had given me the name "Kingsway Custom Homes." Rick was as excited as I was and he told me to come home as soon as possible because he wanted to show me the subdivision called "Woodgate" in Carrollton, Texas, where we were going to build the first home for Johnny Guiterrez. He had been out looking that day and found a lot acceptable to Johnny to build his first custom home on.

"Now the only thing we are going to have to work on is how to find interim financing to build this house with the bank," Rick said to me. So we bowed our heads and prayed that God would open up the right avenues in financing to make this dream become a reality. No sooner did we finish praying than the phone rang. Our good friend Carey Ruyballid from Dallas was on the other line. Rick told him what had been transpiring with the building business and what God had shown me. Carey had told him that there was a gentleman named Joe Schmidt who was looking to invest his money in a new business. Carey was in the financing business and many times knew people who were looking to invest money in various projects. Carey said he would call Joe the next day and let us know.

The following day Rick met with Carey and they went to meet Joe at a local restaurant to discuss the plans. After a three hour meeting Joe decided he was interested and wanted to go take a look at the lot in the Woodgate subdivision. After Joe, Rick, and Carey looked at the lot, Joe turned to Rick and said, "I'm going to go down to my bank tomorrow and see about getting that interim construction loan. In the meantime, I want my attorney's to draw up a partnership agreement which I will then have your attorney look at before signing." They shook hands and the deal was made.

It had only taken a few days from the time we prayed until the Lord speedily moved in opening up the doors for this new venture. We were so thankful to the Lord and we couldn't stop praising Him. God is such a good and a faithful God. If we put our trust in Him, He will never let us down.

Everything progressed very quickly after this happened. Joe's bank approved the interim construction loan, the partnership papers were drawn up and signed, and before you knew it construction began on our very first custom home. I remember watching the tractors as they started grading the lot. Johnny Guiterrez and his wife Karen were also on hand to watch. We were all so excited just seeing the beginning of a new venture in building. Johnny had complete faith in Rick that he could build him a home even though Rick had never built a home before. If you set your mind to do something you can do it if you believe and have faith, work hard, persevere, and see the thing come to pass.

The next step in building was laying the foundation. In Dallas they don't have basements so they put boards around the area where the house is. Then the plumbing is put in before they pour the foundation. It was a great day to see those cement trucks come and start pouring the slab. The workers had to keep smoothing the cement with rakes as the cement came down the shoot. After about eight hours with about ten guys working, the job was finally done.

It was such a wonderful time in my life during the construction of our first home. Every day Rick went to the construction site and made sure all the workers were there and doing their job. At the end of each day I would come over with Christina and Jeremy to see what had been done.

My brother Jack called one day from Minnesota saying that he was thinking of coming down for a visit. Rick told him he needed some help with the crews and asked Jack if he wanted a job. Jack accepted and before I knew it my brother was living with us and working in the construction business with Rick. It was great having family with us. When you move away from your family and relatives there is always a void in your heart. I missed talking to my mom terribly at times. Even though we spoke on the phone often it wasn't always the same as being able to drive over to the house and see someone face to face.

It seemed to help tremendously to have my brother Jack there, especially since I was pregnant again. He helped out a lot with Christina and Jeremy. He loved wrestling and tickling them during playtime. Jack had a special place in his heart for children. He also loved telling stories to them at bedtime and praying over them before they went to sleep. This is something I did every night before the children went to bed. I went by each of their beds and said a prayer over them with my hands on their forehead. I asked the Lord to bless them and protect them as they sleep.

Before you knew it the house was almost completed. Jack was the one putting the roofing on the house. Jack had started doing some construction work in Minnesota when Rick started the company. It was hard work but the money was good.

In the meantime, there were many lots in the subdivision of Woodgate not yet built upon. There was a parcel available a few lots over from the one Rick was building on that had a for sale sign on it. Joe and Rick called on the sign and this led to another exciting opportunity that literally turned our world upside down.

Chapter 10

BIGGER PLANS

"I need to get over to the new lot right away and meet with Joe," Rick said as he ran out the door. Joe had called and said he had some exciting news about the new lot they were looking at purchasing right down the street from the home they were building for Johnny Guiterrez. The last word I heard Rick say before getting in his car to meet Joe was, "Just pray....this could be something big!"

I started to pray and ask God to bless Rick's meeting and whatever was transpiring at the time. I didn't know what was happening, but things had been coming fast and furiously the last year and I was ready for anything at this point.

I waited all day for Rick to come home. The time seemed to drag by not knowing what had happened or what was in the works. All I could do was pray and believe. God sometimes does that to us. We don't know what is going on, but all we can do is believe God is working everything out for our good.

Rick came home that night and said it looked like there was a big scam being put on by the developer. Everyone in the subdivision was told they could only buy lots through the developer of the subdivision, Herman Johanson. Herman was representing buyers from Europe and was selling the lots for $27,000 each. A European from Herman's home country had initially bought each of the lots. But we found out that Herman had sold them the lots for $21,000 and was pocketing the additional 6,000 per lot.

We only found this out because Herman did not bother to tell Rick and Joe not to buy lots from the other real estate broker in the area, Glenda Whitton. Herman figured that Joe and Rick were just first time builders and would probably quit after this one. He did not realize that Glenda would actively solicit Joe and Rick in order to catch Herman in a trap. Glenda knew the European buyers as well and was only asking $21,000 for her few lots that she had. She was going to go back to Europe with this evidence, expose Herman and oust him from the subdivision.

When Herman found out Joe and Rick were talking to Glenda Whitton, he panicked. He wanted them to immediately come to his office in Plano and try to negotiate. At this meeting he tried to bribe Rick and Joe by saying that he would fly each of them with their wives to Europe for a nice trip. Joe and Rick looked at each other and said that would not be acceptable. He then offered to buy each of them a new Mercedes paid for free and clear. Rick was tempted to say yes at this point and clear up the matter but Joe said no.

Rick's partner, Joe, was an ex-New York police officer and did not like to be pushed around. He felt there was a lot more to be made than what was on the table. As he continued to push and demand more in his New York accent, it finally paid off.

Herman said to them that he was going to let them have control of the subdivision. Instead of the lots being sold for $27,000, they would drop to $24,000. Joe and Rick would make a profit of $3,000 per lot. There were still over 100 lots in the subdivision left to be sold. That makes a nice profit of $300,000. They were not to buy any of Glenda Whitton's lots. Herman knew that Glenda was trying to blackmail him and that is one of the reasons why he dropped the price of his lots to $24,000.

Not only would they make $3,000 per lot, but also they would have the pick of any lot in the subdivision. There were over 20 different builders vying for these different lots. In the usual course of events, they would call up Herman's office and see if the lot was available and then put earnest money down on the lot to hold it. In Herman's new agreement with Joe and Rick they would not have to put earnest money down on the lots. They would have any lot that they wanted. Of course, they would have to buy the lot. But before a lot could be sold Rick and Joe would have to give the approval.

By the time Rick and Joe left the meeting they had everything drafted up on paper. They would then take this agreement over to their attorney's for review before the final signing. When Rick and Joe walked out of Herman's office they just looked at each other and shook their heads in disbelief. By playing hardball and not giving in to Herman's initial bribes they were able to walk out of the meeting with control of the subdivision.

When Rick walked in the door that night it was way after midnight. As he crawled into bed he told me an unbelievable thing happened but he would tell me in the morning. I immediately turned on the light next to the bed and said I had been waiting all day to know what was going on and was not going to wait until the morning.

Rick smiled groggily and proceeded to briefly tell me what had happened. As he told me about everything that had transpired that day I just smiled and thought to myself, "How good the Lord is!"

I told Rick I felt we should pray and thank the Lord for the good things He had done today. We turned off the light and each said a prayer of thanksgiving for the provision and faithfulness.

That night as I went to sleep, I went to bed knowing that things were going to drastically change for the better. If God is for you, who can be against you?

Chapter 11

THE GIVING PRINCIPLE

It was unbelievable how fast things moved after the contract was finalized with Herman and taking control of the subdivision. We could not tell anybody that we actually had taken it over. In the contract we were to be silent partners, but everything would have to be ultimately approved through us before any lot could be sold or bought.

Rick and Joe went and had 75 signs made up that said "Kingsway Custom Homes" and put them on every available lot for sale in the subdivision. Many of the builders now had to call and ask Rick and Joe if they would sell their lot. Builders were driving through the area shaking their heads wondering how two guys who just started building homes a few months prior had the financing to have bought all of these lots.

There were rumors going around that Word of Faith Church was backing Rick. No one could understand how this happened, but we knew who was responsible for this sudden change in status: God. We had started tithing ten percent faithfully to the Lord when we moved down to Dallas. There is a spiritual principal that when you give you shall receive. We didn't give the money to get. We did it out of obedience to God's word. In Malachi 3:8 the scripture reads, *"Will a man rob God? Yet you have robbed me! But you say in what way have we robbed you? In tithes and offerings. You are cursed with a curse, for you have robbed me, even this whole nation. Bring all the tithes in the storehouse, that there may be food in my house and try me now in this, says the Lord of Hosts, if I will not open for you the windows of heaven and pour out for you such blessing that there will not be room to receive it."*

In this scripture God says that those who do not give a tenth of their income to the Lord are cursed with a curse. But if you will faithfully start giving, God will open up the windows of heaven and pour out a blessing that you would not even have room enough to receive. That is what God did in this situation. We had not always been faithful in giving because we had many circumstances where we had to pay many bills. Most everyone at one time or another is in this very circumstance. It's easy to start rationalizing as to why you don't have the money to give ten percent away. But that is where faith comes in and believing in God's Word more than your own natural reasoning.

We repented and asked God to forgive us for our unfaithfulness in giving. At that point we made a vow to God that we would pay God first before we paid our bills or ourselves. That's what the word of God means by your "firstfruits." Right when you get your paycheck or commission check, stop and write a check out to the church or the organization that God has you supporting.

As you are faithful in this you will be amazed at how God orchestrates circumstances where you get blessed. I have a good friend, Cynthia, who works in real estate. She has always been a faithful giver to the Lord and God has always taken care of her even though she has had to go through some trying circumstances the last several years.

She went to her accountant recently since he was preparing her taxes for filing and she was amazed at what her accountant told her. She had made several large donations to the church and one very large donation to a Christian Bible college. When she made the pledge at the service and wrote the check I was there that day. I did not realize that the money she had given away was the money she had been saving for a brand new car. In real estate it is very important to have a nice vehicle to show your clients properties.

Cynthia was not giving to get. She was giving because she felt the Lord tell her to give and that it would be a seed faith gift that would bring forth a large harvest. It's just like a farmer who goes out and plants seeds in the soil. As he waters the fields and patiently waits, eventually the harvest will come in. But if that farmer is lazy and does not go out and plant seeds and work in the field night and day, all the harvest he is going to have is a bunch of weeds.

It's important that once we start giving that we work what we have. We can't be lazy and think that things are just going to supernaturally come our way. There is a scripture in II Thessalonians 3:10 that says, *"If a man does not work then he does not eat."* God never condones laziness. But God will reward giving and faithfulness.

Cynthia's accountant told her that she had given away 30 percent of her income last year. The accountant was amazed and told her that it would be an automatic audit unless she photocopied the back and front of the checks she had given and sent them in with her return. Cynthia did not realize she had been giving as much as she had. She was just faithful to give when the Lord told her and always gave more than she needed to.

Because she was obedient to giving, the Lord blessed Cynthia that year more than in the past five years combined. She recently bought and paid for a very nice vehicle and paid cash for it. She also was able to purchase a very nice four bedroom home and having it remodeled. She had to come up with a very large down payment and God came through for her every time.

So not only did she get her new car that she had wanted, but also a new house. She told me the amazing thing is that she has a sizeable amount in the bank even after all of these recent expenditures.

You can't out give God! Cynthia is a prime example of obedience to God. Cynthia works very hard in real estate. She does not sit back expecting the phone to ring. She is a real go-getter. But she has her life in balance with the Lord. She spends ample time with her young daughter and with the Lord as well.

Many people think God is going to drop everything in their lap. That is not the case! We need to be diligent and faithful in the job or position we have. As we are faithful in the little things the Bible says God will make us ruler over much. And tithing is just another area of obedience to God and his word. As we work and are diligent at the tasks at hand, and then are faithful stewards with our paychecks or commissions that we receive to give 10 percent or more in tithes and offerings; you know that God's word says it won't return void. Just as the rain comes down and waters the earth's crops, so will God come down and open up the windows of heaven with such a down pouring of His blessings that we would not have room enough to receive it.

If you are reading this book and have not been faithful in giving 10 percent to the Lord, just repent. Ask God to forgive you for not being faithful in what He told you to do. And then just start giving 10 percent of what you have made from this point on. You don't need to worry about paying back all of the times you have not tithed up until that point; that would take you years to repay. God is a faithful God and as we are faithful to Him, you just watch and see how

Chapter 12

THE BATTLE LOOMS

Within a short period of time after we had taken over the subdivision from Herman, we sold over 20 homes. We had gone from building one home to controlling a subdivision and had contracts to build 20 homes within a six-month period! It was truly amazing!

Because the interest rates had drastically dropped from 18 percent to around 12 percent, everyone who had wanted to buy a home was coming out of the woodwork. As we controlled the best lots in the subdivision and were able to quote a lower price than the other builders in the area, many people were checking out "Kingsway Custom Homes."

The problems we now faced were that we were growing so large and so quickly that we were not able to get interim financing from the banks on all of the homes we had contracts on. We were getting checks from Herman on the overage on the lots every month. Sometimes the checks were in the six-figure range.

We were taking those checks and starting construction on the homes without getting financing from the banks; we were the bank! We didn't have enough money to fund all of these homes that we were building. So Rick's partner, Joe, was visiting different banks trying to get bank financing. When you're a new kid on the block, sometimes this can take a while.

Well, things were going along very nicely up until this point. We had built four homes and were working on another three. We had sold another 13 homes and those buyers were getting their plans drawn and we were grading the lots to start building on. We were just waiting for the banks to give us more money for new loan constructions.

In the meantime, Rick and I were having the times of our lives. Every day Rick would go to the job sites and watch development on the new houses going up. He was working with the crews in getting the houses finished and working with the buyers in getting their new plans drawn up. Rick truly enjoyed his job and was excited about all of the money he knew they were making.

Out of the blue we decided to take a trip over to England. We decided we wanted to buy a vintage Rolls Royce to take the people around to all of the homes in the area. We were also planning on building a few model homes, and since our name was "Kingsway Custom Homes" we thought a vintage Rolls Royce would only add to the ambiance of what we were trying to accomplish.

I was seven months pregnant with my third child at the time. The doctor said that it was okay to travel since I had not experienced any difficulties with my first two children. I remember getting on the jet going over to England. It was a huge jet with more seats than I had ever seen before on a commercial airline. We were flying coach at this point. The airplane was not very full so we were able to stretch out over a few of the seats and make our bed for the night.

They served us a wonderful meal and then we settled down for an in-flight movie. After the movie I tried to get some sleep. It was going to be an eight-hour flight over to England and I had heard about jet lag. Being seven months pregnant on a flight is not very conducive to sleeping, especially in a crunched up position in coach trying to stretch out over three seats, but I didn't care! I was excited about going over to England and being in Europe. I had never been there and I couldn't wait to see it!

Finally, I remember the flight attendant saying we only had around thirty minutes before we were going to land. I looked out the window and saw the ocean beneath us, and, what must have been England, a few miles in the distance. The sun had just risen and it was a bright beautiful day! I was so excited! It was the first time that I had been overseas and I couldn't wait to set my foot on foreign soil.

The plane landed and we all gathered our belongings and started to exit the plane. We quickly got our bags and then had to wait and go through customs. It was a new experience for me and it seemed like the line was very long. But it went quickly and before I knew it we were flagging down a taxi to take us to our hotel.

Everything looked so old and everybody was driving on the wrong side of the road! It seemed like I was on a different planet. It was so great feeling that we were halfway around the world in another country. I almost had to pinch myself to make sure I wasn't dreaming. The taxi dropped us off in front of the hotel and we quickly brought our bags in.

What they tell you about jet lag is really true. Your body clock is trying to tell you that it is night but it is really only morning. We immediately tried to get some sleep but tossed and turned and were not able to get any decent sound sleep. We finally got up and started to make our way around some of the sites in England.

We went on a tour where we saw all of the historical sites in London. I walked into one bookstore and I asked if they had any Bibles. I wanted to buy another Bible because I only had my New Testament with me. There was a large section on the occult. I tried to find the Christian section but was having a hard time finding it. When I asked the sales clerk he gave me a strange look as if I was from another planet. They didn't carry any Bibles and didn't have any Christian literature either.

That incident really spoke to me about how dark other countries are spiritually. In America we are blessed to have many Christian bookstores and Christian influences, not only on radio but television as well. It made me pray for the nation of England that God would send a spiritual awakening to that country.

The main reason we had come over to England was to look for a vintage Rolls Royce, which we could ship back to America. We started looking the next day after we had recuperated and done some sightseeing. We went to several Rolls Royce dealers. We did not want a new one (that would have cost too much money), but we wanted a Rolls Royce that was at least twenty years old and in mint condition - a classic.

We finally found the perfect car. When we walked into this particular dealership, I spotted it immediately. It was beautiful! It was forest green with a beige vinyl top and tan interior. It was in mint condition and ran like a charm. When we turned the engine over it just purred. After negotiating with the salesmen for some time we finally bought the car. We ended up getting an incredible price on it. At that time the pound was greatly devalued compared to what the dollar was worth so our American money was worth three times as much as normal.

We walked out of the dealership ecstatic that we had purchased a classic Rolls Royce. We were going to have the money wired over from our bank in America by the end of the week and then the car would be shipped over within the next few weeks. We would have it by the time our first model home was built.

I was just so excited about everything God had been doing in our lives. We were now building custom homes, had control of a large subdivision, were making a sizeable profit on the lots, and were in England buying a Rolls Royce! It's amazing what a few months time can bring.

The next few days we enjoyed ourselves and went out to eat in some wonderful restaurants. We did some more sightseeing and shopping as well. Since I was seven months pregnant with two small children at home I knew that when I got back things were going to be very chaotic and I should savor this trip.

Before I knew it the time had come to go back to the United States. We were only there for a short five days. But our mission was accomplished and we had found the car we had come to find. As we were packing up our things, I started to reflect on what a special time this had been for Rick and I. God was so good to us and I couldn't wait to see what life had to offer us next. I did not realize at this time that before long we were going to be in for one of the biggest battles of our lives.

On the plane back home I was anxious to get back to Christina and Jeremy. This had been our first extended trip so far away from our children, and i was homesick for them. We had called them a few times when we were out of town. They were staying with a wonderful girlfriend of mine and her family that we knew from the church.

We arrived in Dallas ten hours after we initially took off. It took two hours longer to fly back. It seemed like forever! When we finally stepped off of the plane we got our baggage and went to our car to pick up the children. I was so excited to see them!

When I saw their cute faces I almost cried! They ran up to us and hugged us as if they would never let us go. I gave my friend, Carolyn, a hug and thanked her and Ron for taking such good care of them.

Things seemed so normal and everything was going along so well. Little did I realize that within a week things were going to start falling apart. Rick went back to checking on the jobs and doing his things with building all of the homes. We had purchased the Rolls Royce and it was going to be shipped within the week and should go through customs by the end of the month. We were having a model home built and were going to take various clients around to all of the homes in the subdivision with the Rolls Royce. It was part of the Kingsway Custom Homes charm.

We were in the process of building ten homes at the time that things started to fall apart. Rick's partner, Joe, had basically been taking the proceeds from the monies made on the sales of the lots in the subdivision to start building other homes for Kingsway. They were in committee at various banks to get loans for their new projects, but they were growing so fast and Joe didn't want to wait for approval from the bank. He thought that he could fund some of the building of the homes from the proceeds of the lot sales in the meantime.

Since they had control of the subdivision and the lots, Joe figured they didn't need to close on the lots before they started building on them. Eventually, they would close and get everything finalized so that it would be in Kingsway Custom Homes' name before the deed was transferred over to the new owner of the home they were building.

Joe was basically responsible for the financing and my husband Rick for the building. Rick was not aware of everything that had been going on up to that point with the financial structure. Joe just made him think that everything was running smoothly and the committees were approving their loans for them to build more homes.

One day Rick was at one of the custom homes they were building for a couple moving down from Chicago. The original developer, Herman, came driving up in his Mercedes and started taking pictures of the house that was almost finished being built. Rick asked him why he was taking pictures and Herman answered that the Belgium who originally bought that lot as an investment would sure like to see that a house was now built on it. Rick just looked at Herman with a blank stare not really understanding what he was talking about. Rick told Herman he would get a hold of Joe immediately and they would meet later that afternoon at his office. Herman drove off leaving Rick staring at the back of his Mercedes in awe.

What Rick soon found out when he talked to Joe was incredible. Since they had sold so many homes in such a short period of time, they were not able to get the interim financing from the banks on all of these homes for the construction loan in time. Some of these people had already sold their homes and needed the houses to be started promptly. All of these banks had to go through committees when making their decision if they were going to loan Kingsway money. The original bank that gave them the money for their first home was a very small bank and was not able to loan them all the money they needed. Joe in turn had to seek out other banks that were skeptical of giving this money to a company that had only been around for less than a year. To go from building one home was one thing, but to ask for money for 25 homes put them in another ballpark.

Joe told Rick that he took the money from the sale of the lots in the subdivision and started using it to build the homes. Herman was giving them a check every two weeks for the difference in the price of the lots. They were making $3,000 per lot. They had over 200 lots in the subdivision still left to sell. What had happened in this instance is that the lot was never closed upon. Joe had let Rick start building on the lot without closing it, so in essence when Herman made that statement he was right. They didn't own it technically and in order to close the lot they were building upon Herman had to sign off as the developer and the power of attorney for the Belgium investor.

Rick and Joe were now in a real bind. The couple who purchased the home were being relocated from Chicago and their moving truck was on its way and would be there the next day. Herman knew that he had them in a real bind and used this as a negotiating tool to get back what he had initially been forced to give over to them.

I remember getting the call on the phone from Rick telling me to pray. He briefly went over what had happened and said they had to meet that afternoon at Herman's office. I hung up the phone and immediately started to intercede in the Spirit. It seemed so unbelievable that everything was going so great and now for this to happen!

As Joe and Rick sat in Herman's office there was a look of despair on their faces. Rick was upset that Joe had not told him about the interim financing problems. It was too late at this point because they were already in trouble and Herman knew it. When Herman walked into the room with a smug look on his face they both knew they were in trouble. All Rick could do was silently pray God would lead them and give them an answer to the solution.

Herman sat down in his chair and just looked at them with a wicked gleam in his eye. "So you thought you could play with me and not get burned?" was the first statement out of his mouth. "What are we going to do about this little situation, boys? You have built a house on a lot that my investor still owns?" Herman said coolly.

Rick and Joe sat there feeling like a mouse trapped by a cat in a corner and the cat was just toying with the prey. Joe spoke up and said the bank was going to be funding the money for the other homes at the end of the week and everything would be fine. Herman just laughed and said, "But what about this home? You have not closed on the lot."

There was a long silence in the room and finally Herman said, "I want control back of the subdivision. I will sign over that lot to you and you will be able to close it. But all of the lots now will once again be under my control. He then spelled out all the other conditions he wanted them to do in order for them to finish the existing homes in the subdivision. By the time the meeting was finished Rick and Joe felt utterly defeated.

They immediately went over to one of the most prestigious firms in Dallas and retained the services of a top lawyer. The attorney in turn then put a lis pendence on the lots in the subdivision. A lis pendence is an order that clouds the title so that no lots can be bought or sold. They were in for a big fight with Herman and they both knew it, but they didn't want to give up so easily and so they decided to fight. The retainer that they had to give the law firm was $25,000.

When Rick walked in the door and told me everything that had transpired that afternoon I was in shock. It's amazing what a difference a day can make. That is why we always need to be ready for anything. As we pray daily and put the armor of God on we can withstand the wiles or the tactics of the enemy.

Now in this situation it was important to realize that Joe had made an error in judgment in building on this lot before closing on. Many times we start presuming things and get into trouble. The Bible says, *"Pride comes before a fall"* (Proverbs 16:18). Pride comes before a fall because success many times will blind you to the truth. When you are going through challenging situations in your life you will pray and fast and do whatever it takes to get close to God. But many times when you are going through a success and everything seems rosy, that is the time many people don't seek God the way they normally do in a crisis situation.

They get lazy and start thinking they are the reason for the success. The Bible says all good things come from God. The Bible says the power to get wealth comes from God as well. So when we are going through times of financial blessing we need to realize that ultimately the blessing comes from God. Sure you might have been diligent in working hard to get to where you are now, but God gave you the mind, your body, your intellect and abilities. God opens up many doors for us and it is up to us to walk through those doors with the talents and abilities He has given us.

After the money had been given to the attorneys the fight was on! Every day it seemed like we were on pins and needles as to what the next step in the saga was going to be. Rick and I were praying for God's wisdom and direction. Because Rick was in charge of overseeing the building of all of the homes they had recently sold in the subdivision, when this event happened it caused everything to come to a standstill. It was a major nightmare because we had several homes that were in the process of being built and the construction on these homes came to an abrupt halt. We had to explain to the people whose houses we had been building about what had transpired and that we were in the midst of litigation.

Many of these people said if it didn't come to an end shortly they were going to file suit against us. Some of them had sold their homes and only had a certain number of days before escrow was going to be closed and they had to be out of their existing home and into their newly constructed home. At times I would throw my hands up in the air in utter frustration not knowing what to do next.

There is a scripture in Psalms 61:2 when David prayed to the Lord: *"When my heart is overwhelmed, please lead me to the Rock that is higher than I."* Our hearts were overwhelmed, but as we sought God He gave us refuge from the storm. I tended to read the Psalms during this time of my life and they became very special to me. The Psalms that spoke to me most during this time was Psalms 37. In verse 4 the passage says to *"Delight yourself in the Lord and He will give you the desires of your heart."* This Psalm then goes on to say not to fret when it looks like evildoers are prospering. It says the meek shall inherit the earth and delight themselves in the abundance of peace.

As I meditated on these scriptures, a peace I had never known before seemed to wash over my soul. There is something so powerful about the Word of God. It will give strength to you in times of trouble. Throughout history when men and women have been in trouble they have gone to the scriptures and God has supernaturally sustained them.

I'm recalling the story of Corrie Ten Boom and how God miraculously spared her during the Nazi concentration camps during World War II. Her father had been a watchmaker in Holland and when it was required by Jews to wear the yellow star signifying that they were Jews, it was too much for Mr. Ten Boom. He started harboring these Jewish families in their home and made secret passageways in the walls where they could hide out. Many of these Jewish families were daily being sent away to camps where nobody seemed to know what was happening to them. Little did people know they were being sent away to have their lives extinguished like smoke.

It was a very challenging time and they had to be very careful so they would not get caught harboring these Jewish families or they too would be sent away. They had gotten away with it for a number of months until finally the secret police came and did a raid on their home during the middle of the night without notice. Immediately, not only the Jewish people taken away but also Corrie Ten Boom and her father and other family members.

It was a sad day and there were many tears shed. But they were strong and had been brought up with dignity and respect. They did not plead to the Nazi soldiers to let them go, but willingly went with their captors. They were separated from their precious father who had risked all of their lives to save these Jewish families from extinction. As they saw their father being led away, Corrie did not realize that would be the last time she would see her father alive. What a price he had paid for his beliefs and the cause of Christ!

Eventually, Corrie Ten Boom was released from prison and was able to spread the gospel of the Kingdom and the story of her family's captivity around the world. But her sister and father never made it out of the concentration camp. They died while they were incarcerated. It was a very sad time for Corrie reflecting back on the past. She missed her family tremendously and wanted so much to be able to share the good times they once had in their home in Holland. But it was worth the price they paid because they knew they were doing the will of God by helping the Jewish families.

Sometimes we will also pay a price for our beliefs and ideals. Sometimes we are just going about our normal business when it seems like a catastrophe comes. Another incident of this occurrence is the biblical story of Joseph. God gave Joseph a dream that one day he was going to rule over his brothers. He didn't understand the entire dream but made the mistake of telling his brothers what he saw in the dream. His brothers were very envious and were always saying mean and taunting words to Joseph. One day his father Jacob told Joseph to go down to Shecum where his brothers were tending the sheep to see how they were doing. Joseph was just being obedient to his father when he went. As he was walking down the road his brothers spotted him and conspired amongst themselves. They were jealous of Joseph and wanted to kill him.

They were making plans on how they could do this when the oldest brother, Rueben, said to just put him in a pit, later thinking he would come back and rescue Joseph. Joseph was put in the pit and the oldest brother had to go somewhere for a while to attend to other things. While Rueben was gone the brothers saw some traders on their camels and decided to sell Joseph into slavery instead of leaving him in the pit. They sold him for 20 shekels of silver (even less than the going rate for a slave at that time).

When Rueben came back and noticed that Joseph was no longer in the pit, he tore his clothes in two pieces in total agony. I'm sure he did not know what happened to Joseph, but that his brothers had devised another plan.

Joseph was merely being obedient to his father when his brothers did this dastardly deed to him. How many of you reading this book were just going about your normal, everyday life when circumstances took a dangerous twist for the worse? God is able to get us out of the problem and many times even allows us to go into the trial to get us to a place where He has called us to be. Remember, God led Joseph into Egypt. Also, remember that Jesus was led into the wilderness to be tempted by the devil. God did not tempt Jesus in the wilderness but the Bible says that the Spirit, "led Jesus into the wilderness."

Sometimes it seems like we are in that wilderness experience and we can't understand what God is up to. I'm sure Joseph did not realize God was at work in his life to ultimately save his family from perishing in the years ahead by leading him into the wilderness. It must have been hard to be sold into slavery by your own brothers. I'm sure Joseph pleaded with them to change their minds. He probably even thought they were joking around at first. But alas, it was only too real and now he was on his was into Egypt.

Maybe some of you feel that you have been sold out by those closest to you. Maybe you feel like Jesus in the garden of Gethsemane when he cried to His Father, "My God, My God why have you forsaken me?" God said He would never leave us nor forsake us..

We have to hold onto God's promises that He will come through for us; that there is a purpose to what we are going through. The scripture says "All things work together for good to those who love God and are called according to His purpose." Notice that it says "His purpose" and not "Our purpose"? Sometimes we think that what we want to do, God will just automatically sanction and bless. We need to wait upon the Lord until we see what "His purpose" is for our lives and not just what our desire is.

With everything going on, Rick and I felt like Joseph in the wilderness during this portion of our lives. All we could do was fast and pray. There were days I didn't know how I got through them. I just woke up and kept my mind on the scriptures. The word of God says "That I will keep your mind in perfect peace if your mind is stayed on me."

The more I kept my focus on God and His word, then the more my mind stayed in peace and tranquility. I learned I was able to have peace even though I was in the midst of a storm. It was really a beautiful place to be in. To know that no matter what, God had a plan for my life and as I trusted in the Lord with all of my heart and did not lean to my own understanding, that God would direct all of my footsteps.

God wants to get you to that place today. Are you in a place of turmoil where you wonder how you are ever going to get out of the situation that you are in? If that is where you are today, I want you to put this book aside right now and cast your burdens upon the Lord. In Psalms 55:22 it says to *"Cast your burdens upon the Lord and He will sustain you."* God will give you a peace in the midst of the storm. As you pray and give it to God, He will give you the peace you need until the storm settles down or subsides. Things won't always be this way. God will make a way of escape so you can bear it. Pray this prayer right now, "Dear God, I'm in a situation that I don't understand. Please give me peace during this time and give me the ability to see this through and not to give up in defeat. I know I'm more than a conqueror in Jesus Christ, so please help me to keep my eyes stayed on Jesus and not give into discouragement until the answer comes. Thank you Lord. Amen."

Chapter 13

THE NEW HOME

As we cast our burdens upon the Lord, Rick and I saw a change coming. We were able to sell our portion of the business to Joe and got a settlement. It wasn't a large sum of money, but enough to get us going to start our own custom home company. We prayed about what to call it and decided to name it "Crouley Custom Homes." God had given us the name "Kingsway Custom Homes" initially, but now we could not use the name because it was tied up in litigation.

We bought a couple lots in Plano, Texas and started building a model home. God was good to us and within the first six months of our new company, we had already sold over ten homes. God will give back to you seven-fold what the devil tried to steal from you. Remember, if you are in the midst of a legal or financial battle, just stand your ground, wait for the Lord to speak to you and give you His plan, and then follow it through to the letter until you see the plan unfold. Sometimes God will tell you to stand and fight, but other times he will tell you to get out and do something else. That is what God told us to do and we were seeing fruit from that decision.

We could have gotten bitter. There was a lot of money at stake in the matter. We did not want to have to wait for months or even years through the trials of a lawsuit. We felt the Lord say to get out and get going in His plan He had for us. When you do get out don't look back. Remember, God is able to do exceedingly abundantly above that which we could ask or even think. It's up to you though; you can get bitter or better. We chose to get better. We forgave our enemies and we went on.

I had wanted to build our home for a long time now. Being married to a builder many times you saw other people get their homes built but you had to wait because the homes being built were always being sold to someone else for a profit. When push came to shove my husband would take the profit every time. I finally told Rick that we really needed to start working on our home and he agreed.

We started looking for lots and found a perfect one in a subdivision in Garland, Texas. It was so perfect because it had over 40 large oak trees on it. Now if any of you know anything about Dallas you will know that a lot with 40 large oak trees is a very good lot. It reminded me of the trees in Minnesota. Dallas didn't have many trees of this type. It was so beautiful and the whole street had these types of trees on it. The name of the street was called "Woods Lane." I loved it and we put down some money on the lot and started looking for houses we wanted to have drawn that would fit on the lot and would be to our specifications. I found a home I absolutely loved the exterior of and had our architect come by to look at it. We sat down with him and he started working on the plans so we could start going into the building stage of our home.

I was finally going to get the dream house I had been waiting for! The day they broke ground on the lot was very exciting! They had to take down a few of the trees in order to put the house in the location. The bulldozers and other workmen preparing the land were there. We said a prayer over the land and dedicated it to the Lord. From that point on it went very quickly. The foundation of the house was poured and then we saw the framers come and put up the structure. Before we knew it we were starting to work on the inside. I had picked out all of the wallpaper and fixtures for the house. It was so fun to be able to go and pick out every little detail even down to the doorknobs.

One day I was in the kitchen and giving the wallpaper person some instructions as to where I wanted the border to go when a real estate agent walked through the house with a couple. I heard them oohing and aahing at how they had looked for two weeks for a home and this was the one they wanted. My heart about went through my chest when I heard this. I couldn't believe my ears! What was going on?! My husband came in at that point and said he had gotten a call from a real estate agent and they happened to see our "Crouley Custom Home" sign outside. They walked through the house since it was not locked up and was still under construction. They did not realize it was for us and thought it was a speculation home. Once they saw it they wanted to put an offer in and made a proposal to my husband. The offer was so good that Rick felt he could not refuse it. We were going to make over six figures just from the sale of this home.

As Rick walked up to me outside the home and the other people were still looking at our home with the real estate agent, I thought I was going to start crying. I didn't know why Rick wanted to sell the home that I had been longing for and finally now was able to get. Rick put his arms around me and said, "Honey, this is your home. If you don't want to sell it we don't have to, but the money is very good and we can always build you another home. If we sell this home I will give you enough money from the sale of the home to start producing your album that you have been wanting for so long."

I couldn't believe that I was hearing this from my husband! Have you ever been in a place where you have believed God for something. Now that it was within my grasp I saw that it was slowly dissolving in front of me. That's where I was in this situation. I had two choices that I could make at this point. I could either get bitter or I could move on and look forward to start working on an album I had also been wanting for so long.

God sometimes puts us in those positions. We have been praying and believing Him for something for a long time. We finally get within reach of it only to have to put it on the altar. There is a story similar to this in the Old Testament. Abraham and Sarah were given a promise that they were going to have a son. They had been asking and believing for a long time. When the promise didn't come when they expected, they started to give up.

Abraham and Sarah actually started to stagger at the promises of God so much that Sarah started to laugh. She was getting very old and she felt like it was impossible. But nothing is impossible with God. God actually did come through for them and they had a child and they named him Isaac. Isaac means laughter! It brought such joy to them to see that God actually brought forth his promise even though Sarah had grown beyond her childbearing years.

How many of you long for something and it seems like it is too late? That is where Sarah was. She was old and she thought it was impossible to produce a child at that late stage. But God is a God of the impossible. He brought forth the promised child not in our time schedule but in His.

As Isaac started to grow, I'm sure Abraham and Sarah loved him with all their heart. Isaac was the apple of their eye! There was one point when Abraham actually took Isaac on a journey with him in the wilderness. It was at this point that God had told Abraham to put Isaac on the altar. Abraham could not believe God was asking him to put the promised son on the altar. He had been waiting so long for this child!

Why was God doing this to him at this time in his life? As he laid his son Isaac down on the altar, I'm sure it must have been hard. Isaac's eyes were looking into his dad's and asking him what was going on. He trusted his father after growing up these last few years. He had seen that his father had always been honest and truthful with him. Now he was lying there and his dad had a knife in his hand.

As Abraham started to raise the knife to kill his own son after being instructed by God to do so, God sent an angel of the Lord to stop him. God had put Abraham through a test and he passed it. So Abraham found a ram in the thicket and sacrificed that to the Lord instead. And after Abraham had sacrificed the ram God spoke to him. In Genesis 22:17, God speaks this to Abraham: *"Blessing I will bless you and multiplying I will multiply your descendants as the stars of the heaven and as the sand which is on the seashore and your descendants shall possess the gate of their enemies. In your seed all the nations of the earth shall be blessed, because you have obeyed my voice."*

What a promise from the Lord! The key to the blessing is obedience. What is it that God has asked you to do that you have not been doing? Many times God speaks to us and tells us to do something and we don't listen. As we obey God, we will see the blessings come. God does not want to withhold any good thing from you. But he said in Matthew 6:33, *"To seek first the Kingdom of God and His righteousness and all of these things would be added unto you."*

I know it is not always easy, but if you follow God's word and are faithful to what He has called you to do, God will make a way for you. Pray with me right now, "Dear Father, thank you for your promises. Help me to become obedient to the things that You have called me to do. I lay on the altar any hindrance that may stand in my way. I ask You for the gift of faith to believe what You have told me. Thank you for blessing me and my family. Amen."

Chapter 14

MY FIRST RECORDING ADVENTURE

After we sold the house to the couple from Nashville, God began to open doors for my ministry. WIth the proceeds from the sale of the home, I started on my hearts desire to produce an album. I had met a young man from Word of Faith named Steve Bowers, who was a songwriter and a very anointed worship leader as well. He told me he would write some of the songs for me and knew a talented producer.

Steve set up a meeting with the producer for the following week. I remember the day Tim Miner first knocked on our door. He came walking in our house with his wife and a few friends. I remember looking at him and thinking that he was very young. He had long hair pulled back into a ponytail. He was dressed very casual with jeans and a white shirt. His wife was a very beautiful girl named Cindy. I later learned that her family was a very famous Christian music group called "The Cruse Family." They all sat down in our living room and I proceeded to tell them about the album I wanted to record.

Tim then began to tell us how God had told him to move to Dallas and he was looking at opening up a recording studio. He needed to buy equipment for the studio and told us that if we invested in his studio he would produce the album for me and also help in writing the songs.

After we had discussed the many aspects of this project and the meeting was almost over, I wanted to conclude the meeting with prayer. We all held hands together and prayed that God would give us the wisdom to move ahead with this project if it was of Him. We lifted up our voices in praise to God and thanked Him for the marvelous things He was about to do. After we prayed we felt such a peace that God was about to do something awesome!

As we watched them get in their cars I felt such a peace of God! I knew my prayers for an album were about ready to come into effect. How many of you reading this book have been praying and believing God for your dreams but have yet to see them happen?

I believe we are in the time of *"suddenlies"* when God is going to show up on the scene and the answer is going to come unexpectedly or suddenly.

Disciples and believers were in the upper room and praying as the Lord had instructed them to do before His resurrection. Jesus had already ascended to heaven, but He had appeared to them several times before and instructed them on several things. One of Jesus' instructions was for them to wait in one accord and pray until they would become endued with power from on high.

In Acts 2:1 it reads, *"When the day of Pentecost came, they were all together in one place. Suddenly, a sound like the blowing of a violent wind came from heaven and filled the whole house where they were sitting."*

Do you notice the word "suddenly"? As they were all sitting there in one spirit and in one accord as Jesus had instructed them to do, suddenly the Holy Spirit came into the room and they were all filled with the Holy Spirit. Great power was imparted unto them as Jesus had spoken.

How many of you have had God tell you to do something but have not been obedient to what He originally said? Many times we blame God or others for the answers not coming but it is actually our own lack of obedience which hinders the blessings or promise.

When Jesus told them to go and pray in one accord and wait for the Holy Spirit to come.s I'm sure they wondered what the Holy Spirit was. They had never experienced the Holy Spirit for themselves since the Holy Spirit had not been released yet. Sometimes God will speak something to us, totally foreign to our natural understanding, but as we are obedient to God's call we will experience God's blessing and provision.

The days of suddenlies are indeed upon us. Suddenly you are going to see that son or daughter you have been praying for years come into the Kingdom of God. Suddenly you are going to see that failing business turn around. Suddenly you are going to see your marriage restored and your husband saved after years of standing in faith believing. God wants to bring restoration back to the church in all areas of our lives. He wants to restore families, finances, and favor. But we need to be obedient to what He has called us to do. We need to go back and do the first works He has called us to do in order to get new instructions.

Just believe God today with me that these suddenlies are going to come into your household. Just pray with me today if there has been a hindrance in your life to the blessings that you have believed God for years. "Dear Father, please restore to me the years that the locusts have eaten in my life. Please open up the windows of heaven and pour out a blessing that I don't even have room enough to receive. Bring forth favor on my family and finances for such a time as this you have called me to the Kingdom. Please forgive me for any areas of unbelief or disobedience in not obeying your voice. Restore to me the joy of my salvation. Thank you for your promises and I believe today the answer is at the door and is suddenly going to appear. Thank you Jesus."

After meeting with Tim Miner and his group I didn't immediately rush into any decision about the album. Everything looked good from the natural point of view, but I needed to pray with my husband and wait upon the Lord to get the green light from God.

That whole week I prayed and fasted and sought an answer from the Lord. The answer came in an unexpected way than I had initially thought. We received a call from a friend of mine that I had known from church saying they had some studio equipment that had been bought for a new Christian group. They had spent a lot of money for a drum machine, midi-bass machine, and other equipment that was no longer useful to them since the band was breaking up. It was all brand new equipment and they said we could purchase it for half of what it originally cost. My friend had said when he was praying that my name came to his mind to call and ask if I wanted this equipment. He didn't even know I had just met with Tim Miner about the recording studio. My friend didn't know but the Holy Spirit did and made the connection.

I told my friend I would have to talk to my husband and then get back to him. When I told Rick about it he immediately said that this was an answer to prayer. The studio equipment Tim Miner needed was the same equipment now being offered to us. Through a series of negotiations we were able to buy the recording equipment from the group and arrange a contract with Tim Miner to produce a ten-song album. It was truly an answer to not only my prayers, but to Tim Miners as well.

A few short weeks after we had first met we were now in the midst of seeing a new recording facility open up. At first it started in an office building, but God opened up a door for Tim to eventually move into a brand new warehouse.

Through the equipment we gave him, as well as another investor in renovating the warehouse into a state-of-the-art recording studio, we saw "Knight Light Studio" open up.

I was the first artist Tim was producing. We started working on getting the songs together I would record. That was a tedious and strenuous process to get the right songs for my voice. I write songs, but had not done so for a few years. We did not have the time to spend in writing so Tim and several other talented writers who worked for him started giving me new material to listen to.

It was an exciting but challenging time. Sometimes we pray for something so long and when it finally comes into reality it can become a little overwhelming. I had never recorded an album before. I had recorded some demo tapes in a studio before so I was not totally in the dark on the process. But I was working with such talented and competent people that the devil started to make me feel inadequate and a spirit of fear tried to attack me. I started getting attacked mentally that I was not a good singer. Sometimes I thought I should not be doing this album and just quit and walk away. I knew that these were not my thoughts, but nonetheless I still experienced these nagging thoughts in the back of my mind. There were two things I could do. I could quit and walk away or I could forge ahead and ask God for the grace and the strength to complete the task. God never opens up a door that He knows we don't have the ability to go through. Many times we have to lean on Him for wisdom and strength. But through Christ we can do all things because He will strengthen us.

At the time we were going to a great church in Rockwall, Texas, called "Church on the Rock." Larry Lea was the Pastor of the church and I was involved with the singing group there called "Church on the Rock" singers. Bob and Debbie Mason were the worship leaders and were very good friends and a wonderful prayer support. Many of my friends were in the singing group and they supported me in prayer during this time. It was through the prayers of many strong intercessors that I was able to move ahead to the destiny God had called me to.

We finally compiled all of the ten songs we wanted for my album. I remember the day I was to start recording the first song. I was nervous but I had a peace from the Lord that everything was under control and would work out splendidly. Michelle Letkeman, one of my good friends and intercessor, came with me and interceded for me as I sang. The first day at the studio went fabulous! I had a wonderful time and I sensed the spirit of the Lord with me in such a powerful way!

I continued on recording for the next several weeks. There were days I did not want to go and do this anymore. It challenged me beyond anything I have ever experienced before. There were a few songs on the album that were very challenging to sing. One in particular had a four-octave range. It seems like I heard every note that was not sung correctly magnified ten times. Sometimes I felt like climbing under a rock. Tim Miner was working with some of the most talented people in the Christian recording industry and the devil was trying to intimidate me by comparing myself to these other artists.

How many times has this happened in your life where the enemy tries to make you to compare yourself to others? Maybe God has told you to start a business and things are not going as smoothly as you had anticipated. Some of you may be trying to finish your degree only to have stumbled across some major roadblocks on your journey. And maybe you're a working mother who is struggling to find the balance between motherhood and your career. It is easy during times like this to start comparing yourself to others who seem to just sail through their circumstances. But typically, this is not the case. It may look like they are gliding through their journeys when in essence they have as many challenges and concerns as you do.

It is during these times we need to stay focused and not lose sight of our goal in mind. We need to stay on course and know we will reap if we don't quit. So often we are on the verge of success to quit right before the breakthrough. If you are going through some challenges right now in your life I want you to take a minute to pray and give your burdens over to the Lord. "Cast all your burdens upon the Lord for He cares for you." Cast these cares and thoughts on God and He will remove these burdens and give you peace." Pray with me, "Dear Heavenly Father, I am in a situation where I am over-whelmed with my circumstances (name what you are going through). I release this to you and ask you to give me strength to continue on with the purposes and plans you have for my life. Give me the grace to see every obstacle as only a stepping-stone to something greater in my life. Thank you, Lord. Amen."

As you prayed that prayer with me in faith, God answered you and will give you the strength and grace you need to ful-fill God's purposes for you on this earth. As I prayed that prayer as I was going through the final stages of completing the album, I received such strength and purpose to complete the task. The Holy Spirit gave me a second wind that allowed me to sail past those doubts and discouraging thoughts.

I remember the final day of recording the album. We laid down the last vocal track and I looked at one of the produc-ers, Don, and we both had this look of victory on our faces. It was such a moment of victory and accomplishment that I for-got about all of the pain I had gone through at times to com-plete it.

It was similar to when I first found out I was pregnant with Christina. I was ecstatic that I was pregnant and couldn't wait to hold her in my arms and peer into her eyes. I didn't realize all the months of morning sickness and pain I would have to go through to get to that moment. But when I finally gave birth to her and she was placed in my arms, all the pain just vanished away. Now all that I saw was the gift.

That is the way God wants us to look at the things He places in our paths. There are going to be many times that you are going to want to quit, because quite honestly, it is just plain hard work. But if you persevere and forge ahead you will reap the benefits and the final outcome.

I had persevered through all my feelings of self-doubt and despair. There were good days in making the album; not all were hard. Many times we are the hardest on ourselves. That was the case with me. I was harder on myself than those around me who were producing the album. I had such high expectations and compared myself to others around me as well. This is a dangerous thing to do. You need to keep your eyes on the road ahead. If you're driving up a winding steep mountain road you need to keep your eyes on the road, not the valley below. If you look off the sides you will be more likely to drive off the cliff. Just don't panic; follow the road and you will surely reach the destination without any calamity or mishap.

My album was finally finished and we had a big celebration that night. I had invited several friends over and we had a wonderful barbecue in the backyard. They had shared in my victory because they had prayed me through some of the rough spots. Now I was ready for the other part of the adventure in getting the album mastered and packaged. I could hardly wait to get started!

Chapter 15

A SUDDEN CHANGE OF PLANS

After completing the album the family vacationed for a few weeks at Lake Texoma. I had a wonderful week of celebrating with the kids and watching them swim in the lake. I'm so glad I had that time of recuperating, especially for what lay ahead on the journey.

We got back from our vacation and things were going along fairly smoothly. Rick had several homes he was building and we moved into a home that we had built for ourselves. It was a beautiful brick home with four bedrooms and a lovely pool. I finally thought that things were starting to look up and had never felt better in my life, but there were a few ripples that started to come our way.

The economy in Texas had started to unravel. The Texas economy was tied into the price of oil. The prices of oil per barrel had started to plunge and this produced a chain reaction effect on banks and the economy. Banks were starting to close all over the state. In a matter of a few months our economy had definitely started taking a nosedive. We did not realize this because all of our homes were pre-sold and we were rolling along very smoothly.

We had been hearing for some time from other builders and people in the construction business that we were working with that they had been seeing it slow down quite considerably. We had started looking at some more lots to purchase to expand our building business and taking it to the next level. Rick had an appointment one afternoon with the banker to discuss more interim financing for this project. He went to the meeting as normal and I went about doing some housecleaning and getting the kids ready to take out for a walk.

After we came back from our walk in the park, I noticed Rick's car was home earlier than I had anticipated. We walked in the house and I noticed the bedroom door was shut. This was highly unusual, as normally Rick would be working in the library where his office was. I went into the bedroom and noticed that Rick was lying down on the bed. I asked him if he was not feeling well and he told me what had transpired that day.

He went to the bank and met with his normal banker. The banker told Rick that the funds had dried up and they would not be doing any more new construction loans for the next six months. He said he got his orders from his superiors in another division and because of the unfolding economy in Texas they did not want to risk any more interim financing for construction loans at this time. The banker told Rick he had an excellent track record and that this in no way should reflect on Rick personally. Rick discussed other options with the banker for quite some time but the banker told Rick that his hands were tied. Rick left the man's office feeling totally dejected and not sure of what was going to happen next. That is where I saw him when he was laying on the bed with a headache the size of the state of Texas.

I sat and listened and pondered in my heart what I should say. Rick had worked so hard to get to this position where he felt that things were beginning to look up for us. We had gone through many trials but had prevailed through them all. It seemed like the bottom was dropping from under us again.

How many of you reading this book have had everything going along so great and then all of a sudden your marriage falls apart, or you lose your job unexpectedly, or your son or daughter goes off the deep end? I'm here to tell you that God is still on the throne today despite what it may look like you are going through.   God is a God of the second, third, forth, and fifth chances. If you have gone through a challenge and it seems like all hope is lost, look up! God is on the throne and He is the same today, yesterday, and forever. God will make a way where there seems to be no way. Just trust in Him and don't lean to your own understanding.

I was in a position like this at this particular time in my life. I did not understand why once again it seemed like I was going to have to believe God and trust Him. Why could I not just coast on easy street for a while? I was tired of going through one battle after another. But God was doing something in our lives. He is making us into fine gold and sometimes He has to turn up the heat just a little bit.

There is a story that I want to relate to you about a woman who visited a silversmith shop one day:

A lady decided to visit a silversmith to learn more about the subject. Without explaining the reason for her visit, she asked the silversmith to tell her about the process of refining silver. After he had fully described it to her, she asked *"Sir, do you sit while the work of refining is going on?"*

"Oh, yes ma'am", replied the silversmith, *"I must sit and watch the furnace constantly, for, if the time necessary for refining is exceeded in the slighted degree, the silver will be injured"*. The lady at once saw the beauty and comfort of the expression in the Bible, *"He shall sit as a refiner and purifier of silver."* (Malachi 3:3 - KJV).

Before she left, the lady asked one final question, *"How do you know when the process is complete?"*

"That's quite simple," replied the silversmith. *"When I can see my own image in the silver, the refining process is finished"*.

God sometimes sees it necessary to put His children into the furnace, but His eye is steadily intent on the work of purifying, and His wisdom and love are both engaged in the best manner for us. Our trials do not come at random and He will not let us be tested beyond what we can endure. The ultimate highest purpose for these fiery furnaces in our lives is to make us into the image of Jesus. Remember, Jesus learned obedience through the things which He suffered. God is simply making us more like Jesus through these times and trials in our lives.

God is continually making us into the image of His dear son Jesus. That is why He allows us to go from one situation to another. But there is hope my friend. God does not want you to continually live in the wilderness forever. There is a promised land and we have to believe we will enter that land. Don't ever give up or think God does not purpose for you great things! He does, but many times we quit before we reach our destination. Just before the blessings we often give up. Don't quit and don't lose hope; you will reap if you faint not.

I sat there and looked at Rick with love in my eyes. How hard he had tried to get to where he was. It was not up to me now to try to react in a negative way even though every cell in my body was trying to scream that this was not fair. Life is not always fair and we need to get beyond what we think we should have or the blessings God should be giving us. I told Rick we should pray and ask God for direction. As we bowed our heads in humility not knowing what God was going to do next, we humbly asked Him to direct our footsteps and lead us in paths of righteousness for His names sake. We handed the business and everything over to Him. We thanked God for all that He had done and believed He would make a way in the wilderness for us and lead us out of this situation. We closed the prayer and looked at each other with a feeling that we had touched the heart of God. There are times in your life when you know you have prayed and God has heard you. God always hears us, but there are those special moments when He gives us grace to realize that God has heard our request. We had faith to believe that in a short time we would see God's hand of mercy move once again.

The next morning we woke up and Rick mentioned to me that He felt that we should try to sell our house which we had just moved into and move again. He wanted to move to California! I could not believe my ears! California! Where did he get this idea?! He had heard the economy was going gangbusters there and wanted to start afresh again and move. It seemed like things had come to a standstill in Texas and that God was opening up a door for us to go west. Go west young man! How many of the settlers in the past had heard those words and started out on a journey across the nation not knowing what they were to encounter!

Well, I felt how those pioneer women must have felt when their husband said they wanted to go west and try to find gold or their fortune somewhere else. I had gotten to the point in my marriage to Rick that I learned to trust in the Lord. Often with our natural understanding we can short circuit what God wants to do. I have made it a habit to wait upon the Lord when I come into these times of uncertainty.

For the next several days Rick and I waited upon the Lord for a breakthrough. We prayed and fasted and looked for God to move. One day at breakfast Rick looked up from reading the morning paper and suggested we take a trip out to California with the kids and scope out the land. We weren't sensing anything from the Lord either way and so we decided we would go and visit California and see what the spirit of the Lord would say when we were there.

Sometimes God doesn't give you a direct yes or no. Sometimes God will stay silent on the subject so you will draw closer to Him for direction. That was the case with us in this particular situation. Since it was summer the children were not in school and we decided to leave that weekend. When we told the kids that we were going to be taking them to Disneyland and see California they were very excited. They couldn't wait to go and started packing their bags at that minute. I had to slow them down and tell them that it was going to be a few more days before we were going to leave.

The weekend came and we were all ready to go. We were going to make this a road trip. We packed up our car and started off; what an adventure! It took us two days to drive to California from Dallas. We stayed at a hotel one night and then got up early the next morning and took off again. We had initially decided on going to San Diego first before we would go up to Orange County and visit Disneyland. As we pulled into San Diego we didn't have a clue what we were to do first. We checked into a local hotel, which was near the ocean and had a swimming pool so the kids could enjoy themselves. Once we situated ourselves in the room we then took out a local yellow pages and started looking under real estate offices.

Rick made a few calls to several realtors and made appointments to start seeing properties. He wanted to see what the homes were like in these areas for us to either lease or buy. Rick initially went out with the realtors to view these homes. He came back after viewing these homes and said that the properties were much more expensive than in Dallas. We were very spoiled living in Dallas and being homebuilders. We were used to building beautiful homes with high ceilings, marble floors, winding staircases, and many more amenities.

We decided we would go up to Orange County and look around as well. We took the kids to Disneyland the next day and we had a ball. The children had never seen Mickey Mouse in person and many of the other Disney characters were out on the streets greeting the children from all over the world. We had a wonderful time and went back to our hotel tired but extremely happy after a wonderful day at Disneyland!

The next morning we headed off for south Orange County. We had heard they were building some beautiful homes in Laguna Niguel and other areas in the southern region of Orange County. We prayed that morning and asked God to show us where he wanted us to go. We still had not gotten a direct answer as to whether we were to move from Dallas. We liked California and sensed that God had work for us to do there. We were driving north on the I-5 freeway when we came to Crown Valley Parkway exit. We felt an urge to get off the freeway and turn west. We exited and turned west towards the ocean. As we drove a few miles we started to see the ocean. It was the most spectacular view and we all were in awe at the sight. The sun was shining on the ocean and it looked like sparkles were on top of the water. What a perfect day!

We came to Pacific Coast Highway and we drove down to the beach and let the kids out for a while to play in the sand. Rick and I sat there watching them contentedly. We felt that this was the area God had chosen for us to come to. Rick said he sensed God didn't want us in San Diego but in Laguna Niguel. I was in agreement and that is when we started to look at areas where they were building new homes in Laguna Niguel. It didn't take long before we saw a new housing tract we fell in love with. It had a view of the ocean and the mountains as well from the back yard. It was absolutely gorgeous!

We were in the back yard looking at the mountains and I sensed the Holy Spirit saying to me that this was going to be our next home. I looked at the serenity of the mountains and thought this would be a wonderful place to wake up in the morning and see the sun rising up on the mountains. The kids were playing hide and seek in the back yard while Rick and I were contemplating our next move. We decided that we definitely were called to California and we would go back and put our house on the market. If the house sold in a short period of time then we knew God was indeed moving us out to California.

We finished up our time in California sightseeing and having a good time with the children.

We drove back to Dallas and immediately met with a local realtor that Rick had worked with selling some of his other homes. Within a few days the home was listed in the multiple listing book and there was a big sign in the yard letting the public know that our house was indeed for sale.

Once again, I thought I had my dream home only to be starting out in a new adventure! I was excited about California because I sensed God was indeed moving us on for His purposes. But humans are creatures of habit and change is not always an easy assignment to follow.

We had many people coming over to the house and viewing it over the next few weeks. Everyone who saw it thought it was a beautiful house. There were four bedrooms, a living room and library, as well as a family room and dining room. There was even a telephone booth that we had put in upstairs in the hallway. It was a very beautiful house with spiral stairs, large thirty-foot high windows in the living room that looked out onto the pool in the back yard with a fountain flowing into the pool.

One day we got a call from the realtor saying that there was a couple from Chicago who were being relocated to Dallas and they were very interested in the house. They would be coming by in a half hour and to make sure everything was tidy and looked presentable for showing. We ran around getting everything straightened up and before we knew it the doorbell rang.

As they walked through the house I could tell they really liked it. They didn't want to appear too anxious, but I could tell from the way the women looked at the kitchen that this was the house she was prepared to make an offer on. They left after about an hour and said they would be getting back to us. No sooner did they leave the house when another realtor called and said they were coming by with some clients to view the home again. That couple came and went after about an hour as well. Before the end of the day we had two couples that presented an offer on the house and got into a bidding war. Finally, the couple from Chicago presented an offer we were ready to accept. We sold the house for $5,000 above what we were asking for! God is so good; He knows how to give you the best price if you just wait on Him.

We had a short 30-day escrow on the house since they were being relocated from Chicago and had to be down in Dallas within the month. It was a very hectic time in our lives. We put in an offer on the home in California through a realtor we had met when we were out there and it was accepted. We made arrangements with the moving company to come and pack up all of our belongings and begin our new journey to California.

Moving can be a very bittersweet experience. There were many friends and acquaintances we met in Dallas that had changed our lives forever. We had a farewell party at our home with some of our closest friends the weekend before we were to leave. We prayed at the end of the party and asked God for his hand of protection and blessing to be upon us. Rick still did not know what he would be doing for a job when we moved to California. He wanted to build houses if that worked out, but was willing to take a sales job in the meantime until things fell in place.

Finally, the day had come to move! The moving van pulled up to the house bright and early on Thursday morning. I had many boxes already packed up all labeled with the rooms they were to go into once we got to California. Several friends had come over as well to help with the kids and get things organized. It took all day for them to finish moving the furniture and boxes in the house. We decided we would stay in a hotel that night in Dallas and get a fresh start in the morning. We were going to drive both cars out to California. Rick was going to drive one car and I would follow him.

After staying in a nice hotel suite that night, the alarm woke us up early and we headed out to California. In a way I felt like one of those pioneer women who had decided to go west to find their future!

It took us three days to get to California. We had to make regular stops because of the three children.

The moving van was due get there the day after we arrived. They had the address of the new home and we were going to meet them there as scheduled on Monday morning.

When we got to our new house the moving van was already there. The realtor greeted us with the keys and we started moving in. It took all day for the furniture and boxes to be unpacked. Finally, the last box was unloaded and the beds had been set up for the kids to sleep in that night. We all gathered around in the living room as a family and we said a prayer to bless our new home. It had never been lived in before and we asked God to put His blessing on the home and our family.

After we put the kids to bed, Rick and I went outside in the back yard. The house had such a gorgeous view of the city lights in the valley below. We were in awe that God had brought us to such a beautiful place. The stars were twinkling up in the sky and we felt like God was smiling down on us. We had been obedient to the call to come to California. We had a lot of work in front of us. Rick needed to find work and we had to find new schools for the children as well. Looking back it's hard to believe that we made this move without having a job! But things had always worked out in the past when we were directed by God, so we were going to watch this all play out in time.

The next day we woke up to a beautiful summer day with the sun glistening in the sky over the water. It was if God was smiling on us and saying He was going to lead and guide us to where we were supposed to be.

There are some of you reading this today and God has been directing you to do something and you have to make a big step of faith to do it. What I would encourage you to do is to pray and ask God to give you the courage and the faith to step out into the areas He is calling you. In Hebrews 11:6 it says, "Without faith it is impossible to please God." If we could see it before we do it - then that isn't faith. Faith is the substance of things hoped for, the evidence of things NOT SEEN! Step out by faith into those new adventures and you will be rewarded beyond your wildest imaginations. Abraham was called the Father of Faith because he believed God and stepped out when God told him to go. Believe God today and move out as He shows you. Remember that people just like you started most of the greatest accomplishments in this world today. They had a dream and a vision and they stepped out. Many times they failed at their first attempts, but they learned what not to do the next time. Step out today and see what God will do in your life.

Chapter 16

MY BROTHER - JACK

The next few weeks were exciting, to say the least. I got the children enrolled in a new Christian school and began unpacking and getting the house organized. Rick found employment with a great company and started making a great income right off the bat. We decided not to go into building in California until we learned about the various areas to build in. To build houses in California was a whole different ball-game than in Texas. There were mostly tract homes being built by large developers. The land costs were much higher and there were so many more rules and regulations.

We also found a great church. The pastor used to live in Minnesota and had pastored a church we had once attended there! The weather was always so wonderful and everyday was like waking up on vacation. Sometimes I had to pinch myself to make sure that I was awake!

The autumn came up upon us quickly and Christina and Jeremy started school at Mission Hills Christian School. Jeremy was in kindergarten and Christina was in first grade. Jason (my third child) was only four so he stayed home with me. I was busy with getting my album cover shot in California and found a great photographer up in Hollywood. I also was taking voice lessons up in Hollywood from a very famous voice teacher named Guiseppe Balistari who had been trained over in Italy. He was an elderly man who had trained such celebrities as Mary Wilson, Juice Newton, and many more. I learned many things from him during the season in which I vocally trained with him.

That first year in California we went back to Minnesota for Christmas. We all flew back since it would have taken too long to drive from California. When we lived in Texas we had gotten used to driving home for the holidays and summer vacations. It was a wonderful Christmas! My brother Jack had also come home from Texas. He told us He wanted to come live in California. Since we had moved away from Texas he had no family and wanted to move out west as well. We were very excited to hear that and said he could live with us until he found accommodations.

After we got back from Minnesota things really started moving ahead. I had just received my first shipment of tapes and CD's. My first album was finally out and I had titled it "Out of the Night." I was so excited about this album. It was a promise of God that had finally come into fruition. Now I was starting to get booked into different churches and I was promoting the album. Also, I was working with an agent to try to get a record company to pick up the album for distribution. Little did I realize that just around the corner was one of the hardest experiences that I would ever go through.

I was in the kitchen getting ready to go out the door to pick up the kids from school when the phone rang. I almost didn't answer it because I was on the verge of being late. I picked up the phone hurriedly and said "Hello." When I heard my dad on the other end in a shaky voice saying "Meri," I said "Hi dad, what's up!" He sounded different then I had ever heard him before. All at once he broke down weeping and said "Jack died!" I was in a state of shock. I couldn't believe what I had just heard! I immediately wanted to know what happened. My dad went on to say that Jack had been in his car when it went off the road. They took him to the hospital but could not revive him. There were still so many details that he did not know yet, but he would call me back later and fill me in. Jack was at the hospital in Dallas but was going to be taken over to a funeral home for preparations to come back to Minnesota for the funeral. My dad had made arrangements for us to fly home the next day.

I remember hanging up the phone and just sobbing! My son Jason had heard this whole conversation and was also wailing "My uncle, my uncle died." I had to pick up the kids from school and Jason and I got into the car and started driving. I'm sure it was quite a sight as we were driving along. Jason and I were both crying and if anyone were to have looked over as they were driving by they probably would have been perplexed wondering what had happened to us!

When we got to the school I went over to the daycare room to pick up Jeremy and Christina. If you were late in picking up your children they were immediately transported to the after school care room. I walked into the room and saw a woman I barely knew who was the supervisor of the daycare. I immediately broke down sobbing telling her my brother died. She just started holding me and telling me that God had everything under control. It's amazing how we need other people during times of crisis. God made us in such a way that we need others to comfort us. I also felt God's loving hand of protection on me during this time of crisis. I was so confused and upset. Why did Jack die now? He was only 32 years old! He was planning on coming out to live with us in California; why now God?!

It's amazing how things can change so quickly! I woke up that morning and everything was great. Just a few short hours later my whole world had changed. I had lost my older brother unexpectedly! I was in a state of shock and pain I had never felt before! There are times when the pain can seem almost unbearable, but God will give you the strength if you cry out to Him for help.

I picked up the kids from the daycare and brought them to my car. My youngest child, Jason, was still crying about his uncle. We were both crying in the car before I even started the engine. Christina and Jeremy looked at us like we were crazy. Christina said to me, "You're kidding, Jack did not really die!" It would not sink into their minds that Jack had in fact died.

I drove home and immediately called my husband, Rick, to tell him what had happened.

When Rick heard me tell him the news he got very quiet. He did not react at all on the phone. I thought to myself that it was very strange to react in that way. Jack and Rick were best friends. Rick was really excited Jack was coming out to California for them to start working together. It was almost as if Rick did not even hear what I was saying.

I heard Rick say he would be home soon and we would talk then. As I hung up the phone from talking with my husband I prayed God would give Rick grace. I knew Rick was devastated as well but he wouldn't verbalize it. Everyone is so different as to how they react to death. Some are very emotional and immediately react to the news, while others are more private and want to have their time alone to reflect and come to grips with the death.

I fed the children and gave them their baths and then put them to bed early for the night. It had finally sunk into Christina and Jeremy what had actually happened. Their Uncle Jack was the 'fun' uncle, the one who told them stories and made them giggle. As I tucked them in that night I told them that Jack was now in heaven with Jesus. It gave them some assurance, but they were really going to miss him.

I waited for Rick to come home and finally he walked in. He looked like something the cat had drug in. He told me

that he just drove around thinking. He couldn't believe he
had lost his best friend. He was mad at God for a while and
was arguing with God why Jack had to die. He finally realized
he needed to come home to be with me and comfort our family. He was still numb and in shock when he walked in the
door.

We went to bed that night but I wasn't able to sleep very
well. I remember going outside and looking up at the stars.
It was a clear night and there seemed to be hundreds of stars
up in the sky twinkling. I looked up at the sky and just started to talk with God. I told Him I didn't understand but I
would trust Him. I asked God to give me strength to go
through the next few weeks. I knew we would be traveling
back to Minnesota for the funeral and burial. It would be one
of the hardest things I would ever have to do. I felt God tell
me that everything was going to be fine. God had a bigger
picture than our finite minds could understand. I heard God
speak to me and say, "I have work for Jack to do in heaven."

Now I believe that, as a Christian, God wants us to live a
long life. It is a promise in the Bible to us as believers. But
there are situations and circumstances where many times God
will intervene. It is during times like this that we need to put
our trust in God and know He has everything under control.
Many times we don't understand at the particular point in
time, but later God will give us revelation to show us why.

The next morning I woke up and got a call from my Dad.
He arranged for us to go out on a flight the following morning
to Minneapolis. I had a lot to do to get prepared for the trip.
The children were taken out of school and I was given their
homework for the next week so they wouldn't fall behind.

That day was a very hectic, getting prepared for the trip and
the upcoming funeral. I packed all of the suitcases and got
everything ready for the flight the following morning. We
went to bed early that evening since we had to get up at 4:00

a.m. for a 7:00 a.m. flight from San Diego. Our home was an hour away from the San Diego Airport so we would have to allow enough time to get there.

The next morning the alarm didn't go off! I remember looking at the clock and wondering why the clock hadn't rung yet. Then I realized it was almost 6:00 a.m. Our flight was scheduled to leave in almost one hour. It was going to take us over an hour to drive there. We got everyone up in mere seconds and told the kids to just throw their clothes on. We literally got out of the house in ten minutes flat.

I had never seen my husband drive a car like that in my life. He was weaving in and out of cars on the freeway like a NASCAR driver. The boys thought it was very cool, but I wanted to arrive in one piece. We finally got there and ran up to the gate just as they were ready to shut the door to the plane. Once again, God came through for us.

The flight was a long one! It seemed like it took forever when it really was only four hours. I thought back about how your life can change in just a few days. Finally the long flight was making its descent into Minneapolis/St. Paul Airport. We deplaned and could see my parents at the gate waiting for us.

I ran down to meet them and we just hugged and cried. It was a bittersweet moment for all of us. We got the luggage and loaded all of us into their large Lincoln Towncar. When we pulled up to their house we noticed there was a lot of lights on inside. Several of my relatives were there helping with the meals and supporting our family.

My other brothers and sisters were there as well. They were all happy to see all of us but not necessarily under those circumstances. As we sat down we all started to share about Jack. It's amazing how when someone dies you need to talk about the person. We couldn't get over the fact of how fast it happened!

My parent's minister was over at the house and we all prayed and wept as we celebrated Jack's life. I was amazed when I found out how my parents learned of Jack's death. My dad sat down and told us the story.

Jack had woken up that morning like many others I'm sure. He had been working on a new model home doing the painting and contracting work. He was also employed at a sales job at a local sunbed company where they sold tanning booths to vendors and dealers around the country. Jack had decided to take a break from the painting and head over to his other job to pick up a paycheck that had come in from the corporate office.

He changed his clothes quickly and forgot to put his wallet in his other set of pants. As he was driving to the other company to collect his paycheck, all of a sudden he slumped over the wheel. A car that had been behind him on a local residential street had told my parents this later that day. The road started to curve but since Jack had passed out and was slumped over the wheel he didn't curve with the road but went up a small embankment and ended up in someone's backyard. The woman who lived in the house was a nurse who also happened to be Jewish. She had the Star of David in her window.

Jack had only been driving about 20 mph down the residential street so the accident was not what killed him. They immediately called the paramedics and they were there within minutes. Plano General Hospital was just minutes away from the scene of the accident. The paramedics worked on Jack for over ten minutes. They finally put him in the ambulance and tried to continue to work on his heart to revive him.

At the hospital they continued to work on him but to no avail. They finally pronounced him dead at around 4:30 p.m. that afternoon. When I heard my dad say the time I suddenly realized something very significant. I had put my younger four-year-old son, Jason, to bed for a nap around 2:00 p.m. I layed down for a few minutes as well when all of a sudden at around 2:30 p.m. (Pacific Standard Time), I sat straight up in bed. It felt like something dramatic had happened. I didn't know what it was but it was almost as if I felt my spirit leave my body. I was almost dozing off when I felt this jarring in my spirit and I sat straight up.

I immediately layed back down, but started praying in the Holy Spirit. I knew something significant had happened but didn't realize what. It wasn't until a few hours later that I got the call from my dad telling me that Jack had died. Jack was in Dallas so the time difference was two hours later there. At the same time he was pronounced dead was the time I felt the unusual occurrence in my room.

I quickly told everyone in my parent's living room what had transpired that day. I then asked my dad how he and my mom had found out about Jack. Who had called them? This is where the story gets really interesting.

Since Jack did not have his wallet on him there was no way to identify him. But he did have a business card of a woman named Margo Hastings. She was a good friend of Jack's and for some reason her card happened to be in his pants pockets. They ended up calling Margo and asked her to come down and identify a body of a male down at the hospital. When she got the call she had no idea who it could be, though she had a feeling it could be Jack after they gave her his physical description. Jack was 32 years old and had brunette hair. He was a very handsome young man with bright blue eyes and white sparkling teeth. Everyone who met him was taken with his charisma as well as his striking good looks.

As I heard my dad tell the story of Margo having to identify Jack, I had a visual picture of what it must have been like to have to identify a good friend in a morgue. She was taken to the morgue and they showed her the body. It was indeed

Jack. She couldn't believe it! She had just talked to him the day before. Margo was a strong Christian and she used to see Jack at church often. Margo was able to give the hospital Jack's apartment phone number. He had a roommate named Steve and they called him and told him that Jack had died and they needed assistance in locating his next of kin.

Steve told the hospital he knew Jack's parents lived in Minneapolis and their last name was Jensen, but he did not have the phone number. The hospital told Steve to call the local operator in Minnesota and they would stay on the line with him until they finally located the right Jensen's. So for over an hour the local operator and Steve went through every listing for Jensen in the Minneapolis phone directory. That is a common name in Minnesota since many Scandinavians live there. With each new call the operator asked if they had a son named "Jack." Finally, they came to my parent's residence. My dad answered the phone and the operator asked my dad if he had a son named "Jack Jensen." My dad proceeded to tell him that he did. At that point the enormity of the situation hit Steve right in the face. Now he knew he was going to have to tell Jack's father that his son had died!

"Mr. Jensen, I'm so sorry to have to tell you this, but your son Jack died an hour ago at the hospital," Steve stated solemnly. Once the words were blurted out my dad just sat there for a moment taking it all in and then started to weep. My mother got on the phone and heard my dad weeping uncontrollably into the phone. My mother started to ask what had happened. My dad quietly calmed down and told her Jack had died. Minutes seemed to turn into eternity. It was such a shock for all of them on the phone. My dad asked Steve some more questions about what had happened. Some had thought he got into a car accident. He had been in his car when the ambulance had come and taken him away to the hospital.

My dad thanked Steve for calling and told him they would be in touch. It was after they hung up that my mom and dad sat down and prayed before the Lord. "We knew that Jack loved Jesus so we weren't worried about where he was going to, but we just couldn't understand how this could happen to our child," my parents thought.

As my dad finished telling the story to all of us, we were all in tears. It had happened so quickly! Literally in the twinkling of an eye Jack was gone! We cried many tears that night. But we also had some good memories and laughs about the things Jack had done growing up. It's amazing the memories that will flood your thoughts when someone dies. It is almost as if their whole life passes in front of you. We sure were all going to miss Jack!

We went to bed that night with a hole in our hearts. There was a lot of planning to be done the next few days. My family went through making all of the final preparations for Jack's funeral. Jack's body had been flown up from Texas and was now at a funeral home in St. Paul. The following day we were all going over to the funeral home to view Jack's body. It was something I was not looking forward to. As I got ready to go I prayed to the Lord and asked Him for strength.

As we walked into the funeral home there were already some friends there. My parents know many people in St. Paul/Minneapolis. We were greeted at the door by the funeral director. There were several different parlors in the funeral home. He walked us over to the largest room and it had the name "Jensen" on the sign outside the room. As we walked in, I immediately looked over and saw the casket. I could see the outline of Jack's profile. "How strange," I thought, to see Jack in a coffin. It's amazing what your mind will think during times like that.

My mom and dad had already viewed Jack the day before when they were making the final preparations. I didn't immediately go over to the casket. I was very nervous and didn't want to see him. I knew that he wasn't there anyway. The Bible says in II Corinthians 5:8, *"To be absent from the body is to be present with the Lord."* I knew Jack had gone to heaven to be with Jesus. In many ways I was very happy for him because he was now in his true home. But I knew for closure I should go and say my final farewells to Jack's earthly body.

Nobody was by the casket now and I thought it was the perfect time to go over. I slowly walked up to the casket and looked down at my brother. He was wearing one of his favorite blue suits with a white shirt and tie. But Jack didn't really look like himself. You could tell it was him, but his hair was combed wrong and his face looked puffy. I started softly crying and speaking to him. I knew he wasn't there, but somehow it felt good to say my final good-byes.

"Jack, just last week I talked to you on the phone and you said you were coming to live with us in California. Well, now it looks like you're going to have to wait for me to get to heaven." I can't believe you made it before me! I'll miss you Jack....I love you." As I quietly looked at Jack for several minutes, I felt comforted. I knew that he was in God's arms now. What a comforting thought to know that when you die in Christ you will immediately go into the arms of your Heavenly Father.

My sisters, Jane and Terry, came over to me and we all started looking at Jack. We conversed for a while and then other people started to come up to spend some time alone with Jack so we moved aside.

The rest of the night seemed like a blur. So many people were coming and paying their respects. There were people I had not seen in years. Some of the kids I went to grade school had come to pray their condolences. Everyone was in such a state of disbelief! Nobody could believe Jack had died so suddenly. Everyone had wanted to know what had happened.

From the autopsy we found out Jack had a lower potassium level. This could have caused a heart arethmia and that could have lead to his heart stopping. But the doctor said that was very unusual for a man of his age and physical condition. Jack was in very good shape and played on a few different church softball teams as well as worked out at the gym. I felt God had called Jack home for a very specific reason. Some of these reasons we may never understand. But I knew God would somehow show us the way and give us the strength to go on.

Finally, the night was over and we all said our final farewells to all of the friends and families who had come to support us in our time of grief. We said one final good-bye to Jack and then we went back to my parent's house to get a good night sleep. Tomorrow was going to be the funeral and the burial. "If we thought we needed strength today what is it going to be like tomorrow?" I thought.

The next morning I awoke to the birds singing out of the window of the bedroom I was sleeping in. The Lord immediately gave me the scripture in Matthew 10:29-31 *"Are not two sparrows sold for a penny? Yet not one of them will fall to the ground apart from the will of your Father. And even the very hairs of your head are all numbered. So don't be afraid; you are worth more than many sparrows"*. It gave me comfort to know God is in complete control of our lives as long as we are living for Him. I quickly got up and started getting ready for the day. I knew my mom would need a lot of prayer as well as my dad. It would be the hardest thing they would ever have to do - bury their first-born son. There is always something so special about the first child. Not that every child is not special, but your first child is so special because it is your first experience as a parent. It is such a miracle the first time you see your first child.

I remember when Christina was born. I was in the delivery room and had been in labor for over eight hours. Finally it was the stage where I was supposed to push. After about ten minutes of hard pushing Christina finally emerged. The doctor immediately placed her on my stomach after he cut the umbilical cord. I looked down at this beautiful little girl who was crying very hard and I started to cry tears of joy. What a miracle that God had given to me! I'll never forget that moment. It was so special!

I knew it would be a hard day for my parents! The first-born child they had brought into the world was now going to be laid to rest today in a grave. For those reading this book who have lost a child, I just want to tell you I understand how much pain there is in it. I watched with firsthand experience how painful it was for my parents.

But I do want to share with you that God will be your strength during this time and will uphold you with His mighty hand of grace and mercy. You have gone through one of the most difficult things in this world that will ever have to face you. You are not facing it alone today, though. If you will just call out to the Lord today, He will give you the grace and the peace you need.

My father's sister, Jo Ann Olsen, has lost two children and also has had to watch two of her children suffer with serious illnesses. Many years ago her youngest son, David, was diagnosed with Leukemia. She has a strong faith and believed God for a miracle. When David died at a very early age, it would have been easy for her to become bitter. She didn't; she went on in her life with a zeal and enthusiasm that few people I know have. A few years ago, her oldest son, Billy, died suddenly from a heart attack while he was at the gym working out. He was only 52 years old and in perfect health.

Billy had a beautiful wife, Shelly, along with four young children. Once again she maintained her faith in God. Billy was a strong Christian who constantly was reaching out to the community to mentor and instruct those around him about the ways of the Lord.

It was a devastating thing to watch grandchildren now without a father as well as leaving a young wife behind. But my aunt rolled up her sleeves and did whatever she could to help out at their home. She had faith and prayed God would bring forth His perfect will for these young children and Billy's widow, Shelly. It was a very difficult time for all of them. But a few short years later, Shelly met a wonderful man and they are now married. They have an incredible family and God truly has answered their prayers.

You have a choice during these difficult seasons in life either to become bitter or better. Life is a choice and your emotions are also something you can control. If you will take the advice of Psalms 1 in the Bible and meditate upon God's word day and night, then you will be like a tree planted by the rivers of water. It also says whatever you do will prosper. It seems like the oak trees that are planted in the most difficult areas are the ones that grow the strongest. Just like it is in our lives, it is not the ones who have it the easiest that become the strongest. Usually the people who go through the most challenges are the ones who become the strongest people.

My Aunt Jo Ann is one of those people. Through all of the challenging circumstances I have seen her go through, I have rarely seen her discouraged or depressed. I'm sure she has had her days where she has been extremely overwhelmed with grief. But when she goes out in public she is always reaching out to those around her to bring them joy and strength. My mother and my aunt are two of the women in this world that are examples of the Proverbs 31 woman. They don't let life dictate to them how to feel. They allow the Lord's joy and strength to infuse their lives as shining beacons of hope to all around them. So today if you are in a place where you feel overwhelmed by life's circumstances, call out to the Lord and He will give you strength.

I got up and started getting ready for the day. The funeral was to be held at St. Bonaventure's church at 10:00 a.m. The family was going to get there early since the casket was going to be open before the service for those who were not able to attend the viewing the night before. I quickly dressed all the children in their Sunday best attire and we all piled into the car to head over to the church.

Upon entering the church we had a feeling of peace and serenity. There was music playing and I sensed the angels of God in the sanctuary. I had prayed to God for strength for the day and I knew He was answering that prayer. There were many flowers at the front of the altar from friends and family. The casket was placed in the back of the church and there were a few people in front of it. Once again, the casket was open and Jack was visible to those around us.

People started arriving and taking their seats in the church. There were several more people I hadn't seen for many years come up to me and offer their condolences. All of a sudden I heard a commotion in the back and my sister Jane rushed up to me. She told me that my daughter Christina was crying uncontrollably. She had not seen Jack in the casket yet the night before. She has always been afraid of death and purposely stayed away from the casket at the viewing. But my husband Rick felt that it would be good for her to say good-bye to Jack since they were very close. Christina was only six years old at this time.

Rick was holding Christina and took her over to the casket. When she looked down and saw Jack lying there she immediately started weeping uncontrollably. Rick tried to comfort her to no avail. So he took her outside of the church to try to calm her down. In the meantime, my other son, Jeremy, was watching this whole episode from the stairs leading up to the choir loft. From the stairs you could get a good view of the casket. He was very calm and collected and was watching very intently. My sister Jane told me she walked over to Jeremy and asked him if he was doing okay. Jeremy said to Jane that he didn't understand why Christina was so upset. Jeremy spoke these words at the age of only four years old: "I don't understand why Christina is so upset. Jack is in heaven. That is just a shell that he was in. He is now in heaven with Jesus."

Jane came up and told me what Jeremy had said and was amazed. Truly God had opened a young boy's eyes to see the truth. The Bible says Psalms 8:2, "Out of the mouth of babes have I perfected praise." Even though I was upset about Christina, I was thrilled to know that my son Jeremy was given special grace to see the truth about death. The word of God says that for those in Christ, "death has lost its sting" (I Corinthians 15:55. Though it is painful to lose a loved one, if they are Christians, we have not lost them at all. To be absent from the body is to be present with the Lord. Death actually becomes a celebration of one crossing over into the Kingdom of Heaven.

Jesus spoke to his disciples in John 14:2-3, and said, *"In my Father's house are many mansions; if it were not so, I would have told you. I am going there to prepare a place for you. And if I go and prepare a place for you, I will come back and take you to be with me that you also may be where I am."*. Death to a Christian is a welcome home party! Instead of a funeral service we should have a "crossing over victory party".

Nevertheless, there are still many people who don't understand death. It is a shock to the system to lose someone so suddenly and without warning. As people started to flock into the church and take their seats, I started to feel a sense of anticipation. We were going to get up and read the poem Jack had written to the Lord. Would I be able to read the poem without breaking down?

The church was quite crowded now and the priest motioned that it was time to get started.

All of the family was seated in the front pews of the church. The relatives and friends and families took up the remaining rows behind the family. There was a beautiful organ solo being played by Mark Schultz, the choir and worship leader for the church. As soon as the song was over, Father Terry Rasmussen started the service.

The service moved along very beautifully with several songs being played as well as scriptures being read. It was now time for my sisters and I to go up and read the poem Jack had written the year before. We had printed this poem on bookmarks and gave one to every person in attendance at the funeral.

As we walked to the podium all eyes were on us. We stopped in front of the podium microphone and I started to read the first paragraph. My other sisters each read a paragraph and we would continue on until it was finished. Here is the poem Jack had written:

"Create in me Lord, new desires; your desires. For you said that you would give me the desires of my heart.

And when I am sad Lord, let me reflect, is this sadness for myself and a result of selfishness or is it your heart cry...a cry of intercession and travail for the lost in the world.

I yield myself, my members to you that your Holy Spirit would pray through me, even as through Paul; to give birth in the spiritual realm; spiritual babes. I know birth pangs hurt, but after the labor and when the results of that labor are seen, then that pain is no longer felt; only the fruits of the labor are seen.

So help me to fight 'the good fight of faith,' to be faithful to your calling and to take my eyes off myself, my desires - and to see your desires through my spiritual eyes. And as those souls are birthed into your Kingdom, may I be faithful to pray for the little babes, praying in the Spirit that Christ, the hope of glory be formed in them.

You have taken my stumbling blocks and turned them into stepping stones. And as we walk together on those rocks across torrent waters, I will not be afraid. For my hand is firmly in your hand, and you will not let go and your presence lights up those dark waters so that I can see and you guide my feet so my steps are sure. And if I should slip, the strength of your arm will hold me up. And if I try to go on my own and exhaustion sets in, then discouragement, even the desire to give up and die, then I see you are still there. The one who said you'd never leave me nor forsake me. And I cry out to you and hold my arms out, even as a young child. And you pick me up and carry me so as to rest in your arms and draw strength from your bosom. After, I am rested and as the journey continues, I find that I am stronger now and I know you better. You are my friend. We have made covenant together.

I do know you suffer when the enemy comes and hurts me. It is the only way he can remotely hurt you. These are his only weapons to place doubt and unbelief in men's hearts so as to distrust you and the provision you sent in your son, Jesus.

I thank you for that provision and for the weapons you have given me and that the middle wall of partition has been broken down and the eyes of my understanding enlightened.

I thank you that even as you gave to your son, Jesus, you have given me power through your Holy Spirit to destroy the works of the enemy. The enemy, Satan, the father of lies whose mission is to kill, steal and destroy. But you, Father, have given me life and you restore seven fold that which the enemy has stolen, and the part which has been taken or destroyed.....you give back and restore even seven fold."

As we finished reading the poem, there was a complete hush in the church. The words Jack had written were so filled with such insight into the love of Christ. It was almost like reading an epistle that the Apostle Paul had wrote. I could sense the angels of God throughout the room and the glory of God's power was shining through.

The rest of the service seemed like a blur. There was a closing song and then the casket was closed and was wheeled into an awaiting hearse. The family climbed in a long black limousine and we followed the hearse to Resurrection Cemetery in Mendota Heights, Minnesota, for his final burial.

There were a long string of cars following us with their lights on. It took us about fifteen minutes to get to the cemetery and once we did everyone parked and made their way into a small chapel for another prayer. It was very cold in Minnesota since it was January. The temperature was about zero degrees Fahrenheit. I saw some of my cousins walk up to me with tears in their eyes offering support and strength. We all were in a state of unbelief! After the prayer in the chapel we made our way to the graveside and had a moment of silence. The wind was blowing through the barren trees, surrounding the grave. It was almost as if I could sense God's Spirit breathing on us. I stood next to my mother holding her hand as they said the final prayer before we all departed. It was a long day and we were supposed to go back to the church for a meal prepared by some of the women at the church.

When we arrived at the church we were met by Marti, one of the deacons, who told us he had something very significant to share with us about what he had experienced at the funeral. He didn't want to share it with us at that moment, but wanted to come over to our home later and tell us of the event.

Many people came back to the church and we had a time of fellowship and remembrance of Jack. After a few hours we were ready to go home and speak with Marti.

When we pulled into the driveway, Marti was waiting for us. He was quite shaken up and said he needed to speak to us immediately about what he saw. We were all wondering what it could be.

We all went inside and sat down on the living room furniture. Marti started to cry very softly, exclaiming that he had never before seen anything like this. My dad very gently told Marti to explain in detail what had happened. Here is the story that Marti went on to share as we all sat listening in anticipation.

The funeral had begun and Marti came in a few minutes late. He sat in the back of the church and was meditating upon the music playing. After about ten minutes into the service when they were doing a reading, he felt something very powerful happen in his spirit. He said it felt like electricity was going through his whole body. He looked up beyond the altar and he had a vision of Jack standing there. Jack looked at all of us and smiled. Marti continued on saying that Jack's eyes were so brilliantly blue and sparkling. Then Marti saw Jesus appear next to Jack almost instantaneously. Jack looked at Jesus and it seemed like Jack went over to the Lord. Jesus then began to carry Jack in His arms and Jack and the Lord then disappeared.

Marti told us that when he saw this he immediately started to sob. I remember during the service when I had heard some large sobs from the back of the church. I had just thought that someone was overcome with grief. He told us that when he saw Jack and Jesus together it was so overwhelming to him and he could not contain himself.

Marti then became very quiet as if contemplating something. He mentioned to us that there was a portion in the poem that seemed very prophetic. It was almost as if Jack wrote what had happened that day in church. We brought out the poem and started to read it from the beginning. And then we came to the part that we knew Marti was talking about.

"And if I should slip, the strength of your arm will hold me up. And if I try to go on my own and exhaustion sets in, then discouragement, even the desire to give up and die, then I see you are still there. The one who said you'd never leave me nor forsake me. And I cry out to you and hold my arms out, even as a young child. And you pick me up and carry me so as to rest in your arms and draw strength from your bosom."

We sat in stunned silence as we realized the magnitude of what Marti had said. What a wonderful sign the Lord had given to our family! God had allowed a deacon from my parent's church to have a vision of Jack being held by the Lord. This brought great comfort, not only to my parents, but to the whole family as well.

We started asking Marti questions one by one. We all wanted to know the most intricate details about what he saw. What was Jack wearing? Did he seem happy? How long did he see this vision for?

On and on went the questions until it seemed like Marti was almost exhausted. Finally, after two hours of conversing and going over the vision we felt it was time to call the evening to a close. It had been a very long day for all of us. The Lord had indeed blessed us with something so wonderful to even comprehend. We knew that Jack was with the Lord, but for someone to actually see Jack in the Lord's arms was so wonderful beyond comprehension!

My mom and dad walked Marti to the door and thanked him for taking the time to come and share his experiences with us. After he left we sat around for another half an hour just speaking again of the wonderful mercies of the Lord and his graciousness to our family to comfort us in our time of need.

I went to bed that night with a smile on my face. I was so thankful that God had been with us in such a powerful way at the service and the burial. I could feel God's wonderful hand of protection and comfort on me during the whole day. When I felt I could not take it any more I immediately called out to the Lord and He graciously sustained me.

If some of you reading this today have been going through a time where you have lost a loved one or someone extremely close to you, I just want to say God is with you. He will give you the strength you need during this time of pain. Call out to Him and He will answer you. He may not always answer you in the same way that He did with us. It was so wonderful that God had given us a sign from the Lord, but the Lord says in the word of God in John 20:29, *"More blessed are they that don't see and yet believe."* Jesus had risen from the grave, but had not yet ascended to heaven yet. Jesus had already visited many of the disciples and Thomas was being told about it. Thomas doubted they had seen Jesus and said to them, *"Unless I can put my hand in his nail scarred hands I will not believe."* How often do we ask God for a sign and we don't receive it?

We did not ask God for any such sign. I think we need to be careful about these kinds of things. We need to believe what the word of God says. The Bible does say in II Corinthians 11:14, *"And no wonder, for Satan himself masquerades as an angel of light."* Don't go seeking after signs. Let the signs follow you. In Mark 16:17-18, the Lord says, *"These signs will follow them that believe, in my name they will cast out demons; they will speak with new tongues; they will pick up snakes with their hands; and when they drink deadly poison it will not hurt them at all; they will lay hands on the sick and see them healed."* Don't go looking for signs today but let the signs follow you. God wants to let the power of God flow through you just as it did the disciples after Jesus rose from the grave.

Just trust Him today through all of your circumstances. Pray this prayer of relinquishment to the Lord with me if you are going through a tough time after losing a loved one.

"Dear Lord, please help me through my time of loss. Give me the strength to continue to follow you and let my footsteps be lead of you. Help me to comfort those who are hurting instead of wanting to be comforted. O grant that I may never seek, so much to be consoled as to console. To be understood as to understand; to just love you Lord with all my heart. Make me an instrument of your peace. Give me your peace today. Thank you, Lord. Amen."

The next few days seemed to go by very quickly. There were many friends and family continually stopping by the house to talk and bring comfort to our family. We had a bittersweet time of catching up with many old friends. There were so many wonderful people that came in our time of need. They brought food for dinners, helped with the children when we needed to rest, helped cook and clean, and so many other things that seem overwhelming.

The week passed within no time and soon it was time to get prepared to go back to California. As I was packing my bags for the flight back, I remembered about how things had changed so drastically in just one month. One month prior I had been home for Christmas with my family instead of at a funeral. It had been such a happy time shopping at the mall, opening presents by the Christmas tree, holiday parties and festivities, and so many happy memories. Now one short month later I was packing to go back to California, only this time my older brother Jack was no longer on this earth. I can't call him any time I want like I used to. I won't ever see his smiling face again on this earth. There were so many memories of Jack that started to flood my mind. I started to cry and I asked the Lord to give me strength.

I knew this was only the beginning stage of missing Jack. We had been with our friends and family for the last week and they had supported us every minute of the day. But now I was going back to my home where I wouldn't have all of the support I had up in Minnesota. We all need to remember that when we are dealing with family or friends who have lost loved ones, it is so easy to call them right after the death, but then a few weeks later it seems like people are afraid to call and bring up the name of the deceased family member or friend.

That loved one is still very much alive in the family member's mind. We need to remember them and continue to talk about that person. Talk about the memories you had and the wonderful moments you experienced in this life with them. It would mean a great deal to the family and friends of the loved one who has died.

As I closed my suitcase I gently looked around the room I lived in while going to high school. My mom had redecorated the room and it didn't look anything like it use to. But I felt like a young girl again. I wanted to stay home and not go back to California. I didn't want to face what I knew I would experience when I got back.

I then heard the Holy Spirit whisper in my ear, "Meri, face the pain and it won't remain." I stopped suddenly and said out loud, "Face the pain - and it won't remain?" I then heard the Lord say, "Meri, if you will face the pain of this moment and this situation, it won't remain. It won't be as painful for you if you face it. Many people try to cover their pain with alcohol, drugs, or other replacements. But I made pain for a reason. When you touch a hot stove your hand gives your brain a signal to pull away. Also, when you are mentally hurt you need to pull away and spend time with me. It's important not to isolate yourself totally from everyone. But come away with me, Meri, and let me set you free. Free from the pain of losing a loved one. Jack's not lost; he's been found. Jack is free with me in eternity."

All of a sudden I felt the peace of God envelope me with His wonderful presence. I started to weep tears of joy. Jack was indeed not lost, but found. He was not dead, but in heaven with Jesus. The pity party I had been having was suddenly over. In place was a spirit of joy and peace. I thanked the Lord for this special moment and spent the next several minutes in praise and worship to our Heavenly Father and His precious son, Jesus Christ.

God is so gracious with us. I don't care what you may be experiencing in life at this moment; God is always looking after you. The Bible says in Proverbs 18:24 *"That there is a friend that sticks closer than a brother."* Jesus is the best friend that you will ever have. I don't care if you don't see Him. You can feel his presence and know that He is with you. If you are in a desperate situation today, just call out to Him. He says that He will be with you in times of trouble. He will rescue you out of the perilous pit that you are in. He will help you out of any situation that you have found yourself in. The word of God says, *"Call upon me in times of trouble and I will answer you."* He will surely deliver you from your condition that you have found yourself in. He is an ever present help in times of trouble.

There is no sin too great that Jesus won't forgive. There is no problem too high that he can't reach out and save you. I don't care if you are old or young, rich or poor, fat or skinny, or whatever condition you are in. Jesus is there to help you and bring you into your destiny. It is indeed a journey. Some days are going to be much rougher than other ones. But during those days you just reach out and take His hand. He will walk you through the rough spots. What a glorious God!

Chapter 17

A CALL TO THE MINISTRY

The flight back to California seemed very short. I had a new found confidence in the Lord that everything was going to be all right. After the wonderful experience I had with the Lord back in my room, I had no more fear. I got off the plane with a new sense of purpose and destiny. What great things was God going to do for me in the future? I didn't know, but I knew there were exciting things right around the corner.

The next few weeks were very hectic getting the children back in their routine with school. It had been a very traumatic event for them, but God had given them grace through it all and they were all stronger in many ways because of it.

I was starting to get involved with our church and singing special music. I was also helping leading prayer at 5:00 a.m. in the morning one day a week as well. God was starting to develop some special friendships with a few women in the church. One of these new friends had told me about a meeting up in Los Angeles called "Women of Faith." She wasn't able to attend but said there was a couple speaking named Paul and Joyce Toberty who were used in a powerful way by the Lord. I sensed the Holy Spirit speaking to me that I was supposed to go.

The meeting was the following week on a Wednesday night. I drove by myself up to Los Angeles and was in heavy traffic.

As I drove, I contemplated about what the Lord had for me at the meeting. I sensed that something dramatic was going to happen.

I pulled my car into the driveway of the hotel where the meeting was and then walked into the foyer. A woman at the door directed me to where the Women of Faith meeting was. I walked in and took a seat. The meeting had already started and there was a couple leading the praise and worship. There were many people in the room with their hands in the air and praising God. Such a sweet spirit of worship!

After the worship, a woman named Noreen came to the podium and introduced Joyce and Paul Toberty. The minute they came to the podium I could feel electricity hit that place. They started sharing some stories of faith about their life in the ministry. They were such a wonderful couple and I could sense their love for the Lord. Paul shared for a short time and then Joyce basically took the meeting over and preached a great message. After the message she started praying in the Holy Spirit and she pointed her finger at me and told me to stand up.

She asked me what my name was and I told her "Meri." She then went on to give me a word from the Lord. In 1 Corinthians 12, the word of God talks about the nine gifts of the Holy Spirit. One of these gifts is the gift of prophecy. Prophecy is where the Spirit of God will use an individual to relay a message to another person or group. Typically this message is usually one of edification or comfort. It is something that usually that person already knows. But it is very important to note that this word needs to be judged according to the truths in the Bible. The devil tries to counterfeit this gifting and you see this through the psychics. Psychic hotlines have been flourishing all over this nation and world as people call trying to receive direction for their life. It is not of God and is a counterfeit from the devil. You need to be very careful whom you let prophesy over you. The Bible says in I Thessalonians 5:12 *"To know those who labor among you."*. If someone gives you a word from the Lord it is wise to know something about that person or their ministry. God uses the gift of prophecy to encourage His children and it is a very important gift of the spirit. There are many places in the Bible where this gift is used. That is what happened to me that night and the word changed my life.

The Spirit of the Lord came upon Joyce and she started to prophecy over me that God had brought me forth for the Kingdom for such a time as this. Then she went on to say that God was going to open up many new doors for me to speak and move out in the gifts of the Holy Spirit; that God would make my name known, but there would be much opposition. If I would be faithful, God would continue to grant me great favor. The word continued on for a few more minutes encouraging me in the things of the Lord. Many of the things the Lord shared with me I had already known, but there were a few things I was surprised at. When the Lord spoke to me and said I would be a minister and speaker for the Lord I was surprised. I was a singer and shared often when I sang at events, but I didn't feel I had the ability to speak for the Lord. How often God will speak something to us which we don't feel we are equipped to do.

There are many examples of this in the Bible. Moses didn't feel equipped to go and lead the children of Israel out of Egypt. He made an excuse to the Lord and said he couldn't speak. Moses did have a problem with stuttering and felt there must be someone more skilled than he. But God wanted to use Moses and the Lord told him He would send his brother Aaron with him to speak for him. How many of you today reading this book have been told by God to do something that seemed preposterous? God doesn't want any excuses, but He wants obedience. God often doesn't use the most talented or equipped for the task. He will use the faithful who are obedient. Many times God will use the foolish things of the world to confound the wise. He will take people who don't have certain abilities and use them in the strength of the Lord's might so that God will get the glory. If that is you today, just be obedient to the Lord and say "Yes, Lord; where you lead I will follow."

After the word of the Lord came to me through Joyce I sat down dumbfounded. There was a strong presence of the Lord on me and I was overcome with the Spirit of the Lord. Joyce then went on to pray for others in the room and it seemed like only a few minutes passed before the meeting was coming to a close. They ended the meeting with prayer and immediately the woman who was president of the Women of Faith chapter came over to me.

She introduced herself to me and said that her name was Noreen Owens. She asked me to speak for the next Women of Faith meeting. She explained to me that the speaker they had planned on recently declined due to a circumstance beyond their control and she needed to fill the spot fairly quickly.

I looked at Noreen stunned! Here I had just gotten a word from the Lord that I would be speaking and now the door of opportunity was opening within two hours of that prophesy. I told Noreen I would pray about it and give her a call back within the next few days. I thanked her for the wonderful meeting and I quickly left. As I was driving home I was praying to the Lord about the invitation. I immediately felt my spirit quicken within me and that God was saying He wanted me to step out of the boat and accept the invitation.

The next morning I got on the phone and told Noreen I would speak at her next meeting. She was thrilled and gave me the date and all of the other particulars that I jotted down on my calendar. After I hung the phone up I started praying about what I was going to speak on. I was waiting on the

Lord the rest of the day for an answer. It seemed like heaven was silent at the time. I kept on praying and went about the rest of the week still with no answer about what to speak on.

The following Sunday I was at church praising the Lord during the worship service. I was raising my hands in praise during a song when I heard God speak to me and say, "I want you to speak on the tabernacle." I almost fell over when I heard this. I started arguing with the Lord during the middle of the worship service. I prayed silently to Him saying, "I don't even know what the tabernacle is, how can I speak on it?" I started fussing and complaining in my spirit. Why couldn't He have given me something easy to share on? Why does He always have to do this to me?

How many of you reading this today have been stretched by God. God usually doesn't make it easy, but will challenge your faith when He calls you to do something. He is enlarging your territory and sometimes this means pulling you beyond what you think you can do at the particular time.

Well, this was the place I was in at the moment. I prayed the prayer of relinquishment and told Him I would do what He had asked me to do. I couldn't fight with God anymore. I just needed to be obedient. The rest of the service went along very quickly and before I knew it Pastor Rommel was praying the closing prayer.

As I walked outside I saw a woman I had recently met at the church named Shirley Kunau. She was a minister of the gospel who had spoken at many events over the past few years in California. I had heard about her reputation from a women at our church and she was highly esteemed as a woman of God and a prophet. We had become briefly acquainted over the past few weeks and I thought she would be a good one to ask about this subject. I approached Shirley and quickly told her about my speaking engagement and about what the Lord had showed me to speak on. All of a sudden I saw a look of recognition come into Shirley's eyes and she exclaimed that she had taught often on the tabernacle and had some notes on the subject. She then offered to loan them to me so I could do the research for myself.

Once again God had come through. Here I was arguing with God that I didn't know anything about the subject. God didn't care if I didn't know, but wanted me to learn. It's an important principle of seek and you will find, knock and the door will be open to you. There are so many Christian people waiting for God to drop everything into their laps. I have found continually over the years that God wants us to do our due diligence and seek Him with all of our hearts and we will find Him. If you are seeking a job today you need to go out and be persistent. Keep applying for any type of job you can until the right one comes through. Some people are just plain lazy and then they blame it on the devil that they don't have a job. Or sometimes they even get angry with God for not coming through for them. God showed the children of Israel the Promised Land, but God spoke to them that they were going to have to go in and possess it, drive out the giants in the land and make their habitation there. He didn't do it for them.

So now I was going to have to study and find out all I could on the Tabernacle and put together a sermon as the Holy Spirit lead me. Shirley came by the next day and dropped the notes off at my home. I immediately started studying them and spent the next month steeped in the Bible, concordances, and notes. Finally, I had put together an amazing message complete with a large poster board with a diagram of the tabernacle so they could follow me as I spoke about the various items in the tabernacle.

The day came for me to speak at the Women of Faith meeting. I was prepared and drove up to Los Angeles with my husband. He prayed with me before we got out of the car and helped carry my poster board and notes. Upon entering the room I again experienced a feeling of anticipation. I knew God was going to do something spectacular for me. I had been obedient to speaking on what the Holy Spirit had showed me. I had spent countless hours praying and studying. Now it was finally time to share my message.

There were quite a few people who had come to the meeting. I set up the poster board on an easel at the front of the room next to the podium. Noreen and her husband prayed with me for the anointing to be strong as I ministered the word of the Lord. The meeting started right on time with some wonderful praise and worship. It seemed like an eternity before they called me up to the podium. I was very nervous at first but didn't show it. I walked up there like I had spoken hundreds of times before.

I opened the meeting with prayer and then started sharing with them the story of how I came to speak on the tabernacle. One thing I have always found out about speaking in front of others is that it is good to be transparent. People want to know that you are real and not someone who is untouchable. I did relate the story of how I didn't want to speak on that subject and had an argument with God. Everyone started to laugh when they heard that part of the story because everyone can relate to fighting with God over something He sometimes calls us to do.

But then I got down to the meat of the message. I went into detail about the tabernacle and the history of how it came into existence. I then shared on every item in the tabernacle and the symbolism behind it. Before I was done every person in the room was mesmerized by what God had me share. It was a compelling message, but went into great detail about the plan of God for our lives. At the end of the message I had people come up for prayer and there was a long line. It took over an hour before I had finished praying with all who were in the line.

When it was finally time to pack up and leave, the husband of the woman in charge came up to me and said it was the most well prepared message that he had ever witnessed. I felt good knowing I had done everything God had told me to do. I went away from that meeting knowing that God had challenged me to speak on something totally foreign to me. I had to research and study for many hours to get to the point where I felt I could speak with any authority on the subject.

I had prayed and fasted and done my due diligence to get to that point. Now God had to take over from there - and He did. As I left the meeting that night with my husband, I knew this was only the beginning of many more meetings where I would be obedient to what God was showing me to speak on. This was another journey of faith and I didn't know where it would lead me, but I did realize that where He leads, I would follow.

Chapter 18

A NEW BEGINNING

A few more months had passed and things were going along fairly smoothly. The children had adjusted to coming back and getting back in school. They were sad that Jack had passed away, but they knew there was a purpose in everything. I sensed very strongly in my spirit that God wanted me to start a women's group of some kind.

I had recently met a good friend when working at Bullock's at the Mission Viejo Mall (Bullock's was sold to Macy's a few years ago). She was a make-up artist and her name was Kristen Renfree. We had become very close and she was also a Christian. I felt the Lord had put it upon my heart that Kristin was to be involved in this women's group.

One day I attended a Women's Aglow meeting up in Costa Mesa and shared my vision of this women's meeting with the area board president. When she heard my idea she immediately said she needed to speak with me after the meeting.

I sat down with her at a table and she shared with me that one of the Women's Aglow Chapters was ready to close their doors, but they were looking for someone to take it over. She immediately thought of me when they were discussing this earlier. Then when I shared with her that I felt God had spoken to me about setting up a women's group only confirmed it.

She basically was offering me to step into the office of president of the Huntington Beach Chapter of Women's Aglow. I told her I would pray about it and get back to her. It seemed like God was always putting me in these positions where I was on the cutting edge of what He wanted to do at the moment.

I discussed what had happened in this meeting with Kristen and we prayed. After our prayer we both felt it was ordained by God that we should forsake our own endeavors and go with taking over the chapter of the Women's Aglow in Huntington Beach.

We went to the first meeting as the president and vice-president. We were introduced by Shari, the president of the area board. There were about 20 women present and most of them were senior citizens. They were all very lovely, beautiful women of God who had walked with the Lord for a long time.

As I stood up to share about the vision God had given me about setting up a women's group, I stood back in awe. Here only 30 days ago God had spoken to me about starting a women's group. Now I was standing in front over 20 women who were wonderful women of God who wanted to be taught.

I shared with these women about the vision God had given me and that I would be there for them to help them with whatever God had wanted for their lives. It was another new beginning for me and I had no clue where God was going to take this thing.

After I shared for another ten minutes we had a buffet lunch. The women crowded around me thanking me for taking over the position of president. Until that point I didn't realize that if I did not step in as president, their chapter was going to close. I knew God had arranged this whole thing. As I mentioned earlier, God has a way and means committee above what we can ever even think. This was a set up from God!

After a few hours of fellowshipping with these wonderful women, Kristen and I finally left. As we left in our car we had great anticipation of what was going to happen with our little chapter of Women's Aglow. We had some seasoned women who knew how to get a hold of God in prayer. I knew we had a lot to learn from these women. It was only the beginning; hold on for the ride!

We started out with a great big bang! The past president had been having their meetings at the Claim Jumper in Fountain Valley. Well, we would continue on there until God showed us otherwise. At the next meeting of Women's Aglow we were formally sworn in as president and vice-president. There were over 75 people who attended and everyone was very excited about what God was going to do.

We were very young women with a vision and we knew nothing could stop us. If God be for us who could be against us!

Every week we got together for prayer and Bible study at the home of Ruth Hapke. Ruth is a wonderful woman of God who has the gift of hospitality. Every Tuesday morning we would meet at Ruth's home and have a time of Bible study. After the Bible study we then went into a time of praise and prayer. These meetings were powerful and this is where the foundation of much of the ministry that I have today is founded on.

Their chapter had been ready to die but was now thriving and many new people were coming into the Bible studies and monthly breakfast meetings. We were seeing the gifts of the spirit flowing out of these meetings and the women were growing and moving out by faith.

For the next year I watched as God continued to expand this ministry and began healing and transforming women's lives! It was a wonderful time to see the Holy Spirit move in such a powerful way.

However my journey was about take an unexpected detour. One day I had to go to the Department of Motor Vehicles and get my licensed renewed. When I finally got to the clerk I paid my fees and was told I needed to take an eye examination since four years had elapsed. I stepped up to the line and was told to cover my right eye and read the first line on the chart. I covered my eye but I didn't see anything. I must have started to move my other hand away from the eye so I could see with the right eye. The technician immediately corrected me and said I had to keep my right hand over the right eye. I had not realized that I had subconsciously moved my right hand. So I put the hand back over my right eye and looked again at the line on the top.

To my amazement I could not see anything! I was totally flabbergasted! I had always had 20/20 vision. Now I couldn't even see out of my left eye at all! The technician told me I needed to go and get my eyes checked out at an ophthalmologist's office and gave me a temporary license. He could not give me the permanent license until I had done that.

So I walked out of the Department of Motor Vehicles with a confused look of bewilderment on my face. What is happening to me? I've never had any vision problems? Do I need glasses or is it something far more ominous than that, I thought to myself.

I called my husband who immediately assured me that it was probably nothing. But deep down inside I felt that it was indeed something that I needed to jump on right away. I made an appointment with an eye specialist and went to the appointment the next day with anticipation. I explained to the doctor what had happened at the DMV and he started looking in my eye with an instrument. He told me this would allow him to see into the eye itself. After looking through the lens for several seconds he finally made a comment. The doctor told me that it looked like my optic nerve on my left eye had withered. Withered? "What does that mean?" I anxiously thought!

The doctor sat me down and told me I needed to go see a neurologist immediately. It could be a number of things that would affect the optic nerve that way. He didn't want to discuss any of these possibilities with me, but gave me the name of a neurologist that worked at Mission Hospital right down the street. He even called and made the appointment for me to go right down and see him that day. I thanked the doctor and left for my next appointment with the neurologist.

The spirit of fear tried to immediately hit me as I walked out of the door. "You're going to die, something is really wrong with you," I heard a voice say to me. I knew this was not the voice of God so I immediately pushed the thought from my mind. I prayed to the Lord softly and asked Him to give me strength.

As I walked into the medical building where I had the appointment I went and saw that Dr. Johnson was on the third floor. I took the elevator to the floor and walked into the nicely furnished office and gave my name to the receptionist. It seemed like I had to wait an eternity until I was finally ushered into his office.

Dr. Johnson was a man in his mid-fifties who had a very kind expression on his face. He asked me many questions about what I had experienced. He asked me about my family's medical history. I answered everything he asked and then he finally sat down and leveled with me.

"There are a number of things that this could be," Dr. Johnson stated. "We don't want to get into any type of speculation until we have a MRI of your brain. Then we will be able to determine exactly what this is and why you cannot see out of your left eye." I tried to question him about what were some of the possibilities of why this was happening. He didn't want to frighten me, but he told me that it could be multiple sclerosis or some other autoimmune disease that attacks the nervous system. "Or it could be something entirely different," Dr. Johnson patiently told me. "We won't know until we have the MRI taken," he stated. So once again we scheduled an appointment for the MRI at the end of the week. I thanked Dr. Johnson and left the building with a heavy heart. Things had been going so well the last year and now I had to deal with this!

It seemed like a lifetime until I had that MRI. My husband, Rick, was very supportive and prayed with me every night. "It's probably nothing," Rick would cheerfully say to me. But I could see in his eyes a look on concern on his face when he thought I wasn't looking. Finally, the day came when I was to have the MRI.

I had to go to another medical building right across the street from Mission Hospital. I again signed in and they led me into a room where there was a long tube like machine. "What is that contraption?" I asked the nurse.

It is a MRI machine, which stands for Magnetic Resonance Imaging. MRI scanners do not involve x-rays, but work on the principle of atomic nuclear-spin resonance. They use massive magnetic fields, so far thought to be harmless to the body, and radio signals to deflect atoms and cause them to emit tiny signals that can be localised. These produce computer-constructed images of amazing detail. MRI scanners can resolve detail in the brain and spinal cord so fine that the individual plaques in multiple sclerosis, for instance, can be seen.

The nurse instructed me how to get into the machine and then told me it would take an hour for all of the images to be recorded. She turned and walked out of the room and shut the door quietly behind her. I was left inside of this long hollow tube with a feeling of total isolation. Many people get claustrophobic when they are inside the MRI machines. I was starting to feel the same way but I started praying to God.

"Lord, please give me the strength I need to get through this today," I pleaded gently to the Lord. As soon as the prayer left my lips I felt a sense of total calm come over me. The rest of the hour in the tube I quietly sang songs of praise to the Lord. Before I knew it the time was over and the nurse came into the room and let me out of the machine.

I signed all of the forms they needed and was told the doctor would be calling me after they reviewed the images. It would be a few hours for all of the images to be processed. I thanked the nurse and quickly left the building and rushed to my car. I was just glad to be out of that place!

I drove up to our office in Santa Ana where my husband's business was located. Rick and I went to lunch and I told him about all that had transpired from my visit with the MRI machine. We had a great lunch and I was feeling very happy when the phone rang. I cheerily answered the phone to hear a voice I didn't recognize. "This is Dr. Johnson, is Meri Crouley available?" "Oh, hello Doctor Johnson, this is Meri!"

"I have been reviewing your images taken from the MRI and it shows that you have a brain tumor," the doctor repeated slowly.

There was silence on the phone as the words hit my mind...."Brain Tumor?"

"Did you say a brain tumor?" I repeated back to him in a state of shock. "Yes, Meri, we have detected a brain tumor and we need to do more tests immediately! I need you to come down and check yourself into Mission Hospital. I have ordered many tests to be taken on your brain. When can you come down to the hospital?" the doctor asked.

I told him I would go and pack a few things in an overnight bag and then go down to the hospital within the next few hours. I quickly thanked the doctor and hung up the phone with a look of shock on my face. My husband had heard part of the conversation and also had a look of dismay on his face.

For a few minutes we just sat there and didn't say a word. A spirit of fear began to hit my mind with destructive thoughts of death. I heard voices in my head saying things like, "You're going to die," and other horrible thoughts. Then I started to hear words of faith come into my heart and I knew it was the voice of God. The Lord was bringing to my mind all of the scriptures from the Bible I had learned over the past few years as a Christian. "Don't be afraid of sudden fear", "Trust in the Lord with all of your heart and don't lean to your own understanding," "By Jesus stripes you were healed". The Holy Spirit was bringing all of these verses to my remembrance. God was telling me not to be afraid, but to trust in the Lord.

Instead of a spirit of fear taking control of my mind - now a spirit of faith was rising up in my heart and giving me the strength to overcome any challenge. We quickly left the building and went home and packed up a few items in an overnight bag to take to the hospital with us. I called a good friend of mine who came over to the house and was going to watch the children for a few days while I was at the hospital.

We didn't try to frighten the children and so we just told them that mom was going to have some tests done at the hospital. They were concerned but didn't seem that upset since Rick and I both seemed so calm. I kissed the children and told them I would see them soon and call them from the hospital. I even told them they could come see me tomorrow and possibly have Daddy take them out for ice cream. They were overjoyed at hearing that and squealed with delight. After hugging them one more time I turned and quickly left the house. I had tears in my eyes knowing I was not going to be home with them that night in my own bed. "What kinds of tests was I going to have to go through at the hospital?" I thought.

Rick drove me to the hospital and we were silently thinking to ourselves the whole way. When we got to the hospital we parked and walked into the entrance. I asked a matronly looking woman at the front desk where I was supposed to go. I gave her my name and told her my doctor's name as well. She told me to go to the third floor and check in with the nurses at the station there.

When I arrived at the third floor the nurses instructed me to fill out some forms for insurance purposes. Then they led me to my hospital room where they instructed me to change from my street clothes into a hospital gown. I was given a blue hospital gown that only tied at the back with strings. I was told to put it on quickly because there were x-rays that needed to be taken as soon as possible.

A young nurse came into the room a short time later and told us her name was Melinda. She had a fresh face with freckles sprinkled across her nose. She could see that I looked worried and she smiled and told me not to be afraid. She told me these tests wouldn't take long and everything was going to be fine. I felt like God had sent an angel in that room to reassure me. Melinda told me Rick would have to leave the room because they were going to be sending me down for tests for the whole afternoon.

Rick reluctantly kissed me goodbye and said he would come by later to see how I was doing. When Rick left the room I started to feel isolated again. What were all of these emotions going through my head? Why did it seem like I was on a rollercoaster? One minute I felt like I had the faith to slay Goliath and the next thing it seemed like I wanted to run into a corner and hide?

Some of you reading this chapter may be in the same situation that I was. At this moment you need to take some time and give all of your fears and concerns over to the Lord. *"Call upon Him in times of trouble and He will answer you"* (Psalms 50:15). Now is the time when you need to trust in the Lord with all of your heart and not lean on your own understanding. God is with you but you need to push aside all of your own fears and rest in the arms of the Lord. God will not leave you nor forsake you. I know it may seem hard now but this is only going to be a part of your testimony. In order to have a testimony you need to go through a test. In order to have a message to share you need to go through a mess. If you are in a test or a mess today call out to the Lord. He will deliver you from these trials and give you a testimony and a message. He will give you the testimony to share with others who are going through similar circumstances. The Bible says, *"They overcome by the blood of the lamb and by the word of their testimony"* (Revelations 12:11). As other people hear you share your testimony it will give them the strength to overcome their tests and trials as well.

Rick had gone and I was all alone in the room waiting for the nurse to come and take me down for the afternoon of tests. She cheerfully peeked her head in and asked if I was ready and I told her I was. Another male nurse came in the room and took me down to the x-ray room. He chatted light-heartedly with me as he was wheeling me down the hall to the elevator. At this moment in time I did not even feel like conversing with anyone and almost wished that he would be quiet. However I was too polite to say this to the young man at the time so I kept my mouth shut. Once in the elevator he pushed the button to the floor we were going to and we immediately started heading downward. I too felt like I was in a downward spiral and prayed again to the Lord that He would rescue me. *"When you pass through the fires you shall not be burned, the floods shall not overflow you"* (Isaiah 43:2).

Finally, we got to our destination and the nurses that worked in that area started getting me prepped for the tests. They gave me a special robe to wear for these tests and started giving me directions as to what they wanted me to do. They got the machine all ready to go and then left the room while they started taking the x-rays. It seemed like I was in that room for an eternity before they came back in. All alone in the room with the whirring noises of x-rays being shot through my body, I again felt a feeling of isolation. Tears starting streaming down my face and I wondered why this was happening to me. But then the Holy Spirit started comforting me with His presence. I felt a warmth come all over my body as if arms were being wrapped around me. And then I realized for the first time that this was Good Friday. Jesus had died on the cross for me two thousand years ago. He died not only for my sins but also for my sicknesses. Easter Sunday was coming in two days! I had been so caught up in everything I forgot about Easter weekend.

Normally, I would be getting ready for a big Easter celebration and preparing for people to come over and celebrate the holidays with us. But this time Easter would be a different time for my family and me.

As the last few x-rays were being taken I suddenly had a revelation of Jesus on the cross. It was almost as if I could see Him on the cross with all of the pain and suffering he experienced. And I heard the Lord say to me in a gentle soft voice, *"I would have died for you even if you were the only one." Again, tears started to flood down my face, but this time it was not tears of self-pity but of joy. What a refreshing revelation to know that God sent us His only son that whosoever would believe in Him would not perish but have everlasting life"* (John 3:16). My soul was flooded with a glory I had not known before. What is it about suffering that seems to bring forth the glory of the Lord in our lives? Once I got beyond myself and really saw Christ, I could see the clear picture. The devil, or even your own flesh, will get you to focus on the pain or the problem, but if you will look past your pain and look into the face of Jesus you will be transformed.

Even as Jesus was on the cross, His mother, Mary, was weeping and crying. He had compassion on his mother but knew He must go to the cross so we could all be free. He could have willingly come down from that cross and even called 10,000 angels to His side to deliver Him. But that would have only brought temporary relief for him and Mary. He endured the cross, despising the shame, so we could all have life. If you are in a time of pain today, reach out to Jesus. He understands your pains and your problems. Call out to Jesus today and He will give you the strength and the faith you need to face any situation you may be going through.

In my time of isolation and pain the Lord gave me a whole new revelation of Jesus. It was as if I was going through the cross with Him. In the Bible it says, *"Take up your cross and follow Him"* (Luke 9:23). I did not sign up for this brain tumor. But now I had to trust in the Lord and follow Him. It wasn't a fun thing to do; I wished I could run out of the hospital and not ever come back. But I had to face this cross and I knew the Lord would be with me during the whole problem.

Finally, the nurse came back in the room and shut off the machine. Next she took me to another room for some CAT scans of my brain as well. That took another few hours but this time instead of having a pity party I now was having a praise party. The revelation of Jesus on the cross so touched me that I was in awe of His glory and majesty. It's amazing at how things can change by just changing your attitude. If you look at the problem you will be in pity, but if you look at Jesus you will be transformed. *"Be ye transformed even by the renewing of your mind"* (Romans 12:2).

The tests were finally over and I was brought back to my room. Rick called on the phone and said he was coming over in an hour and bringing the children with him. He asked how the tests went and if I was doing all right. I told Him the revelation that God had given me while I was having the tests done. Rick rejoiced with me when He heard about my experience with the Lord during the x-rays. Indeed I was being x-rayed not only by the machine but also by the Holy Spirit. The Lord was examining my heart and had shown me my fear. But as soon as I looked at Jesus the fear left. Face your fears and they will disappear. Face your pain and it won't remain. If you are experiencing fear or pain today, either through a circumstance or something going on in your life, just turn it over to the Lord. Don't run from it, but face that pain or problem. Look to Jesus who is your hope of glory.

"At the cross, at the cross, where I first saw the light, and the burden of my heart rolled away. It was there by faith, I received my sight, and now I am happy all the day".

Chapter 19

THE BRAIN TUMOR

I was resting in my room after the tests when my husband Rick peeked his head into my hospital room and announced that I had company. The next thing I knew all three of my children came rushing through the door with flowers and candy in their outstretched hands. It was so cute to see how excited they were to see me.

After giving them all big hugs and kisses they started asking me questions. "Mom, what are you doing in the hospital?" my daughter Christina asked me with a worried look on her face.

I compassionately spoke to the children about the tumor that they had discovered while doing the MRI. I gently said to them that the Lord had this whole situation in His hands and we were not to be worried but to have faith in Him

"But what if you die?" my son Jeremy asked me with a look of fear on his face. I reassured Jeremy I was not going to die and that God had everything under control. That answer seemed to reassure him and he happily plopped down on the hospital bed next to me. We all had a wonderful time for the next few hours just sharing and being together as a family. After a few hours the nurse came in and said visiting hours were over and everyone needed to go home. Reluctantly, Rick told the children it was time to go and everyone proceeded to kiss me goodnight and leave the room.

All alone now I again reflected on the events of the day. I was getting very tired and knew there would be more tests tomorrow, which might even be more demanding on me emotionally. I finished the day by praying and reading my Bible. Before I knew it I had drifted off to sleep and the next morning I awoke with a nurse telling me breakfast was being served.

After breakfast I was again wheeled down the hall to have another series of blood work and tests done. Finally, I was again wheeled back to my room where a doctor wearing a white coat met me. He introduced himself as Dr. Willard and he said he was the surgeon going to be handling my case.

He sat down next to my bed in a chair. In his hands he held a file with the results of the tests. For the next hour Dr. Willard went on to explain what needed to be done with my brain tumor. "You have a brain tumor which is called an meningioma. That particular tumor grows out from the lining of the brain called the Menges. It has probably been there for several years and has been growing very slowly. It started growing into your optic nerve and that is why you have loss in your eyesight. There are several different ways of operating to remove this tumor. One way is to go in through the roof of your mouth. The other way is to go in through your skull from your forehead area. There can be complications from both of these procedures and we have to use caution in how we will proceed from this point."

"But what about using radiation to shrink the tumor?" I cautiously asked Dr. Willard. He said that was a possibility, but the tumor had grown to the size that they needed to remove it before it did any more damage to my eyesight. "Years ago people with your condition would have eventually gone blind," he said, "But thank God that technology has developed to the point where we are able to operate and remove these tumors."

"Is the tumor cancerous?" I asked not even wanting to say the word. The doctor replied, "Most tumors in the brain are benign, but some can be cancerous. We won't actually know until we operate and are able to go in and take it out and then test the tumor for cancer." He assured me that I was not to concern myself with cancer at this point.

We spoke for several more minutes about the ramifications of the surgery and then Dr. Willard told me I could get a second opinion The minute he spoke those words I felt the Lord indeed wanted me to get another opinion on this brain surgery. All of a sudden Dr. Willard's pager went off and he checked it. He rushed off in a hurry saying he needed to go into surgery but would talk to me later in the day. I thanked him and watched him scurry out the door to his next surgery.

Once again I sat in my bed pondering all I had just heard. "Lord, I don't want to go through a brain surgery! Please heal me miraculously so that all of this can be behind me!" I pleaded with the Lord.

It was at that minute my husband came walking through the door with several of my close friends. John and Pattie Worre were the first people I saw walk through the door and I shrieked with delight as I saw them. They are from Minnesota and were in town visiting some relatives. I was so surprised to see them there! There were some other friends who came to visit also and we all sat around in the room fellowshipping while I told them what the doctor had just spoken to me in our conversation.

Patty spoke up and said she felt God wanted us to have a time of prayer while we asked Him for wisdom in this situation.

Several of my friends along with my husband gathered around my hospital bed and we started praying. I sensed the peace of the Lord come into the room in a very dynamic way. Then they laid hands on me and started to ask that God would supernaturally heal me. After several minutes of praying we finally concluded our prayer and shortly thereafter everyone went home for the evening. Easter Sunday was the following day and everyone was preparing to go to Easter Sunrise service in the morning.

I was still scheduled for a few more tests in the morning and would be released on Monday. I was going to have to spend Easter in the hospital! But I knew I was not alone; Jesus was going to be more real to me that Easter than any other year. I had such a revelation on Good Friday in the hospital that it totally changed my outlook on what I was going through. I went to bed that night with a song in my heart. I had such an expectancy of faith that the stone was going to be rolled away in my life and a miracle come forth.

Chapter 20

THE OPERATION

I awoke on Easter Sunday morning to a beautiful sunny day outside of my hospital windows. He is Risen! He is Risen indeed! What a glorious day to know that Jesus, my Savior, had rose from the grave! He had overcome death and was now raised in all His glory. What a revelation to know that as Christians we now live through Christ. It is no longer I who live but Christ who lives in me (Galatians 2:20).

After breakfast I was taken down for my final session of testing and probing. After a few long hours of this, I was again wheeled back to my room. Waiting for me in the room were my children and John and Patty Worre. They had brought me an Easter basket loaded with gifts. We had a wonderful day of fellowshipping in the Lord. Time seemed to fly by and before I knew it visiting hours were over with and they were being told to leave. As I said goodbye to my family and friends I was again grateful that God had given me such a wonderful life.

I went to bed with a smile on my lips knowing that tomorrow I would finally be able to go home to my own bed. We never realize how much we miss home until we are away from it for a while. I missed tucking my children into bed for the night and telling them stories of faith from the Bible. There are so many things we take for granted in a day. I couldn't wait to get home and start being a wife and mother again.

Monday morning rolled around sooner than I imagined and Rick had come early to pick me up to take me back home. We signed all the release forms and the doctor once again sat us down for a final chat before leaving the hospital. He reiterated my circumstances with the tumor and told me I should get a second opinion from another surgeon. I thanked Dr. Willard and told him we would be in touch within the week. Rick and I walked out of that hospital and I said to Rick, "I hope I never have to step foot in these doors again as a patient." My stay was short but it was long enough for me!

I went about my day getting the house back in order and attending to things that had gotten a little out of control. Thank God for mothers and women who know how to take care of a house! Rick had tried his best to keep everything under control when I was gone, but the house was in disarray and everyone was happy I was home.

That afternoon I received a call from a good friend of mine, Dorothy Johnson. She was the area president of the Women's Aglow in Orange County. I had known her for a few years and someone had told her about the brain tumor. She was calling to give me a piece of information that would radically change my life.

Dorothy knew a good friend of hers whose daughter had a brain tumor. Dorothy mentioned that this girl had a wonderful brain surgeon and she went on to give me this girl's name and phone number. "I felt the Lord tell me to call you and give you this information," she said. "I don't know if you have a doctor or not but you might as well call her." I thanked Dorothy and proceeded to call the girl immediately.

I remembered what Dr. Willard had said about getting a second opinion and I felt this was a divine appointment of the Lord. The girl who I called was named, Kari, and she told me about her experience with a brain tumor. "I had a wonderful doctor up at UCLA who performed brain surgery and I am completely fine today," she told me. She gave me the number to her doctor and I thanked her profusely.

As soon as I hung up the phone with Kari I called Dr. Becker's office at UCLA and made an appointment to see him on Wednesday. I was told I should bring my MRI slides and any other information the hospital had on file. I immediately made a call to the hospital and had them set aside these things for me to pick up on my way to UCLA.

On Wednesday, Rick and I made our way up to UCLA Medical Center in Los Angeles. We had the MRI slides and a medical chart Dr. Willard gave us. After we parked, we found Dr. Becker's waiting room and told the nurse we were there to see him for my 11:00 a.m. appointment. She showed me into a room and told me Dr. Becker would be in shortly.

In about ten minutes Dr. Becker came in and started look-ing at my MRI images on the screen on the wall. After looking at these images very intently for several minutes he turned and said to me rather abruptly, "You're a very lucky girl that you found me. People come in from all over the world to have me treat them for their brain tumors."

At first I was a little taken back with the audacity of that statement. But then the Lord showed me this was the faith this man had been given by God. He was an extremely gifted surgeon and the word had spread about his talents all over the world.

"You have an meningioma tumor. We need to operate immediately. When are you available so we can select a date for surgery?", Dr. Becker boldly stated.

Dr. Becker spoke with such authority that I was stunned. He knew it needed to be attended to immediately and not put off any longer. We scheduled the date right then and there for three weeks later. I thanked Dr. Becker and left the hospital in a state of disbelief. It was only a week ago when I had received the news of the brain tumor. Now I was going to be undergoing brain surgery in three weeks. Brain surgery! I still was in shock thinking about it.

I drove home and when I got there I called my parents. I told them what Dr. Becker said and they said they were going to book a flight and come out and be with me for the surgery and help me recuperate afterwards. It is so wonderful having Christian parents who believe in God and walk in His ways. We prayed together on the phone that God would continue to lead and guide my path during the next few weeks. When we hung up the phone, the Lord once again instilled in me a sweet sense of His presence.

The next few weeks went by with a blur. Many of my friends called and were praying for me. The Women's Aglow ladies called a special time of prayer and anointing over me. They anointed me with oil and prayed God would supernaturally heal me. I believed God would cause the tumor to disappear and when we did the final CAT scan before the surgery was to take place that it would be a miraculous event. I have seen God move this way in many instances and didn't want to limit what He could do.

A few days before the surgery, my parents arrived at John Wayne Airport in Orange County. Rick and I picked them up at the airport and we hugged each other like we hadn't seen each other in years. During times of crisis it causes you to grow closer together in many ways. My family and I have always been close. It was wonderful they were there for one of the hardest challenges I ever had to face.

We drove back to our home and had a wonderful time with all of the children who were getting time to spend with their grandparents. We had a wonderful meal together and we laughed and shared stories of precious moments we had all experienced in the past together. Finally, it was time to tuck the kids in bed and after everyone was asleep I spent some quiet time with the Lord. I prayed, "Lord, in a few days you know I'm going into surgery. If it be your will, please take this cup from me, but nevertheless, not my will but yours be done." I prayed the prayer of relinquishment to the Lord. Even as Jesus was in the Garden of Gethsemane before He was going to the cross, He prayed the same prayer. Jesus knew the pain He would suffer for our sins. He prayed God would take the cup of suffering from Him, but ultimately He relinquished it to God and said He wanted to do God's will.

I knew that when Jesus died he bore all of my sins and sicknesses. But I also understood that God uses doctors and indeed I had one of the best surgeons in the world operating on me. I went to bed that night with thoughts of the operation and how long it was going to take. Before I realized it, I dozed off to sleep and woke up with the birds again chirping in my window.

If the Lord knows every time a sparrow falls to the ground and also knows how many hairs are on each of our heads, He surely will take care of me through this surgery tomorrow. It was the day before the surgery and my mom and I went up to UCLA for the final tests and CAT scans before the operation the next day. I still believed that when they got the test results back from the scan I would be healed. It took all day for the tests and we went from one floor to the next for various blood tests and examinations.

Finally, we were finished and the head nurse told me I was to come the following day for the surgery at 5:00 a.m. Dr. Becker wanted me as the first surgery on the schedule in case there were any complications. Five o'clock in the morning? I would have to get up by 3:00 a.m. just to get ready since it would take an hour to drive up to Los Angeles from Orange County! Well, you don't argue with the head nurse and we told her we would see her the next day. She gave me very specific instructions not to eat anything after midnight and to come with an empty stomach. They didn't want me getting sick during the anesthesia. She gave me a list of things I was to bring for the week since I would be staying in the hospital afterwards.

My mom and I walked out of UCLA knowing that the next morning we would be back bright and early. The rest of the day flew by as I prepared my suitcase and got the children all situated. My parents would be staying with them while I was in the hospital. I had a good friend who was going to come over at 4:00 a.m. in the morning and stay with the children since my parents were going to be with me at the hospital during the surgery.

I tucked the kids in bed for the night and said a special prayer over each of them. I knew I would be leaving before they awoke and I wanted to reassure them that everything would be fine. Children are very sensitive to our emotions and can read through these situations. As I was praying over my daughter, Christina looked up at me and asked me, "Mom, what if you don't come home. What if you die during the surgery?"

I was startled to hear her ask me that question. I hadn't even thought about dying during surgery. It is always a possibility when you are facing surgery that you might not wake up. That question hit me like a ton of bricks. I smiled down at Christina and gently reassured her that Jesus was going to be with me and that everything was going to be just fine. I gave her a final hug for the night and quickly left the room with tears in my eyes. It was hard to look at her when she asked that question with such fear and trepidation. I wanted to hold her and never let her go. I didn't want to leave early in the morning for the hospital. But I remembered the prayer of relinquishment to the Lord and once again asked the Lord for strength for tomorrow.

The alarm clock sounded at exactly 3:00 a.m. "Well, this is the big day!" I thought to myself. I dragged myself out of bed and quickly got ready to go. I put on a sweat suit that zipped up the front so they wouldn't have to pull it over my head. The nurse told me to come with a freshly scrubbed face with no make-up or perfumes on. By 4:00 a.m. all of us were ready to go. My friend Tommi Thornberry had come over to watch the children for the day. The kids were still sleeping and I peeked my head into their rooms and said a prayer over them before we departed.

We quickly got in Rick's car and made our way onto the freeway for the long trip up to UCLA Medical Center for the operation. My mother and father were also in the car with us, and my mom suggested we say a prayer for the day. As we started praying, the sweet presence of Jesus flooded the car. After praying my mom suggested we start singing some praise songs to the Lord. So here we are at 4:30 in the morning singing to the Lord about his goodness and mercy. I'm sure some people would have thought we were crazy if they really understood the repercussions of it all. Here I was going up to have my brain operated on and we were singing in the car at the top of our lungs. *"In everything give thanks for this is the will of God in Christ Jesus concerning you"* (I Thessalonians 5:18).

Finally at 5:00 a.m. we arrived at the UCLA Medical Center where Rick dropped us off at the front entrance while he went to find a place to park. I checked in at the front desk and was escorted to another wing in the hospital. My mother and father were told they would have to wait in the lobby while they prepped me for surgery. I hugged my parents and they once again said a prayer to the Lord for protection over their daughter.

The nurse gave me some hospital garments to put on and told me to place my clothes on the chair where they would be moved later to my room. As I was getting changed, Rick came in the room. He had parked the car and had been told where

I was. Even though my parents could not come in at that time my husband was allowed.

I'll never forget the next thirty minutes or so before I was to be wheeled into surgery. I sat in the hospital bed with my gown on while Rick sat in a chair next to me. Rick looked very scared and I gave him a smile and told him it was going to be all right. We sat and talked about many things and finally the nurse came in and said it was time to go into surgery. Rick gave me a kiss and told me everything was going to be fine. I smiled at him as I was being wheeled down the hall.

There were two male nurses escorting me to the surgery. I remember not having any fear at this time, but only a sense of great peace in the Lord. As Psalms 23 says, *"Even though I walk through the valley of the shadow of death, I will fear no evil. Thou art with me O Lord."* I truly knew Jesus was going to be with me in the operating room and I had no need to fear.

The last thing I remember were the nurses hooking me up to a variety of machines in the operating room. Everything was very sterile looking and precise. The anesthesiologist came into the room and started telling me he was going to put me to sleep during the operation. He explained the procedure briefly and then started having me count backwards from ten. "Ten, nine, eight, seven, six...and before I knew it I was in a deep sleep induced by the drugs.

Now I was not aware of anything going on because I was asleep, but there were many people that day praying for me. I know it was the prayers of these wonderful friends and family members that gave me the complete victory which I will later tell you about.

That morning at 9:00 a.m. about 20 women came together for their normal Bible study at the Methodist Church in Huntington Beach. These precious women prayed all morning for me while I was in surgery. I would later find out that everything they prayed came to pass.

My parents and husband were waiting in the lobby of the Medical Center. Several of my friends had come down to be with them as well. My good friend, Cynthia Shakarian and her mother, Vangie, came for the day. Cynthia's parents, Richard and Vangie, are the presidents of the Full Gospel Businessmen's Fellowship. Kristen Barbato was another close friend who came down to spend the day with my family as well. There were some who stopped by for a few hours to show support to Rick.

It was very hard for Rick during this time of the surgery. Rick trusted in the Lord, but it must have been difficult knowing that your wife is in another part of the hospital having her brain operated on. Rick later told me he thought he was going to lose it emotionally a few times. But with the strength of the Lord he was able to make it through.

After several hours it started to get grueling for my parents in the waiting room. Every time they saw a doctor come out of the door they were hoping it would be Dr. Becker with news of the surgery. Finally, they received the news that they were waiting for. Dr. Becker came out and went up to my father and my husband.

"Well, we have good news!" Dr. Becker passionately stated. "Everything went much smoother than I had anticipated. The surgery should have lasted eight hours but we were able to cut that down by half. There had been a major artery running through the tumor, which could have caused a stroke. But when I went to take out the tumor it came out just like plucking out a grape. The tumor is being tested for cancer but most of these are benign and that is what we expect this one to be. Meri will be wheeled into ICU in the next half hour or so."

Everyone was elated when they heard this information! It was as if a big weight had been lifted off of them all and they started rejoicing in the Lord. My dad thanked Dr. Becker for everything he had done. They spoke briefly for a few more minutes and then Dr. Becker excused himself since he had some other patients to attend to.

All of a sudden I could hear someone calling my name, "Meri." I had been in a deep sleep and someone was calling my name; who was that? Then I awoke and it felt like a truck had run over my head. And then I remembered! I had just had a tumor removed from my brain! Well, thank God I was alive! The nurse started asking me what my name was and who the President of the United States was. I thought it was a little foolish to be asking me those things, but then I realized they were only asking me because they wanted to see if my brain had been adversely affected in any way.

I answered the questions correctly and the nurse smiled and told me everything had gone very smoothly with the surgery. She then explained they were going to be wheeling me down to intensive care while I was in recovery. I told the nurse that my head hurt badly and she said they would be giving me morphine for the pain once I arrived in intensive care.

As I was being wheeled down the hallway all of a sudden I heard some heels running after the gurney down the hall. My good friend, Kristen, had seen me being wheeled down the hall and exclaimed to all of those in the waiting room that she was going to say hi to me and see how I was doing.

"Meri, how are you doing?!" Kristen excitedly blurted out. I looked up at her and the first thing I said was, "How much hair did they take Kristen?" Here I had just gotten out of surgery and the first question out of my mouth was, "How much hair had they taken?"! Looking back now it is a little comical. But at the time it was a huge thing to have half of your hair shaved off when you had long hair.

I didn't realize my whole head was wrapped with a bandage and she couldn't even see my hair. She gently looked at me and said, "They didn't take that much." She saw how groggy I was and didn't want to alarm me by what she couldn't see. The nurse handed her a bag and told her it was mine. Kristen looked down and saw this small brown bag filled with something inside. She thought it was my hair and was thinking to herself, "Poor Meri, they took off all of her long hair." Only later when she looked in the bag did she realize that they were my undergarments and she had a good laugh at that one.

They continued to wheel me down to intensive care and told Kristen that she couldn't talk to me now but would have to wait until later. Once I got to my room I was introduced to a wonderful male nurse who was going to take care of me for the evening. His name was Joe and he had such a sweet and gentle spirit. He started hooking IV's up to my arm and started administering the Morphine for the pain. It seemed like nothing took the edge off of the pain for the next few hours. I had never felt such pain in my life and I prayed the Lord would give me the strength to endure it.

Joe gently told me it wouldn't be long before the pain would go away. He explained that I had gone through such an extensive operation that my body was in a major healing mode. No one was allowed in the intensive care unit for the first few hours; not even my husband. But there were several of my friends that somehow had gotten patched through from the operator to Joe's extension at his desk. Everyone was worried and wanted to know how I was doing.

I had been dozing and Joe needed to take some vitals on me. This procedure woke me out of my slumber and he started telling me about the various friends of mine who had been calling the last few hours. Donna Eagan had called from Minnesota and was very worried, Joe calmly told me. Donna has been a friend since childhood and I smiled to myself as I thought of all of the mischief we had gotten into as kids. Wasn't it just like Donna to be the first one to get through?

Joe explained that he had patiently told them my condition and that I was doing fine. Several of them wanted to call back later and get updates on my status. Joe told them that he would gladly talk to them and give them my condition when they called. I thought to myself how blessed I was to have the Lord give me such a wonderful nurse to watch over me during my recuperation. Even though I was starting to feel a little better, I knew it would be a while before I was going to be back to my usual self.

My husband Rick was finally allowed to come in and see me. Rick took one look at me all bandaged up and you could see a look of pain in his eyes. He immediately tried to cover up his reaction and told me how great I looked. I knew he was lying but it was good to see my husband and have him right next to me. We all sat together for a while and Joe went on to tell Rick that I had come through the surgery just fine and my vitals were normal. I was able to share with Joe about my faith in the Lord and was able to minister to him even while I was in a weakened state.

It was evening now and Rick kissed me goodbye as he went home to be with our children. My mom and dad were also going to go home with him but would be back the next morning with the children to visit. I would be moved from ICU in the morning to my own room. As I drifted off to sleep I thanked God I had made it through the day and the tumor had been successfully removed.

The next morning I noticed Joe was gone and there was another nurse who had taken his place. This one wasn't as friendly and I silently thanked God that Joe had been the nurse on the shift before her. At about 9:00 a.m. I was wheeled down to the hospital room that I would be sharing with another patient. It was a big room and there was a curtain that could be rolled down the middle of the room to give me privacy if needed. There was no one in the other bed at the time but they would be coming in shortly.

The nurse helped me change into a clean hospital gown and moved me onto the hospital bed, which would now be my home for the next five days. As they were finishing getting me situated all of a sudden I heard my mother's lovely voice. I had not gotten to see my mother since I had come out of surgery and I'm sure I must have been a sight for sore eyes. As we embraced I could feel the arms of Jesus around me as my mother hugged me. There's nothing like having your mother there when you are going through situations such as this. In fact, I felt like a little girl again and that my mom had come to take care of me during recovery.

During the next few hours my mom helped unpack some of the items I had brought with me since I was going to be staying in that room for five days. She had bought me a lovely new black satin set of pajamas and also a black turban that could be placed on my head to cover up the bandages. My mom knows me so well and knew I would want to freshen up once I was starting to feel better.

At around noon the person who was going to be sharing the other bed in the room was wheeled in from intensive care. It was a woman in her thirties who also had surgery done on her head as well. They closed the drape between our beds as they got her situated. It was quite a large room so I was not at all uncomfortable with the situation in the slightest.

Visiting hours for the day were going to be between 3:00 and 5:00 p.m. I was very excited because my children were going to be coming down for the first time since the operation. I had spoken to them on the phone, but I missed them dearly and couldn't wait to see them. The morning of the surgery I was told they were all very upset and Christina had cried for fear that I was not going to be coming home. It was going to be important for them to see that I was fine and God was very gracious to me.

I started getting prepared for the afternoon visit with some close friends and family. I put on the new black pajamas that my mom had bought for me and went in the bathroom to freshen up. When I looked in the mirror I was startled to see I had black eyes and my face was swollen. There was a white bandage wrapped around my head so I couldn't see how much hair they had taken off. That didn't bother me at the moment; I was thankful to be alive and kicking.

I started to wash my face very gently and then tried to put on some concealer to cover up the bruising. I put on a little lipstick and then placed the black turban over the bandages. It was quite a transformation from just a few minutes ago. I now felt presentable for the children and my other guests. It was important the children not be startled when they saw me and that I put on as bright and happy face for them.

I walked back to my bed and my mother's face was beaming when she saw I was wearing the items that she brought me. "You look wonderful," she exclaimed excitedly. The nurse came in at that same moment to tell me the doctors were making their rounds and that my mother was going to have to leave while they examined me. My mother went out into the lobby and the doctors came in for their visit. The surgeon who had performed the surgery, Dr. Becker, was not among them. There were four doctors present and I had never seen any of them before. They were going to be doing the post-operative care.

They each had a chart in their hands and the first doctor looked at the chart with a puzzled look on his face. He looked at me again and with a startled look said, "Is your name Meri Crouley and did you just have brain surgery two days ago?"

I knew that he was amazed by the way I looked after just having brain surgery. I told the doctors that I indeed had the surgery and was in fact Meri Crouley.

The first doctor who initially spoke introduced himself as Dr. Hameran. He told me there were a few medical students with him for observation and asked if I minded if they sat in on the visit. I told Dr. Hameran I didn't have a problem with that.

So Dr. Hameran started asking me various questions in relation to the year, date, how old I was and other pertinent information to see if my brain functions were working correctly. After he was satisfied with my answers he then took my blood pressure, checked my pulse, and did a routine examination of my vitals. After about ten minutes he looked at me and said I was recovering faster then he had ever seen a brain tumor patient recover before.

He did advise me to take it very careful as to the amount of visitors who came and to also watch what I ate over the course of the next several days. "Even though you feel better now, your body is still in a major recovery mode which will take time to heal," he said. He told me he would be coming by later in the evening for another visit. Then they thanked me and left quickly to visit another patient.

As they exited I saw one of the medical students looking at me with an incredulous look on his face. He still could not figure out how I was able to look so refreshed after only a few days after surgery. God was indeed doing marvelous wonders all around me. Through all the prayers of my friends and family I was indeed recovery faster than even I had anticipated.

After the doctors left, my mother came back in and I told her about how amazed the doctors were with the transformation and my recovery. We both praised the Lord for His wonderful goodness and mercy. I took a short nap while my mother read in the chair next to my bed. Visiting hours were coming up in a few hours and I needed my strength for the rest of the day.

I was gently dozing when I heard voices in the back of my mind, "Mom, wake up!" I groggily opened my eyes to see my three children peering at me around my bed. Rick and my mom and dad were also there. I lazily smiled and they started to each give me a hug. It was a wonderful reunion and for the next few hours we went over the whole ordeal with the children. We told them about how God had done such a wonderful miracle and that I was recovering quicker than they had ever seen a brain tumor patient. It was a glorious time and before I knew it the nurse came in and told us they would have to leave for the evening.

I reluctantly kissed them all and said I would see them again tomorrow. As I went to bed that night I said a prayer of thanksgiving to the Lord for the marvelous things He had done. I had gone through the fire and I was not burned! There are times in life that you will face incredible trials and situations that seem beyond your ability to cope. But that is when you need to cast your burden upon the Lord and He will sustain you.

Studies have been done and they say that 90 percent of the things we worry about never come to fruition. We need to trust God with what He has said and let Him take the fear from us. Don't lean to your own natural understanding, but have faith and trust in the Lord with all of your heart. God will lead you through the most difficult of all circumstances if you allow Him to. Remember, Jesus is the good shepherd and He knows you. He made you and knows every fiber of your being. He understands your thoughts and all of your fears. That is why Psalms 23 is so special to me. *"Though I walk through the valley of the shadow of death, I will fear no evil. Thy rod and thy staff they comfort me."* Sometimes God has to use His rod of correction on us. Sometimes the shepherd out of mercy for the sheep will use the rod. The hireling will use the rod to beat the sheep into submission. The true shepherd will use the rod to lovingly correct the sheep so they don't go off in a direction that is not good for them.

His rod and staff are both instruments to bring correction as well as comfort to the sheep. And it should bring comfort to you that Jesus is always watching over you as the good shepherd. He knows you by name and will make sure you come through this trial.

Remember, Jesus also makes you to lie down in green pastures and leads you besides the still waters. Many times sheep will continue to just keep going unless the shepherd will force them to lie down and rest. God knows our bodies need rest and often allows circumstances to come into our lives where we are forced to rest and get rehabilitated. God will restore your soul. That is ultimately what God wants, fellowship with you. So if you are in a place today where you seem totally abandoned and bewildered, let the good shepherd, Jesus, lead you besides still waters and restore your soul today. Just rest in the Lord.

The next few days went by in a flurry. Between having several visitors a day and doctors coming and doing check-ups regularly, it wasn't too long before I wanted to go back to my own home.

Dr. Becker came in on the fourth day of my stay at the hospital and sat in the chair next to the bed. "Well, young lady, it looks like the angels are smiling on you today," he said with a twinkle in his eye. "You are to be released a day early since you have been such a fantastic patient." I let out a whoop and we both laughed at my burst of emotion.

"I know it is not an easy thing to go through brain surgery. It can be very traumatic on both the physical and emotional parts of the body. But I have never seen anyone come through a brain surgery and recover as quickly as you have. You are a remarkable young woman and it has been wonderful meeting both you and your family this week. Please stay in touch with us here at UCLA and let us know how you are doing!" He gently shook my hand and then made his way out the door to visit other patients.

I sat there stunned for a few minutes knowing I was going to be leaving tomorrow. I was excited to be going home, but at the same time knew there would be a long road to recovery. As I contemplated everything that had gone on the last few days, my parents came in the room. They had just gotten back from eating in the cafeteria at the hospital. I told them the good news and they said they thought we should celebrate with a little party that evening during visiting hours.

My mom and dad went out and bought a few appetizers and brought them back in time just as my husband Rick and the children came bouncing into the room. The children were very excited when they heard I was going home the next day and started to jump on my bed as they hugged me. We all laughed at their enthusiasm and for the rest of the evening had a wonderful time enjoying each other.

Over the course of the next few hours several other friends came by. We ended the visiting hours by having a time of prayer and thanksgiving to the Lord. He is a gracious and merciful God and I thanked Him that He was always with me during the times I most felt alone. Looking back to when I first was in the MRI machine and they did the tests for the brain tumor, He had never left me nor forsaken me. What a great God!

We all said our goodbyes for the evening and I kissed my husband and family goodbye. As the lights were being turned out I said my final prayers and fell to sleep with a smile on my face.

Chapter 21

COMING HOME

The sun started streaming through the window earlier then usual, it seemed. I awoke slowly but then almost jumped out of bed. "I was going home today!" I was so excited that I almost fell out of my bed. The nurse came in to give me my breakfast and she laughed as she saw how exhilarated I was! "You better slow down or you'll be back in here at the rate you're going!" she stated as she set my food on my bed.

"At least I won't have to put up with this food anymore!" I good-naturedly jested with her. We talked for the next several minutes about the procedures for being released from the hospital and I was given some forms to complete before leaving.

After breakfast I started putting on my clothes that I had brought with me to the hospital in a little satchel. I was almost finished when my husband came in and said he was ready to take me back home. I gave him a hug and said I was packed and now all I had to do was change and get out of Dodge.

It literally only took me a few minutes to get changed and Rick laughed when I came out of the bathroom. "Have you turned into a quick change artist?" he repeated sarcastically.

I was just so excited about leaving the hospital and going home! I quickly looked around the room to see if I had forgotten anything that I should bring with me. There were several bouquets of flowers people had sent to me lining the room. I decided to take two of them with me and leave the others for my roommate to enjoy.

My roommates name was Marsha and she was not scheduled to leave for another few days. I walked over to her bed on my way out and gave her a peck on the cheek. A tear started to fall down her cheek and she said how much she was going to miss all of the activity in the room from my family. We had exchanged numbers earlier and I told her we would be keeping in touch with each other and not to be upset. I had been able to witness to her about the Lord while sharing the room. She was not a Christian yet, but the Lord had used me to plant many seeds in her life. I knew that her conversion was not far off.

I walked down to the main nurses station and said goodbye to all of the staff that had taken care of me for the past five days. There were so many wonderful people that I had met during my stay. It was a bittersweet moment because on one hand I was ecstatic about going home, but it was hard to say goodbye to some new friends that I had gotten to know during my ordeal. I signed the last papers for my release from the hospital and Rick and I got in the elevator and made our way to the first floor.

As I walked out of the doors of the UCLA Medical Center, I said a prayer of thanksgiving to the Lord. It was under a month ago when I had initially made my way to meet with Dr. Becker and show him my MRI slides. Now I was walking out tumor free and ready to face the world again! Free at last, free at last, thank God almighty I'm free at last!

The ride home was uneventful, but the traffic was the usual bumper to bumper. My mother was at home with our three children. My father had gone home the day before since he needed to get back to his job, but my mom was going to stay on for another week to help me while I recuperated. As I walked in the door all of the three kids came running and gave me hugs and kisses. It was so good to see them all in my home! We never realize how blessed we are just to be surrounded by our own families sometimes!

My mom came out of the kitchen with a big smile on her face! She had done an incredible job of keeping the children on their routines while I had been in the hospital. The kids had already eaten dinner for the night and were now getting ready to take their baths and get ready for bed. It was around 7:00 p.m. and their bedtime was 8:00 p.m. I had not eaten dinner yet and Rick said he wanted to prepare a special meal for me so he went into the kitchen and started rustling up some food to prepare.

I took the next half and hour and played with the kids and caught up on all the news at school and the neighborhood. All of a sudden I heard the doorbell ring and some of our neighbors, Andy and Barbara Adler, were at the front door. Andy coached the boys in baseball and they wanted to see how I was doing. They had brought some chocolates with them. My mom escorted them inside and they sat down and we had fellowship for a short time.

In the meantime, Rick had prepared a feast for my first meal home. He made swordfish with special seasonings and a beautiful salad with some rice. A meal fit for a queen! Since everyone else had already eaten, I sat and ate in on the couch while we finished visiting with the Adlers. For dessert I had a few pieces of the chocolate they had brought me.

We let the kids stay up a little later than normal and they sat with us as we chatted with Barbara and Andy. Finally, it was time for them to go home and we said our goodbyes and thank yous. The kids went up to their rooms and Rick said he was going to tuck them in for the night and say their prayers.

I stayed downstairs and my mom and I chatted for another fifteen minutes before I started getting sleepy. It had been a long day since I had gotten up before the crack of dawn that morning. I kissed my mom goodnight and went upstairs. I peeked in on Rick as he was saying prayers with the boys. "We're so happy that mom is home, Dad!" I heard Jeremy say.

"Yeah, God really answers prayers doesn't he?!" Jason chimed in. It was so cute to see their little faces peering out from under their covers as Rick tucked them in. I didn't want to disrupt their prayer time so I quietly slipped down the hall to my room. I was very tired now from all of my company and the excitement of coming home. I took a quick bath and then slid beneath the cozy sheets. Before I knew it I was sound asleep.

At about 2:00 a.m. I awoke with a serious headache and felt as if I had to throw up. I nudged Rick and told him I was not feeling well. Rick helped me to the bathroom and I started to vomit repeatedly for the next ten minutes. "What was happening to me?" I thought. Only a few hours prior I had felt wonderful. Rick woke up my mom and she came into the bathroom and tried to be of assistance. Finally, after another ten minutes where I was repeatedly getting sick my mom told Rick to call the hospital. Rick frantically called UCLA and got a nurse on the phone. She told Rick to bring me in at once. I could have brain swelling and they needed to do a CAT scan to see what the source of my problem was.

So at 3:00 a.m. in the morning Rick hurriedly placed me back in the car and we raced back up to the UCLA Medical Center. There were very few cars on the road and it was pitch black in the dead of night. Rick was very worried as he looked over at me. I had brought a bucket with me to use as I continued to vomit. By this time everything that I had in my stomach was gone and I was dry heaving. I felt like I was going to die. I was not afraid, but just deathly ill and told Rick to hurry and get me to the hospital.

It seemed like Rick was going 100 miles per hour and soon we were pulling into the entrance of the medical center. Rick double-parked the car and took me through the front doors of the building. I was wearing my pajamas with a robe over it and slippers. I did not even have time to change. The nurse at the front desk saw me and suddenly looked alarmed. Rick told the nurse that I had just been discharged the previous day and gave her the history about just having brain surgery a few days ago. The nurse listened intently as he proceeded to tell her how I woke up violently ill a few hours ago. She ordered a wheel chair to come and get me to escort me to the emergency room.

As I was being wheeled down into the emergency room I felt that I was going to die! My head was pounding and my stomach was nauseous. I know this sounds a little melodramatic but at the time it was real to me.

They wheeled me into the emergency room and transferred me from the wheelchair over to a gurney with curtains around it. There were several other gurneys in the main room I was in. The nurse started questioning Rick what had happened and he proceeded to tell her everything that had transpired over the last several hours. She asked what I had eaten the last few days and Rick told her about the supper he cooked for me the night before. When she heard that Rick had cooked shark with many seasonings she immediately told Rick that I was only to eat bland food for the next several days once I got home from the hospital.

She was amazed that Rick had not been told that I was to remain on a strict diet with the types of foods I was to eat. After scolding Rick for having not adhered to the rules that were supposed to have been given to him she started hooking me up to IV's, which she said would calm me down and help curb the nausea.

There was a lot of commotion going on in the emergency room at the time. It was the middle of the morning someone had been brought in who was on the gurney right next to me beyond the curtain. I could hear him groaning and found out that he had been in a fistfight with someone. He was pretty banged up and they were working to calm him down as well.

The last place you want to be when you feel as bad as I did was in an emergency room with all different types of scenarios going on all around you. I wanted to die and crawl under a rock somewhere and scenes from the show ER were happening all around me. What drama!

Finally, a doctor came over to me and said they were going to be taking me down to another wing in the hospital where they were going to be giving me a CAT scan. This is where a machine will scan your brain to see if there is any swelling or problems happening. Their main concern was that my brain might be starting to swell and was rejecting the drugs that were supposed to stop that occurrence from happening.

Once again I was being wheeled down the corridors on another gurney to get a CAT scan. Would this ever end? I had just checked out of the hospital a day ago and here I was going through some of the same routines again. They hooked me up to all of the monitors and got the CAT scan all ready to start scanning my brain. The nurse said she would have to leave the room when the scanning started but that she would be back right after the tests had ended. I briefly acknowledged what she said with a nod and quickly turned my head to the wall praying that somehow this nightmare would end. The door closed softly as the nurse left the room and I heard a whir of activity start to go into effect.

The machine started scanning my brain and I laid there in total silence praying that nothing was wrong. I was starting to feel a little better now since they had put some drugs in the IV's. It wasn't too long before the tests were completed and the nurse came back into the room with a cheerful smile. "We'll have the results back soon and then the doctor will come in to visit with you about the report," she said with a melodic tone in her voice.

I started to drift off to sleep and then I heard the voice of someone from afar off in my mind. It was the doctor who had come in to report the findings of the CAT scan. "Good morning, Mrs. Crouley, I'm Dr. Anderson. I know this has not been a very pleasant night for you so far, but I have good news for you. There is no swelling of the brain and everything appears to be normal. It appears to us after looking at your file that what has happened is that you had a reaction to the dinner when was prepared for you by your husband. With the drugs we have given you it should calm down your nausea and you should be able to go home in a few hours after some more observation to make sure everything is in order." He made a few notes in a file and he was gone before I could even blink an eye. I didn't feel like talking anyway and so actually I was glad he had left so quickly.

They wheeled me back to the emergency room and told Rick that everything appeared to be normal. They wanted to monitor me for another hour or so and gave me some more IV's with medication to calm any more nausea that might try to appear again. For the next hour or so I dozed and was able to get some sleep. It was very early in the morning and most of the night I had been up vomiting. I was finally now starting to feel like myself again.

It was about 5:00 a.m. when the nurse told Rick we could leave the emergency room. She gave Rick some papers to sign and said we would have to check out at the front desk before we would have clearance to leave. They propped me up on the gurney and an attendant brought the wheelchair over again for me to make my exit from the hospital. I was gently helped into the wheelchair and transported to the front desk where Rick signed some last remaining papers before we made our exit.

A nurse was with us as well and when Rick went to get the car to pull up to the front of the entrance she waited with me. We sat there in silence as we waited for Rick. I had nothing to say at that point. I was exhausted but thankful to God that everything was fine with me physically. Finally, the car pulled up to the front doors of the medical center and the nurse wheeled me gently to the front door of our car. After helping me in the car she said goodbye and we thanked her for helping us get situated.

Rick put the car in drive and he slowly pulled away from the emergency room entrance and made our way down to the freeway. What a night!

As we pulled into the driveway I was thankful to once again be home from the hospital. How often do we think that we are at the end of a trial only to have something else hit you in the face unexpectedly? This is a lesson that we always need to be on guard and ready for whatever may hit us in the face.

We walked into the house and my mother came running down the stairs thanking the Lord I was fine. It had been a heart wrenching night for her to see her daughter come home and then have to be rushed out again to the hospital. We praised the Lord for His goodness and then I went upstairs and fell immediately to sleep. I was exhausted from this last ordeal but thankful that everything was normal with all of the tests they had done at the hospital. Bless the Lord Oh my soul and all that is within me, bless His holy Name!

Chapter 22

RECOVERY

I woke up the next morning and I felt like a new woman. They had given me some drugs that would take away the nausea. My poor husband wasn't trying to kill me, but only bless me with some wonderful foods I hadn't eaten in a while. Thank God that it wasn't something life threatening and I was starting to feel like my old self again.

The next few days went by quickly as the children went to school and I slept and recuperated. My mother was at my side feeding me and watching over me like a hawk. It felt like I was a child again and it was so good to have my mother there nurturing me back to health. I slept several hours during the day and my body was slowly regaining the strength I once had.

The children would come home from school and come running into my room to see if I was awake. I tried to be awake by the time they got home so I could talk with them about how their day went and go over any schoolwork they might need help with. We started getting back into their regular routine and it felt wonderful.

My mother stayed with me another week and got the house in tiptop shape. She scrubbed everything from top to bottom to make sure our house sparkled. She wanted to make sure everything was sanitized and clean so I wouldn't have to be doing much housework after she left. Finally, the day came when it was time for my mom to go back to Minnesota. She had already been out in California for almost three weeks.

I did not want to see her go and I shed a tear just thinking about putting her on the plane. But all good things must come to an end and I knew it was time for her to go back to Minnesota to attend to her own responsibilities. Rick put my mother's suitcases in the car and I kissed and hugged my mom for at least two full minutes. I told her I would never forget what sacrifices she had made to come and help me during this time in my life. We both cried and laughed at the same time! How wonderful it is to have such a godly mother! I walked her to the car and waved as my husband and mom drove down the street to the airport. I didn't have the strength to go and still needed to rest and get my health back. The children were at school and Rick was going to pick them up on the way home from the airport.

I went into the house and everything seemed so still now that my mom had left. I broke down and sobbed! It's hard when you live in another state from your mother sometimes. I knew that God had led us to California, but I missed my family in Minnesota as well. Even though we would go home and visit a few times a year, there were some times when it was almost unbearable without them. This was one of those times.

I cried out to the Lord for strength. "Lord, I feel all alone right now. Please give me the peace and strength that I need to recuperate and continue on in the call that You have on my life and for my family." I immediately felt the peace of the Lord envelope me and give me strength. The Lord says in Psalms 46:1, *"God is our refuge and our strength, an ever-present help in time of trouble."* There may be some of you reading this book today who are going through very challenging circumstances and you feel all alone. You may feel that way but you are not alone. Just call out to the One who created you. He is an ever-present help in time of trouble. God knows just what you are going through and Jesus can relate because He experienced loneliness and pain as well. When Jesus was dying on the cross, He looked up to heaven and with a loud voice He declared, *"My God, My God, why have you forsaken me?"*

Jesus felt forsaken at that moment because Father God turned His back on sin. Some of you today may feel like God has forsaken you too. God has not forsaken you but He is birthing you through into a new thing. I remember when I had my first child, Christina, and when I was in labor I thought I was going to die. The labor pains were so intense that sometimes I almost couldn't breathe. But before too long the baby was ready to come forth and I had to push for her to come out. After several pushes Christina arrived and was put on my belly for me to bond with her. All of the pain of the labor did not compare to the beauty of the birth.

Some of you are going through some severe labor pains. But don't be distraught because you are going to bring forth a wonderful birthing of a ministry. It will be from your trials that will come your triumphs. It will be from your tests that will come your testimonies. It will be from your messes that will come your messages. So just remember, you are a work in progress. God is not done with you and praise Him during this time that you are under construction.

Many times when I would walk down the street when I was growing up in St. Paul, Minnesota, they had construction sites they were working on. They sometimes would put a big sign that would say, "Men at Work". Well, God is doing some construction in you today and some of you need to put a big sign around your neck saying, "God at Work, please proceed slowly."

We get impatient sometimes when we are on the freeway and a few lanes are closed down. As we're stuck in traffic we start wondering, "What is going on; is there an accident or what?" Only to find out after a half hour sitting there that it is construction going on. We get very upset thinking, "Why didn't they do this in the middle of the night or something."

Construction is never convenient for anyone. It slows everything down and causes inconveniences for people. That is the way tests and trials are for us. It slows down our plans and makes us have to stop and move a little slower. But this is a good thing because God is doing repair on our roads. He is doing construction on the inside of us oftentimes.

But once the construction is done things start opening up again. Many times faster and more efficient than it was before. In 1 Peter 1:6 (NIV) it says, *"In this you greatly rejoice, though now for a little while you may have had to suffer grief in all kinds of trials. These have come so that your faith - of greater worth than gold, which perishes even though refined by fire - may be proved genuine and may result in praise, glory and honor when Jesus Christ is revealed"*. You are being made into fine gold! God is making you a genuine person who will be able to relate to others. This will bring great glory to the Kingdom of the Lord.

This too shall pass and before long you will feel like yourself again. Learn to praise God throughout all of the tests and trials. Before you know it you will once again be sailing along in the glory streams of the Lord. *"In everything give thanks, for this is the will of God in Christ Jesus concerning you"* (I Thessalonians 5:18).

Chapter 23

A NEW CALL

The next few months flew by as everything in my life returned to normal. My health had completely recovered and I was getting back into my usual activities. While most of my hair remained long, I had three inches around the hairline completely shaved off during the surgery. It was stapled back together after the surgery and then eventually the staples were removed a few weeks later. My hair was growing in slowly and it would take almost a year before I would not have to wear any type of hat or headband.

I was one of the most fashionable women around during that year. I had hats for every outfit. It was actually quite fun to wear various hats with my clothing. I felt like Princess Diana for the year.

I started resuming my activities not only as a mother, but also my responsibilities as president of Women's Aglow. The Spirit of the Lord was moving in our chapter meetings and many new women were starting to attend the monthly breakfast meetings we were holding. I started to get invited by other chapters to speak about what had happened to me in reference to the brain tumor. Word had spread about what the Lord had done and I was inundated with phone calls.

For the next few years I spoke throughout Southern California. I was also starting to speak up in Los Angeles and down in San Diego. The Lord really started to teach me during this time about preparing a message and then moving in the Gifts of the Spirit afterwards in praying with various people. It was exciting to watch and many people were encouraged as God spoke through my ministry to them.

I was at a conference in Anaheim when the thought started coming to me about once again reaching out to young people. It had come to me so suddenly in my thought processes that I dismissed it after a few moments of pondering it. I thought to myself, "I'm too busy to start getting involved in that." It's not that I didn't want to obey God; I wasn't sure where the thought came from and should have known that God was starting to put these seeds in my mind to get me prepared for what He was going to ask me to do.

That is the way the Lord works many times in our lives. He will start dropping thoughts in your mind as well as other people who will start making suggestions to you about certain things. He is getting you ready and prepared for the calling that He is placing on you. These thoughts started popping into my mind quite regularly now and God was starting to get my attention. I started praying and asking God to show me what He wanted me to do about the young people. I waited on the Lord, but it seemed like He was silent about the subject for the moment.

So I continued on with my life and one morning I was down in San Diego speaking at a woman's conference. I was sitting there as a woman was sharing some of the announcements for upcoming activities with their organization. She started speaking about a youth outreach they were going to be having the following month. I was listening but also thinking about the message I would be sharing shortly when all of a sudden the Holy Spirit dropped a bomb on me. I heard the voice of God say to me, "Now is the time that I want you to start working with the youth." It was almost as if God had spoken audibly to me and I sat there stunned. This wasn't just a thought that He had placed there as before. This was a direct command, and I knew that it was the time to really start moving out in this realm.

But what was I to do about this? I wasn't sure, but one thing I have found out from walking with God the past several years prior was that I was now going to seek and I would find. I got up and shared the message God had put on my heart for the day and finished out with praying for a few hours over many women who had come forward with various needs. The Holy Spirit ministered to them in a very profound way and the conference was finished later in the afternoon.

After the conference many women were talking in the lobby and I walked up to Jane - the woman who had given the brief announcement about the youth outreaches that had been going on in San Diego. I went up to her and shared with her about what the Lord had spoken to me during the conference about getting involved with youth outreaches. I asked her if she would be willing to get together within the next few weeks and strategize as to the types of outreaches that we could do to best reach the youth of California. She agreed and gave me her number and I said I would be contacting her within the week.

As I drove home from San Diego that afternoon I again was dumbfounded as to what God was doing! The Lord is so amazing that you never know what He is going to drop in your lap at any given time. When God does give you a new direction He doesn't tell you the full scope of what you are going to be doing usually. He just gives you a broad overview and then expects you to start seeking. Many times if God were to show us the full outcome of what He wanted us to do, most of us would never even attempt to step out because of all of the obstacles that we will encounter.

The next day I called my good friend, Dorothy Johnson, area board president of the Women's Aglow Fellowship in

Orange County. I told her about the incident that took place in San Diego and how God had spoken to me about reaching out to the youth. She immediately was excited and told me that she wanted to be a part of whatever I was going to do.

I then called Sandy Weisman who was also in Women's Aglow. We had spoken the past two months about this very thing at an earlier conference in Orange County. She also wanted to be involved and told me to let her know what the next step would be.

I picked up the phone and called Jane. We set up a meeting for us all to get together at the Denny's restaurant in Oceanside. Oceanside was a good place to meet since it was about equal driving distance from San Diego as well as Orange County.

The following Friday I drove down to Oceanside with Dorothy Johnson and Sandy Weisman. Jane met us there at the Denny's restaurant at 9:00 a.m. We all got there about the same time and were seated in a booth. We ordered some orange juices and all started talking at once, it seemed. There was anticipation in the air that God was doing something unique. I asked Jane point blank, "Jane, you have been doing these outreaches to youth the past couple of years. What is the most effective way of reaching out to the teenagers?"

Jane looked at me directly and spoke with an authority saying, "Concerts are the most effective way I have seen the young affected by the gospel!" She then went on to tell stories of how they had done several concerts in various areas of the country. A few hundred came to the concert and often many came forward to accept the Lord at the end after a message had been given by a youth pastor or band member.

We all started asking questions about various things that pertained to the outreaches and Jane was very patient in answering everything that we were picking her brain on.

We all started brainstorming on various venues and types of concerts for the next hour or so and before we knew it the time had flown by and it was almost noon. We had to break up the meeting since we all had places to be shortly. We knew the meeting was productive and thanked Jane for the information she had shared. We told her we would keep her informed about what was transpiring and we would keep in touch.

As we drove back we started to talk about getting together and praying over this matter. Dorothy Johnson spoke up first and said, "If this is the Lord we need to start bathing this in prayer. Why don't we start praying at my house beginning next week on Wednesday morning?" Well, it sounded good to all of us and we made a date to start praying the following week on Wednesday.

Dorothy didn't want too many women to come at first. She felt we needed to keep this prayer meeting to a smaller group of women that really had the vision for the outreach. And so it was decided that we would start praying next week. We marked our calendars and as I dropped off Sandy and Dorothy I again was excited that we were at the beginning of a new venture where we did not know where it was going to lead.

The week seemed to fly by and before I knew it the following Wednesday was already upon us. I dropped off the children at school that morning and I drove over to Dorothy Johnson's home in Mission Viejo. I parked my car and walked up to a beautiful home and knocked on the door. Dorothy opened the door with a big smile and said "Come on in." Sandy was sitting at the kitchen table with a cup of coffee in her hand. There were a few other women there as well who Dorothy had invited that I did not know but who had a heart to reach the youth.

We chatted for several minutes while we got coffee and made our acquaintances and then Dorothy called the meeting to order. She gave a brief overview of what had transpired the following week and said we were all there to pray for direction from the Lord as to what we were to do in getting this youth outreach started.

We all were sitting at the kitchen table and held hands as Dorothy opened with a word of prayer. "Dear Father God, we ask that you will direct us as to where we are to go and what we are to do for the youth of California. Please give us wisdom and guide us in the way that we are to go." Dorothy started the prayer and then we all started to pray for the things which God had placed upon our hearts. We were praying for almost an hour when the Holy Spirit came upon us in a very dramatic way. The fire of the Holy Spirit seemed to descend upon us almost as if we were in the upper room on the day of Pentecost. The spirit of prophecy started to come forth. The word of the Lord started to speak through us that there indeed was going to be a revival among the youth, greater than in the days of Azusa Street.

For those of you reading this book not familiar with Azusa Street revival I will give you a brief overview.

This worldwide revival began in downtown Los Angeles on April 9, 1906, in a small private home at 216 North Bonnie Brae Street in a tarry meeting. A "tarry meeting" is where people would wait upon the Lord for the baptism of the Holy Spirit with the evidence of speaking in tongues. Brother Lee was the first to receive the baptism of the Holy Ghost, followed shortly by several others including the revival leader, William Joseph Seymour. As the news began to spread around the city, the little house could no longer accommodate the crowd. Brother Seymour, directed by God, located and purchased an Azusa Street building that was being used for storage. The building was owned by First AME Church, the city's first black Christian congregation. First AME had moved to a larger location.

The movement began quietly in a small black prayer group yearning for the restoration of Christian life together as experienced by the apostolic church at Jerusalem on the Day of Pentecost. Glossolalia (or speaking in tongues) appeared and virtually every race, nationality and class on earth was immediately attracted to the revival.

Racial prejudice miraculously disappeared with profound social implications. Growth exploded exponentially and by 1909, it took root in over 50 nations. Less than 10 years after the revival's start, by 1914, the Pentecostal movement was represented in every American City and around the world from Iceland to Tasmania. The event was published in 30 different languages, its adherents turning the world "upside down" as Jesus' first disciples were reported to have done.

And now we all just sat there at the kitchen table after we heard the Word of the Lord come forth about what God wanted to do in this area. We sat there amazed knowing we had heard something very significant and that it was time to move. We didn't really know what to do at the time, but we just felt that before long God would show us.

We concluded the prayer meeting that day and made another date for the following week to pray as well. We all made a covenant to each other that we would continue to pray throughout the week and write down anything significant that the Lord would show us in prayer.

Before we knew it a week had passed and we were back again at Dorothy Johnson's house to pray. The same group of women were there and we all sat at the table and started to converse about what God had been showing us. We all decided we needed to just get right to prayer and we did. We prayed for about an hour when the Holy Spirit once again descended down on our little prayer meeting. We sensed such a sweet presence of the Holy Spirit in the room! Once again the spirit of prophecy descended upon the group and the word of the Lord came forth. God spoke to us to "Start looking for venues; faith without works is dead!"

It was such a direct command and we knew it was the Lord. In the natural realm, I'm sure most of us wanted to just keep praying about this for another few months. But God was very specific that we were to start looking for places to have this outreach at.

For the next few hours we started brainstorming about various venues in the area that we could hold this concert at. One place that Dorothy suggested was the Amphitheatre in Laguna Beach where they hold the Pageant of the Masters every summer. This theatre is located in the heart of Laguna Beach. Many tourists come to Laguna Beach throughout the year and enjoy the art galleries and culture. It is a very beautiful area located right on the Pacific Ocean in Southern California.

We all thought that this would be a great place for a concert and Dorothy Johnson said that she would make a call to see how much the venue charged and also to see what dates were available for booking. It was May of 1996 and we felt that the concert should take place in the fall just after school had started. This would give us four months for preparation and promotion of the concert. We concluded the meeting, and we all determined that we would continue to pray about this, and scheduled another meeting for the following week.

In the meantime, I started looking into various Christian bands that could perform at the event. Southern California was a melting pot for many different types of Christian groups. One sound emerging was punk and Ska music. It wasn't the secular style of punk, but a new version which Christian bands had gotten a hold of. It was starting to take off in many of the local churches. There were also several new Christian record labels which were promoting and producing these new bands. One such label was called "Tooth and Nail" records.

I had met someone at our church who told me about this record label and said that there was a management company who represented many of these artists on this label. The name of the company was called Davdon Management. They said the owner of Davdon was a young man named Dave Bonson and they gave me his phone number to call about booking bands for our concert. I called Dave up on the phone and he was a very pleasant but businesslike young man.

I told him about what we were attempting to do and he said that he would send me out a roster of the artists that he represented. He said that one of the up and coming bands that he represented were called "The Supertones." "They are a Ska band and they really rock," Dave declared enthusiastically. I asked Dave what a "Ska" group was. Dave replied that Ska was a type of music that used horns in their sound. It was a very happy sound and had a very distinct upbeat style in their music. Dave told me to listen to their demo tape, which he would send. He mentioned that their new album was being released very soon and they would be a great band to book. Especially since they were just getting ready to be launched nationally.

I thanked Dave and told him I would be contacting him as soon as I listened to their tape. As I hung up the phone I sensed the Lord telling me that this was one of the bands He wanted us to book. I closed my eyes and prayed that God would continue to guide us in all of the decisions that we were going to make. This was new territory for all of us since we had never put on a concert before.

I called Dorothy and told her about my success with finding a contact for booking various artists. She was thrilled and encouraged me to keep up the good work. That week the Lord continued to open up doors with divine contacts that would eventually help with the concert. I met a man who worked in the printing department at Saddleback Church in Santa

Margarita. His name was Larry and he told me he had a business that could help print the flyers for the event. He gave me his business card and I tucked it away for future reference when the time arrived when we would need to print flyers and posters.

We once again met at Dorothy Johnson's home the following week for prayer and Dorothy said she had some bad news. We were all set on booking the venue at the Laguna Amphitheatre but when the attorneys looked at the contract they said there was a clause in the contract not worded correctly for them. We would have to put up a million dollar insurance policy, which was standard procedure for putting on an event. But the clause in the contract stated we would still be liable even with the policy. It was a clear sign to us that this was not the venue to hold the concert at. Now we were going to have to keep praying and ask God to show us where we should now hold the concert at instead.

We prayed more fervently than ever that day and we got the green light from the Lord to continue in prayer and not to quit. After we prayed we were once again sitting around brainstorming about places when Dorothy cried out with delight and said, "I know the perfect place! Melodyland!" We all stopped and looked at her in amazement. Melodyland was a church across the street from Disneyland and in the sixties and seventies had been a very dynamic and thriving church. Over the last several years many changes had come to the church and Ralph Wilkerson was the current pastor. Dorothy knew some people over at Melodyland who worked in the office and she said that she was going to give them a call and see if we could book that venue.

The minute we left, Dorothy called and talked to one of the secretaries who worked in the office at Melodyland. She told them she was with Women's Aglow and we wanted to do a youth outreach. The woman was very receptive and Dorothy told her we wanted to find out how much the church cost to rent out. Melodyland had an unusual style church seating. There was a circular stage in the middle of the church and the seats went around the stage. It was an excellent venue for a concert. It had about 3,500 seats in the church and was the right size for a concert.

Dorothy told her we wanted to do the concert in the fall - preferably in September. When the secretary looked on the schedule she said that September 14th was available and gave Dorothy the price for the rental of the church. It was within our budget and Dorothy told her to place a hold on that date. After she conferred with us, Dorothy said she would get back to her no later than the following week. As Dorothy hung up the phone she sensed this was God moving and that we had a new venue. The first thing she did was call me and tell me about this new development. I was very enthusiastic about this and told her I would go into fasting and prayer for the new few days. Dorothy mentioned she would call the others as well and have them pray.

The next few days we all were praying and when we finally came together for prayer again we all sensed this was the right venue. We all prayed for the next few hours and by the time we were finished, we clearly knew we were to call the church and book the date. Dorothy mentioned that they needed a deposit to hold the date. That's when we started realizing we were going to have to raise money to start launching out into this arena.

"I have some extra money that was given to Aglow which we were trying to determine where to put it," Dorothy suddenly shared. It is about $500 and I feel that we should use this money for the concert. I will call a meeting with the Board and we will have a vote to make sure that everyone agrees.

Now we were really excited! God doesn't lead you down a path that He does not provide for. There is an old saying that

"Where God guides, He provides." Indeed God was providing through these circumstances that were now coming forth. All of us said we would start looking into fundraising for this endeavor. What was God going to do next?!

Dorothy called the church and booked the date for the concert on September 14th. After meeting with the board later that week it was unanimously decided that the money indeed would be used for the outreach to the youth. Dorothy was able to write a check to the church for the deposit on the venue. It was decided through the International Office of Aglow that we would run all of the funds for this event through the Aglow International non-profit foundation. This way we could use all of the resources that Aglow International had access to. We would also be protected legally since we were coming under their non-profit umbrella. That was another major answer to prayer as well!

The month was now June and we only had a little over three months before the concert was to take place. There was so much to do in getting ready for this. First of all, we needed to book the bands that would be playing. Then we needed to make the flyers and posters so we could start promoting this to the churches and the teenagers in the surrounding areas. What good is an outreach if there are no people in attendance?

As I mentioned earlier, none of us had ever attempted anything like this before. And on such a large scale as well! We had now booked a venue that could hold 3,500 kids! How in the world were we ever going to fill that auditorium? I was thinking initially of reach 300 teenagers. But God had enlarged our territory. So often our vision is too small. God wanted us to stretch our faith and believe Him for something big to happen!

I called Dave Bonson over at Davdon Artists Management and told him we had booked Melodyland for September 14th.

I told him I wanted to book the Supertones for that date. Dave looked on the schedule and said they were just coming back from tour the prior week. He mentioned that they would be back in town and available on that date. The price to book them was $1,800 and he would need a deposit of 10 percent.

I told him that it would not be a problem to send in the deposit for $180. Dorothy had already committed $500 from the Aglow funds to handle these expenditures and I knew God was supplying all of our needs according to His riches in glory. Things were going along so wonderfully it seemed almost too good to be true. We still did not know what to call the concert though. We had been praying and knew we were going to have to go to print soon. Little did I realize that God was going to give me the name sooner than I thought.

A few days after we had been given the initial money from the Aglow fund I was coming home from church with my family. Everything was going smooth until there was an incident with my 15-year-old daughter, Christina, who was upset over a minor incident that we were discussing. It ended up, by the time we pulled into the driveway, to be a major blowout and we all got out of the car very agitated.

I had to blow off some steam so I told everyone I was going to go to the gym for an hour or so. I worked out very vigorously that day complaining to the Lord that I didn't know why I had to go through these things with my children. How often do we bring these little things up to the Lord?

I was driving home from the gym and once again was complaining about the situation with my daughter. When will I ever learn to shut up?! All of a sudden the Spirit of the Lord spoke to me in an abrupt fashion. God spoke to me in my thought processes, "There is a bigger move of God coming than in the seventies with the Jesus movement; There is a new wave coming. I want you to call this concert series

"Youthwave" and the slogan is "Be a part of the new wave." You and your daughter are going to be right in the middle of it."

As I drove down Crown Valley Parkway, I was stunned at the significance of what God had spoken to me. I had been asking God for a name for the event we had wanted to do. When I heard the Lord say that the name was "Youthwave," I was totally flabbergasted! What a great name! "Be a part of the New Wave." I was totally excited about what God had said to me. My little problem with my daughter was no longer even relevant. I heard God speak to me that He was going to do a bigger thing than in the early 60's and 70's with the Jesus movement! I could not wait to get home to speak with my daughter first and reconcile what had happened during our argument. God said that Christina and I would be right in the middle of it. Somehow my daughter and I would be used very significantly in this next move of God in California.

I drove down the street pulling into my driveway thanking God for speaking to me in such a distinct fashion. Isn't that like God to talk to you when you least expect him to? Here I was upset at a situation on the home front and God had dropped a bomb on me to just start believing Him for a great move of God on the youth!

The name "Youthwave" rang out in my spirit. I could not wait to get home to speak with Christina about what God had said. I also could not wait to call Dorothy Johnson and give her the name that God had spoken to me about.

I walked in the door and Christina was in her room sulking. Teenagers are so difficult sometimes when you get into arguments. I knocked softly on her door and she didn't answer at first. I knocked again and I heard a little voice on the other side of the door saying, "What do you want?" I could hear the anger and the frustration in her voice.

We have to be so careful as to how we handle the teenagers in our life. They can be so difficult at times that you just want to shake them. But they are going through so many things hormonally and in other areas that you need wisdom in order to get God's mindset on the matter.

I spoke to Christina very softly and told her I wanted to speak with her. She didn't answer at first but then I heard the door unlock and slowly the door opened. I sat down on her bed for a moment and saw her as she shrank back under the bed sheets on her bed. Her eyes were swollen from crying and she had a very defiant look on her face.

I smiled slowly and felt the presence of the Lord flood the room. "Christina, I'm sorry for anything I may have said that offended you earlier." I then went on to share with her for several minutes about how her father and I loved her so much. After we got through with the situation and cleared the air, I now wanted to speak with her what God had spoken to me about Youthwave.

I gently started to share with her about my encounter with God on the way home from the gym. She sat up in bed eagerly when I shared about the experience. After I finished the story I had her attention in a big way.

"What do you think God meant about a "bigger wave than in the seventies?" she asked. I then went on to explain about what had happened during the sixties and the rebellion with the drugs and the free love movement. I spoke about my own rebellion in the seventies and how I came to find the Lord in a very dynamic way in the late seventies. There were thousands of young people who came to the Lord all over the nation during that time in history. But now God was going to send His Spirit in such a dramatic way that more people would come to God than even during that time in history.

We sat and talked for several hours about this situation. Christina was enthralled with the history of the Jesus movement and asked questions about many things. Finally, it was getting very late and time for her to go to bed since school was early the next morning. I said a prayer over her as I tucked her into bed. Even though she was a teenager, I loved to still pray over her at night and bless her upon retiring.

I laid my hands on her forehead and as I concluded a nightly blessing over her I sensed the Spirit of the Lord resting upon her in a more powerful way than usual. "Dear Lord, I thank you for my daughter, Christina, who is going to be used so significantly in this final move of the Holy Spirit. Please give her grace and protect her against any spirit of the enemy trying to distract her from the things that God has called and planned for her. Thank you Lord."

Chapter 24

YOUTHWAVE

The next morning I called Dorothy Johnson and told her my experiences driving home from the gym. I explained about getting the revelation from God about the name and calling our outreach event "Youthwave." Dorothy was also very excited and we were ready to start moving full steam ahead. Since we had the venue and the date, we could now start printing flyers for the event and start promoting the concert.

It was almost the end of June and we only had a few months before the concert was to take place. We had to start moving quickly to get the word out to the various churches and youth groups in Orange County. I called Larry - the printer - and told him we were ready to meet and give him all of the specifications so he could start printing our posters and flyers. We set up a meeting for later that day at 3:00 p.m. at his office. I hung up the phone and was happy that finally we were ready to roll!

I had a lot of other details to take care of that day and before long it was 3:00 p.m. and I was pulling up to Larry's office. The meeting only took about fifteen minutes. I gave him the outline of how I wanted the design. A friend of mine who worked in graphics had designed a crowd shot that was on the shore with a big simulated wave, which looked like it was going to crash down on them. Also, on the top we had in big text: "Youthwave '96 - Be a part of the New Wave." Larry thought everything looked great and I gave him a deposit check that Dorothy Johnson had given me for our initial fifty percent deposit. As I left, Larry said the printing would be done within a week's time. I thanked him and left with a song in my heart knowing that I would be able to start distributing these posters and flyers to many pastors and youth around Orange County.

The week sped along and that weekend our family was scheduled to go to Las Vegas. My husband had a business there and there were several business meetings planned. Many times we would go as a family to Las Vegas when he had these meetings and stay at a nice hotel. Las Vegas had changed over the past several years and tried to appeal to a more family-friendly atmosphere. The hotels we would stay at would typically have a nice pool and areas where the children could enjoy themselves as well. We went for the weekend and had a great time! It was coming home from our little short trip that God once again spoke to me in a very dramatic fashion.

We were driving home from Las Vegas and the traffic was horrific. I was contemplating about Youthwave and all of the things I needed to do when I got back. All of a sudden, God spoke to me again very suddenly and direct. "Meri, this concert will not be successful unless you have 24-hour prayer at least two months prior to this event."

It took me by surprise that God would say that we needed to have 24-hour prayer at least two months prior! That seemed almost impossible to try and coordinate. How was I supposed to put together a 24-hour prayer team? I had enough to do with all of the promotion and planning of the event. I started to argue with God about doing this, but one thing I have found out is that you don't argue with God; He always wins. God started to show me I was not the one to be in charge of this but gave me the name of a lady I knew from Aglow named Rosalee who would be the perfect person for this job. I didn't know Rosalee very well, but I had her number and knew I was to call her when I got home from my trip.

The drive home didn't seem to take as long after God started to speak to me. After arriving home I put the kids in bed since it was quite late and they all had school the next day. When I awoke the next day I got the kids out the door for school and then immediately called Rosalee and told her what the Lord had shown me on the way home from Las Vegas. She seemed very interested and said she had been praying more frequently than she ever had before. She told me God had indeed been drawing her out to pray more fervently for the youth and our nation. I was ecstatic that this indeed was a divine appointment and that God's timing is always the right one.

I invited her to meet with Dorothy and the other team when we had our weekly prayer time the following day. She gladly accepted and said she would be there. Later in the day Rosalee called back and she said she had been praying about this and felt God was calling her to do it. But she said she had no idea of where or how to start this. I told her I would come up with some kind of plan as the Lord revealed it to me and I would see her the next day at Dorothy Johnson's home.

I hung up the phone and went into prayer immediately. "Lord, you have told me to set up 24-hour prayer two months prior to the concert. I need to know how to do this and what Your divine plan is?" I sat waiting and contemplating this question when I once again heard the voice of the Lord reveal the answer to me. "Meri, there are 24 hours in a day. You need to break this down into eight people who will have three hours a day to pray. Break the three hours into six time slots at half hour increments. Then rotate the shifts so that every eight hours the prayer coordinators hour will change. That way every prayer coordinator will have three different hours to fill in three different time slots."

I again was stunned as I saw how simple this plan was. I got out a piece of paper and started writing the hours of the day. I put coordinator one from midnight to 1:00 a.m. Then I wrote coordinator two and put 2:00 a.m. to 3:00 a.m. on the piece of paper. I continued doing this until I reached 8:00 a.m. in the morning for coordinator eight. Then I started again from 9:00 a.m. to 10:00 a.m. that would be coordinator one's time slot and so on and so forth until the whole 24-hour schedule was filled in. The Lord gave me an ingenious plan. It was so simple when you did it this way! We now had our outline for the 24-hour prayer network. I immediately called Rosalee back and told her the plan God had given to me. She was amazed as well and told me it was an incredible outline. Of course it was - God gave me the plan!

Once God had given us the plan, it didn't take long before we were in full gear getting the 24-hour prayer team launched. I was scheduled to speak during the next few months at many meetings all over Los Angeles and Southern California. I was driving up to Thousand Oaks one morning to speak at a Women's Aglow Fellowship meeting when I heard the Lord speak to me that I was to ask the women to volunteer to pray for the concert.

"But Thousand Oaks is not even in the area of the concert, Lord," I protested. The Lord told me that it didn't matter the area that they were in - it was still in the same region. The Lord told me to ask for volunteers to pray and that He would take care of the rest.. So I told the Lord I would do as He asked and continued driving praising the Lord for His good-ness and mercy.

I exited off the 101 Freeway and started turning down the streets. I pulled into the parking structure and started walking up to the Civic Center Building where the Aglow meeting was scheduled that morning. I normally came with an intercessor who accompanied me for support, but this morning I was alone. I pushed the elevator to floor two and slowly I started to move upwards. "Give me wisdom and strength Lord," I prayed silently.

Once I exited the elevator I made my way into the room where the Aglow was meeting. The women were very friendly and hugged me as I entered the room. The meeting got under-way quickly and before long I was given the microphone to speak. The Spirit of the Lord started to quicken me that I was to share with them about the Youthwave concert immediately. So I changed my direction of where I had initially started speaking and shared with them about the Youthwave concert and everything that had transpired up to that moment in time. I told them about driving in my car and the Lord speaking to me about a bigger wave of the Lord coming to the youth than in the seventies with the Jesus movement. I then told them about the mandate that God had given me for setting up 24-hour prayer. The Lord showed me that it would not be suc-cessful unless I did this. No sooner had I gotten done sharing this with the women when all of a sudden the Spirit of prophecy came upon me and the Lord started speaking, "If you will pray for this Youthwave concert then I will personally go after your lost children and relatives. The youth are my heart and if you put this first, then I will put your family first. Come to the front now and make a commitment. I am wait-ing."

We all sat there stunned as we heard the word of the Lord come forth. All of a sudden the women rushed to the front of the auditorium. There were many women kneeling and pray-ing silently in front of the podium. Some of them were weep-ing and others were praying in the Spirit. We all knew that something very significant was happening!

The Lord told me to lay hands on them and anoint them for this prayer service that they were committing to. So I told them that God spoke to me to anoint them and that is what I did. For the next fifteen minutes I laid hands on them and anointed them with oil.

After I was finished praying with the women, I then told them that each women who volunteered for prayer was to write their name, address, and phone number on a legal pad. I told them we would be contacting them within the next few days about the times where they could commit to pray for the next few months.

The rest of the meeting flew by as I gave a powerful message that God had given me earlier in the week. After the meeting the women flocked around me asking questions about the concert. Several of the leaders went to lunch and were very supportive of what God had done that day at the meeting. One of the women said God had told her the same message about a wave of the Lord coming and hitting Southern California in a very significant way. We were all very excited about what God was going to do!

I drove home that day again thanking God for His great wisdom and plan. Our prayer list would be completed before we knew it. When I got home I called Dorothy and told her about the women in Thousand Oaks and how God had moved in a very dramatic way. There were 20 people that had volunteered to pray. We both decided that we needed to have a prayer meeting at Melodyland and invite many of the women who were already involved to attend. We called the church and got permission to meet there and scheduled the day for a Wednesday morning the following week.

We got busy on the phone inviting everyone we knew to come. We called all of the women who were already scheduled to pray and told them to invite others as well. It was a very busy week preparing for the prayer meeting as well as attending to the other details of the concert. We had printed out the flyers and posters that we were going to hand out at this meeting as well.

Wednesday morning was finally here and I arrived at 9:00 a.m. to find that there were already 50 women present. Everyone was very excited about what God was going to do, and within the next half-hour another 50 women showed up. We had over one hundred women who were eager to pray and do what the Lord had called them to.

Dorothy Johnson opened up the meeting with prayer and thanked them all for coming. She gave a brief overview of what had transpired up to that time and then introduced me. I got up and gave them the outline of what God had shown me with the 24-hour prayer schedule. I told them that I needed eight coordinators who would be responsible for three hours per day. Each shift rotating every eight hours so no one person had any one time period. It would be evenly divided up in sections as the Lord had shown me.

I once again brought forth the prophecy that God had said in Thousand Oaks at the Aglow meeting that whoever prayed for the Youthwave concert, God would personally go after their unsaved loved ones and family. The Lord had spoken to me that it was something that would continue all the way through to the concert. If God spoke it to one group, He meant it for everyone. I needed eight women who would commit for the next few months to lead this prayer movement.

I asked for eight volunteers and slowly the women started coming to the front of the auditorium. Before I knew it we had eight women standing there looking at me with anticipation in their eyes. Dorothy Johnson and I were both standing at the front of the podium and we closed our eyes and prayed for the women. "Thank you Lord that these women have heard your voice and answered the call to pray. Nothing is done but through prayer and supplication before you, Lord. Please bless them and give them the wisdom to fill the prayer times they will be allocated. Thank you Lord!"

Before we closed out the meeting I had everyone come to the front and we all gathered around the stage. I told them that we needed to pray for the Youthwave concert and see if the Spirit of the Lord would bring forth a word of prophecy. About fifty women joined hands together and started to pray in the spirit. There was an excitement that you could feel in the air as we all united ourselves in prayer in one accord.

"There is a revival coming to this land which is going to far surpass Azusa Street," I heard one voice shout out under the anointing of the Holy Spirit. There were several "Amen's" that came forth from the women after hearing that proclamation. Then the Lord spoke through me in a dramatic way to the women present, "My children, I have called you for such a time as this. Now is the appointed time when I will once again pour out my Spirit upon all flesh, your sons and your daughters shall prophecy. This is a new day when I will raise up the sons and daughters of God. There indeed is a great wave which I am going to send to California. It will hit California first and move its way across this nation. I am going to totally anniliate the spirit of perversion and pornography, which has a grip on this generation. I will break the spirit of addiction from this generation and you will see a generation that will arise that will boldly proclaim and declare that Jesus is Lord. Have faith and move out boldly during this time. The Kingdom of Heaven suffers violence and the violent take it by force. You will see me move in a way as you have never seen. It will be a much greater move of the Spirit than in the seventies with the Jesus Movement. But it will also be greater than the Azusa Street outpouring and anything that you have seen even in the book of Acts. Believe me and watch and see the salvation of God. Now is the appointed time to move. You are called to pray, and as you pray you will see My hand move across this State and Nation."

After the Word of the Lord came forth we all stood there praising the Lord. God was so great and we had such an anticipation that we were on the threshold of something very dramatic about ready to come into our state. A few more women came and said God showed them something as well and the next half hour was taken up by other people sharing scripture and visions God had given them to confirm the word of the Lord which was brought forth.

We wrapped up the meeting by giving each of the eight prayer coordinators their prayer packets with time slots, posters, flyers, and anything pertinent that they would need to facilitate their responsibilities as prayer coordinators.

Before I left Melodyland, Dorothy Johnson and myself stopped by the office and gave some posters and flyers to the secretary. We told her to give them to the youth pastor and that I would be contacting him later to go over some ideas about promotion with him since he wasn't in at the time. We thanked them and walked to our cars in total amazement about the power of God we experienced in the prayer meeting.

I drove home and was just about to start dinner when I got a call that was going to rock my world to the very core. Dorothy called me and told me that the church office had just called her and said the concert was cancelled. I couldn't believe my ears! Cancelled! There must be some kind of mistake, I said. Dorothy explained that after we gave the posters to the secretary, she brought it to the youth pastor when he came in. The youth pastor told the secretary that the bands that were going to be playing were rock bands. For some reason initially when we had booked Melodyland they thought it was going to be a nice little youth outreach. We clearly explained we were going to have music, but since it was

Women's Aglow who was initiating this request, they didn't have any clue that it was going to be alternative music.

When the pastor came into the office later that day, the secretary explained about this event to him, including the rock music and he immediately said that he wanted the concert cancelled. That is when Dorothy received the call about the cancellation and then she immediately called me. I was in total shock! We had all of our printing and posters already done! We had spent a lot of money in getting this concert underway as the Lord had instructed us to do! Why was this happening?

Now I want you reading this book to understand a very important principal. God will give us plans to do for Him, but I have found out over the years that Satan will try to oppose those plans. Sometimes by people very close to you and even in the church. We need to be diligent during these times and get the mind of the Lord on these matters. In I Samuel 30:1-6 the Bible tells us how David had been off fighting with his men and then returned to Ziklag after a long battle. When he returned he found that the enemy had stolen everything. They took all of his possessions including wives and families. What David did was not panic, but he went in and inquired of the Lord. Immediately the Lord told him to pursue the enemy for he would recover all. David did pursue the enemy and not only recovered what the enemy had stolen of his, but he also obtained the spoils of the enemy.

When we come under attack we need to first stop and inquire of the Lord. And then when we get God's mind on the matter, we need to pursue as the Lord instructs us. So many quit during the time of opposition and just lay down the fight. That is why the Bible says in Matthew 11:12 *"The Kingdom of Heaven suffers violence and the violent take it by force."* We need to violently possess God's Kingdom and not let anything get in our way. I was facing one of these times and now I needed to inquire of the Lord.

I told Dorothy I was going to call the office and talk to the secretary. There must be some kind of mistake! She gave me the number and I immediately called her. A receptionist answered the phone and I was directed to the secretaries phone extension.

When she answered the phone I explained who I was and told her I would like to come in and speak with her and the pastor. She was very cordial but said that the pastor did not want to have any concert which was going to have an alternative style of music. But she told me I could come by in the morning and see what we could work out. I set the time for the following morning at 10:00 a.m. and thanked her as I hung up the phone.

I called Dorothy back and told her about my meeting the next day. In the meantime, I got on the phone with all of the head intercessors and prayer coordinators. It was an urgent prayer alert and we got the intercessors to start praying immediately. I also told them to fast as well, if possible. I was going to call a fast since this was such an important request.

Many times in the Bible when there were special circumstances or events that were happening, the people would fast to obtain favor from the Lord. Fasting means that you abstain from food. There can be several variations of fasts in the Bible. Most often fasting consisted of drinking water only. But in the book of Daniel there was a situation in which Daniel told Shadrach, Meshach, and Abednego to eat only vegetables. Throughout history many Christians have embarked on this fast known as "The Daniel Fast." In Daniel 1:12-17 (NIV), the scripture reads,

"Please test your servants for ten days: Give us nothing but vegetables to eat and water to drink. Then compare our appearance with that of the young men who eat the royal

food, and treat your servants in accordance with what you see." So he agreed to this and tested them for ten days. At the end of the ten days they looked healthier and better nourished than any of the young men who ate the royal food. So the guard took away their choice food and the wine they were to drink and gave them vegetables instead. To these four young men God gave knowledge and understanding of all kinds of literature and learning. And Daniel could understand visions and dreams of all kinds."

You can see that by fasting God gave them wisdom and understanding into many things. That is the purpose of a fast. To abstain from either all foods and drink only liquids, or to abstain from certain types of foods as they did in the "Daniel Fast". There are many examples of fasting in the Bible when they needed wisdom from God.

Another situation in the Bible occurred in the Book of Esther. Esther had been chosen queen over all of the other young girl's in the Kingdom. But there was a wicked noble man named Haman who had a plot to destroy all of the Jews. Esther's cousin, Mordecai, had heard about this diabolical plot and informed Esther that she needed to go in front of the King and inform him about this. She was instructed to go in and petition the king for mercy. Esther pleaded with her cousin that if she went to see the king without first being called she could be killed. When Esther's words were reported to Mordecai he sent back this answer, *"Do not think that because you are in the king's house you alone of all the Jews will escape. For if you remain silent at this time, relief and deliverance for the Jews will arise from another place, but you and your father's family shall perish. And who knows but that you have come to royal position for such a time as this?"* (Esther 4:12-14).

Esther immediately called a fast for three days along with her maidservants. After she fasted three days she went before the king and was immediately granted favor. King Xerxes extended his scepter toward Esther and told her that he would give her half of his Kingdom. What was it that she was petitioning him for? Esther didn't immediately state what her problem was. She had been given wisdom by God to invite the King to a banquet she was giving later in the day.

She told the King to invite Haman to the banquet as well.

So the King and Haman went to the banquet Esther had prepared. As they were drinking wine, the King again asked Esther, "Now what is your petition? It will be given you. And what is your request? Even up to half my Kingdom, it will be granted."

Notice again that Esther did not blurt out what she wanted at this time. The Lord had given her wisdom and she invited them to another banquet the following day. "Then I will answer the King's question," Esther replied.

That night the King could not sleep, so he ordered the book of the chronicles, the record of his reign, to be brought in and read to him. It was found recorded there that Mordecai had exposed two of the King's officers who guarded the doorway, who had conspired to assassinate King Xerxes.

"What honor and recognition has Mordecai received for this?" the King asked. "Nothing has been done for him," the attendants answered. The King said, "Who is in the court? Now Haman had just entered the outer court of the palace to speak to the king about hanging Mordecai on the gallows he had erected for him.

His attendants answered, "Haman is standing in the court." "Bring him in," the king ordered.

When Haman entered, the king asked him, "What should be done for the man the king delights to honor?" Now Haman thought the King was talking about him, but he had been speaking about Mordecai. So Haman asked for a royal robe, one the King had worn, and a royal horse, one that the

King had ridden upon, and then to be lead on the horse through the city streets, proclaiming before him, 'This is what is done for the man the king delights to honor!"

"Go at once," the king commanded Haman. "Get the robe and the horse and do just as you have suggested for Mordecai the Jew, who sits at the King's gate. Do not neglect anything that you have recommended! Haman must have been furious! He thought the King meant to honor him!

But the King had meant to honor Mordecai. Haman then had to do all that the King requested and Mordecai was honored throughout the town.

God will use the plots that the enemy has planned for you and turn them around. Instead of Mordecai being hung on the gallows, the wicked Haman's plot was exposed by Esther at the banquet the next day, and Haman was hung there for all to see. So you can see that is was from the three day fast that God gave Esther the wisdom she needed before she went to the King to petition the King.

I felt that I was in similar circumstances. I was in dire circumstances where I needed an immediate answer and I was going to fast and petition the pastor for mercy. I knew God would grant me my petition as long as I was obedient. The rest of the day I fasted and prayed. I waited before the Lord and He gave me great strength to go before the church the next day.

The next morning I drove up to the church by myself. Dorothy had a previous commitment and she could not get out of it. I was not afraid, though, because I knew the Lord was with me. I parked my car and walked up the stairs to the church office. I told the secretary I was there to see Susan, and she told me to be seated for a few moments. As I waited to be let into the church office, I silently again prayed for favor.

The church door opened to the offices and Susan came out. She walked up to me and told me to follow her into the office. We chatted casually as we strolled down the hall about how nice the weather was that day. I know I was making small talk but I had wanted to break the ice and put on a friendly countenance. I sat down at a chair by her desk and she gave a little sigh and started to tell me that Pastor Wilkerson was not available that morning. Something had come up and she had discussed this concert at length with him. He still did not want to allow the concert to proceed at this time.

I persistently tried to tell her that we already had spent money for posters and flyers. I also told her that this was going to be an evangelistic outreach where possibly hundreds of kids could be saved. I went into detail about what the Lord had showed us and she listened patiently. But after all was said and done, she still said that her hands were tied and there was nothing she could do about it. She thanked me for coming down and I reluctantly got up to leave. I thanked her for everything she had tried to do for us and slowly walked out the door and went to my car.

As I started up the car and started to drive out of the parking lot I was in shock. God had brought us this far so why had this happened to us? Discouragement and defeat started to slowly creep into my thinking. This was indeed a moment of great humiliation. I could almost hear Satan saying, "Where is your God now? He led you down this path only to fail you!" But I knew God had told us to do this and there had to be another way.

An idea came to my mind to call Richard Shakarian, the President of the Full Gospel Businessmen's Fellowship. His daughter, Cynthia, is a good friend of mine and Richard knows many people. Maybe he would have a solution to this problem in locating another venue. I called his office and was put through to him. I explained the situation and Richard told me to drop by the office and we would go over the details. Their office is located in Irvine and I drove there as fast as my car could get there. I parked my car and went up to their beautiful offices in a high-rise building. I was escorted into Richard's office and he greeted me warmly.

I sat down and told him everything that had transpired the last few days. I told him about the vision the Lord had given me about the youth and a great wave of revival God had wanted to touch them with. Richard went on to share about how he had done many youth revivals when he was younger. His father, Demos Shakarian, had started the Full Gospel Businessmen's Fellowship many years prior. Demos was a great businessman, but also a wonderful man of God. God instructed him to start an organization for businessmen and Demos was obedient to the Lord. You can read the testimony about this great organization in a book called, *"The Happiest People on Earth"*.

It was after we had talked for a while when Richard suddenly stated he was going to call Ralph Wilkerson and tell him that he should continue on with this concert. "I've attended the church many times and I'm sure I can put a call into Ralph and something can be done," Richard declared boldly.

I thanked Richard and knew that God was going to have His way. In the meantime, I also had many more friends who were also worshippers at Melodyland Christian Center and they were going to contact the pastor as well. I just knew something great was going to happen and the Lord was going to open up the Red Sea. It was going to be as miraculous as when Moses came up to that great Red Sea and the Egyptians were close on their heels. It looked as if all was lost and the people were murmuring and complaining that God had brought them out in the wilderness to die. But when Moses raised his staff, God opened the Red Sea and they were able to cross over onto dry land. When the Egyptian soldiers tried to follow them, the Red Sea swallowed them up. Praise God! The Lord was going to do the same thing for me.

The next few days passed and I was expecting a call giving me a good report. No phone calls came in. I finally called Richard Shakarian and he told me he had put in several phone calls to the church, but no returned phone call had come back. My good friend, Mel Tari, who is an international evangelist and wrote an incredible book, "Like a Mighty Wind", which is the story of the revival in Indonesia many years ago, also tried to call and got no return phone call. What was happening? Why was the Lord allowing this to go on? It was torture.

All of the intercessors kept praying and fasting. We were on a mission and we were not going to stop until we heard from God. It was several more days and we had not gotten any response and suddenly I felt the Lord say, "The cloud is moving, I want you to look for another venue." It was as simple as that. Now I understood. It wasn't about what I was doing, but it was a test that Melodyland was going through. God was giving them a chance to allow His Spirit to move in their midst and for whatever reason they were not allowing this to come into their church.

I called up Dorothy Johnson and told her that we should stop trying to knock down a door that would not open. God said to start looking for a new venue. She agreed with me and now the race was on to find another place to hold a concert of that magnitude. I immediately got on the phone and started calling around different churches and concert halls. I had gotten a few leads, but none of them panned out. I was talking with a youth pastor of a large church about my dilemma. He told me to call the Anaheim Vineyard. He said they had a large auditorium with state-of-the-art facilities like none other in the area. I had not been to the Vineyard in several years. They used to meet in a cafeteria when I first went there. But since that time they bought this property in Anaheim and it was an incredible venue! This youth pastor gave me the phone number of the church and also a contact person as well. I thanked him and immediately made a call to the church.

I was put through to the contact person whose name was Dave and he immediately told me about the venue and the cost. It was affordable to us at that time and we set up an appointment to meet with him the following day.

As I drove over to the church I prayed in the Spirit that God was going to open up a door for us to hold this concert. "You have not brought us this far to just drop us, Lord. Please open up a new door," I fervently prayed.

I pulled into the parking lot and was surprised by the building. When I had initially went to the Vineyard it was in a different location, meeting in a cafeteria. Now I was looking at an impressive building with a large bookstore right across the way from it. The Vineyard also owned the building and it looked like many of the other buildings around it.

I walked through the front doors and saw a receptionist seated behind a desk. I gave my name and told her I had an appointment with Dave. She made a call on her phone and told me to have a seat, Dave would be out shortly. As I sat down in the foyer I noticed that there was a lot of activity at the Vineyard. People were coming in and out of the offices. Everyone seemed so happy and full of the Spirit of the Lord. A few people noticed me sitting there and said a cheery "Hello" to me as they walked by. I felt a sense of peace come over me while waiting.

Dave came out shortly after that and we went into the auditorium to take a look at it. It was massive! It held over 4,000 people and was set in a theatre style seating arrangement. It had a state-of-the-art sound system and a massive stage as well. As we walked around the auditorium, Dave continued to talk about the building and the different features that it offered. I told Dave about what had transpired with our concert being cancelled at the last venue. I explained we needed a new venue to now hold the concert. "Do you have a problem with alternative music," I hesitantly asked. Dave replied that they did not and often they used that venue to hold outreach concerts. I breathed a sigh of relief. "Let's go back to my office and look at the schedule," Dave replied.

We sat down in Dave's office and I told him that the concert date was scheduled for September 14th and immediately Dave said that would be a problem. "We have church on Saturday night at the Vineyard and we use the large auditorium for that," Dave said. "But what about Friday night, September 13th?" I was silent for a few moments as I pondered the question. "Well, I never thought about that night since we initially planned for a Saturday. But let me see what I can do. I will have to call the Management Company and see if the bands are free that night." I told Dave I would call him as soon as I knew something within the next few days. He told me he would put a hold on the date for us for September 13th. I thanked Dave and left the building and got into my car.

As I drove away from the Vineyard, I looked back in my rearview mirror and saw the church sitting there in the parking lot. "God you are amazing! You only give us something better when there is a change, don't you!" I knew the change in date might be a problem, but I was going to believe that God had something better in mind.

Once I got home I called Davdon Artists Management and talked to Dave Bonson. I told him about everything that had transpired recently with the change in venue and date. He looked at the concert calendar and said that the Supertones would be able to perform on Friday, September 13th. Valu Pac was another band I had booked and he said they were also available. I told him to change the booking date and send me the new contracts. He agreed and as I hung up the phone I let out a loud holler to the Lord. "Thank you Jesus." God had indeed moved in a big way again. It seemed like all of hell was trying to stop what we were doing but God made another way.

I want to impress upon those of you reading this that when the Lord tells you to step out and do something for His Kingdom, you will experience opposition. The enemy immediately comes to try to steal, kill, and destroy that dream God spoke to you to do. You need to fight for it. You need to stand and not give up during these times of trials. The problem with most people is that during times such as these they quit and give up the fight. We can't back down during those times when it looks like all hell has broke loose upon us. We need to stand and fight the good fight of faith.

God told me to put on a youth outreach concert and we did everything we were told to do. I believe God originally wanted us to have this concert at Melodyland, but for whatever reason, we had to change the venue because of lack of response from the leadership. In this next move of God the Lord is going to be speaking to many leaders about certain things. God is going to change things and it is going to happen very quickly. We need to be obedient to the Holy Spirit as He speaks to us.

There are some leaders out there who are building their kingdoms and not Gods. They are building bigger churches, but not building people. It all comes down to the bottom line: are we listening to God and doing what the Lord says to do? It doesn't matter how large or small the church is. Anything that is healthy will eventually grow so I am not attacking large churches. We just have to be careful that when the churches or ministries start to grow that we don't forget the Lord.

It's often easier to serve the Lord when we are going through trials. We have to stay on our knees praying before Him to get the strength just to finish the day out oftentimes. But once the blessings start to come that is when many people forget to pray, forget to read the word, and/or don't spend the times necessary with the Lord any more. We need to actually pray more when the blessings come so that the spirit of pride does not creep in. Remember the word of God says in Proverbs 16:18 *"Pride goes before destruction, a haughty spirit before a fall."*

If you look in the Old Testament you will see a continual pattern that the children of Israel developed. They served the Lord and then blessing would come. But then they would forget the Lord and God would raise up their enemies to come in and overtake them and bring them into captivity. Then they would cry out to the Lord again in humility and once again God would deliver them out of the hands of their enemies. It would continue on like this back and forth.

So we need to be very careful not to quit during times of opposition and trials. Press on toward the mark of the prize of the high calling in Christ Jesus. But also learn during the victories that we are not to gloat and start thinking that we have done this. Stay humble and worship the Lord for the good things He has done.

Chapter 25

A NEW VENUE

Now that we had a new venue and date for the concert, things were back on track full speed ahead. The Lord started supernaturally bringing forth the money for new flyers and posters, which we printed immediately. I also started meeting with many churches in the areas telling them about the concert.

Dorothy Johnson had told me about a Foursquare church in the area where there were two young youth pastors who had a fantastic youth outreach. Dorothy gave me their number and told me to call them up because they had some specific ideas about marketing the concert.

I called them and made an appointment to meet these youth pastors the following week. When I drove up to the church and parked my car, I sensed the Holy Spirit come all over me. I knew there was a key here for something very strategic that God was going to implement. I sat down with these two young men whose names were Doug and Brian. I quickly went into everything the Lord had spoken to us about this concert and how we had been promoting it.

For the next two hours Brian and Doug gave me very specific ways of marketing this concert with the churches locally. Doug said I needed to go and start meeting with the local youth pastors. He told me there were several meetings all over Southern Orange County where youth pastors meet together for gatherings just to praise and fellowship. They usually met once a month and they were divided up by locations. He told me he had a list of all of the leaders name and phone numbers. This list also had the location of the churches and what times and dates during the month they met.

After they gave me the list, we talked for the next several minutes about some other issues. Then I thanked them and took the list with me out the door. This was indeed something I had never thought of before. Sure, I had been calling some local churches, but this would be significant because I would have several in front of me at one time. It would really help facilitate the time!

The next few weeks literally flew by! With the list of local youth pastors, I started contacting them all and telling them about the concert. I set up a team of people who helped me distribute the flyers and posters for the event. I found out where all the monthly youth pastor's meetings were and attended as many as I could. At most of these meetings I was able to speak for several minutes about the event.

I also was given the name of a young man who had locally promoted several large events. His name was Juan Cassis and we met for breakfast early one morning in Corona Del Mar at a local restaurant. After I sat down with Juan, I started telling him everything I had been doing to promote the concert. He looked at me amazed after listening for several minutes! "I wouldn't do anything different than what you are doing," he said. "You are right on track for where you need to be." There were issues of security that we needed to discuss. There could be several hundred kids present and we needed to know that things would be handled properly if anything got out of control. Sometimes kids will come into these concerts looking to stir up trouble. Juan urged me that we should search their purses and pat down the guys before they enter the venue.

I started wondering what I was getting myself into! Pat down these kids? What are we looking for - guns or knives? Juan mentioned to me that one incident can ruin the event and we needed to be cautious and aware of everything that could transpire. There were many areas of expertise Juan had experienced that I had not. I told Juan I wanted him to help me with various parts of this concert such as the stage manager and security issues. We wrote up a contract and I told him I had to get it approved by the board. I thanked him and told him I would be getting back to him within the next day.

I spoke with Dorothy Johnson and other members of the board and they all unanimously told me that Juan would be a good addition to our group. He also mentioned that we should do some radio ads and take out ads in certain Christian alternative publications. We had some money that was allocated for promotion, so we agreed to place these ads. I made the calls and got the artwork in place to get this rolling along.

The time was slipping by quickly and now we only had a week to go before the concert was to take place. We were doing everything within our power to promote this concert. We also had all of the intercessor's in place who were praying for revival and that the Spirit of God would come forth in a mighty wave on that night! I had called Rosalee, who was the head intercessor for the Youthwave concert. I told Rosalee that she needed to contact all of the intercessors to come and pray at the Vineyard the day before the actual concert. We needed to have one final prayer meeting where we could get this thing prayed through until completion. She agreed and started making calls immediately. She called me back and told me that many people were going to be there for the final prayer push.

All along we had been giving the intercessor's weekly updates on what to pray for. Rosalee would contact the head coordinators who would in turn contact the prayer partners in their time slots. It all seemed to be working like clockwork. Everyone was diligent to pray during the times they had signed up for. Some of the time slots were a lot more challenging than others to fill. The slots between 1:00 a.m. and 4:00 a.m. were always the hardest time slots to fill in with people who would faithfully pray. But we found them one by one. It takes a very committed person to get up at that hour and be obedient to the call. "Could you not tarry one hour?" were the words so often used to challenge those to take up the call to pray.

The day before the concert came and I drove over to the Vineyard to meet with all of the prayer coordinators and intercessors. Dorothy Johnson came with me along with Sandy Weismann. As we drove we talked about all of the details that needed to be attended to the day before as well. We were only charging $7.00 for the price of admission to the event. Group tickets of ten or more people would only have to pay $5.00 per person. We would have loved to just have free admission but we had too many things to pay for. We not only had to pay for the venue, but also for the bands, insurance policy of one million dollars per incident, security, etc., etc., etc. We had all of the costs budgeted out and Dorothy made a comment to me that we needed at least 500 kids there in order to break even financially. This was not a money issue but a ministry event. But so often money is a key factor in what you do for the Kingdom. That is why I believe that the business person is as much of a minister as a pastor or evangelist.

It is important for you reading this book gifted in business to see the responsibility you hold in your hands. There are many ministers of the gospel who cannot do what they do without finances. In this next great move of God I believe God is going to turn the wealth of the wicked and give it to the godly (Proverbs 13:22). Business is a high and holy calling and you need to be faithful with what God has blessed you with. As stewards of what God has placed in your hands, if you are faithful in the little, God will make you ruler over much. I believe in this next great move of God there will be many who will be raised up in business to help facilitate the church in doing what they were called to do.

God had used various people to bless us in getting out the printing, promotion, and other aspects of this concert. But there were still many other expenditures and we tried to make it as affordable a price as possible. Some of my own children even told me that if it were free, then kids wouldn't think it was worth going to. I had to mull over that one for a while. But I understood the reasoning. If the bands played for free, they must not be any good. We were trying to evangelize here and many of these kids who were going to come maybe had never heard of these bands before. They would be coming with friends or neighbors who had invited them to go. Hopefully, the plan was that the friend would buy their ticket. Many youth groups were buying up group rates and purchasing extra tickets.

I had set up a concert hot line and youth groups could call in and reserve their tickets. Things were going along fabulously and now it was almost time for the event itself. We had all gathered together for a group time of prayer and intercession for the concert. The last time we did this at Melodyland the concert had been cancelled. I was not going to get gun shy, though. I knew God had His way in what was happening. There were about 20 women who showed up for this time of prayer on Thursday, September 12th. Some of the first prayer coordinators who signed up in Thousand Oaks, had driven down. People from all over Southern California were there and ready to do battle for the Lord. We were in the main sanctuary down by the stage. We all gathered together and held hands in prayer. "Lord, tomorrow night there will be many children here who need to have a touch from you. I'm asking that You pour out Your Spirit upon these children even as you promised in the book of Joel. Send forth that great wave of revival that You promised You would send. Open their eyes so they will know You and experience your power and glory," I fervently prayed.

One by one each women brought their petition before the Lord. We had done our part in doing what the Holy Spirit had asked us to do. Now it was up to the Lord to do His part. We continued to pray for the bands that would be playing and their families. We asked God for protection over the kids who would be coming and that there wouldn't be any security problems. One by one we came and brought forth our requests to the Lord. After quite a while of praying, the Spirit of the Lord came down in a very dramatic way. We felt His presence so strong that a few of the women got down on their knees in worship. There was silence in the sanctuary now. We had an air of expectancy that God was going to indeed do something very powerful tomorrow night.

The Spirit of the Lord spoke through one of the women present, "I am going to do a new thing and you shall see it break forth in a wonderful way tomorrow night. I am indeed going to bring a wave forth in the youth of this nation. My youth are going to be on the front lines of the greatest move of God this world has ever seen. I'm calling them from the north, south, east, and the west. Tomorrow night I call in the youth from all over this county. I will call the youth in from all over Southern California. Even as I moved in the sixties and seventies by a new wave of the Spirit I will begin to move again. Where the land had been dry and cracked spiritually, I will bring fresh rain. By my Spirit I am going to move. For it's not by might, nor by power, but by my Spirit, says the Lord."

The spirit of prophecy came forth in a refreshing way and one by one the Spirit of the Lord spoke. After several minutes there once again came silence. We sensed that the time of prayer was over. God had heard our prayers and we were ready for tomorrow night! We concluded the prayer time and made arrangements with several of the women who could not attend tomorrow night to hold a prayer vigil from their homes or churches.

Several of the women had to leave and get back home and we said goodbye to them and thanked them for coming. The youth pastor came down to meet us and we went over all the particularities for the next evening. We walked through where the ticket counter and booths were going to be. He showed us the room where we could bring the young people after the altar call for prayer. We went through the backstage area and we determined where we were going to set up the food and beverages for the band members during the concert. Dorothy and I went down the list we had drawn up and checked off each one as we went. There is so much to do to prepare for an event such as this that it can become mind-boggling!

After a few more hours of running through all of these last minute details, we finally felt we had covered everything. "Go home and get some rest," Dorothy said as we walked out of the Vineyard Church to our cars. I didn't think that was going to be possible, but I told her I would try. My mind was racing and I still was thinking of all of the things I had to do.

A pastor friend of mine from Arizona, Robert Choate, had come into town and was going to film the event. He had felt very strongly that God had wanted to capture this event on film and had donated his time to come. Also, Tim Miner, wrote a song for me to sing at this event. I had not really expected to sing at this event. But one day in prayer I sensed the Lord saying He had a new song for me to sing at this concert. I argued with the Lord telling Him that we already had several bands playing. But the Lord impressed upon me that he wanted this special song so I called up Tim Miner and he said he would pray about writing a new song. The next week he had called me back and said he had written a song for the concert and would overnight it to me with a scratch track so I could learn the vocals. I had been practicing for several days and felt confident that I knew the song well enough to sing for the event. The most important thing was that the Lord anointed it when I sang it.

As I went to bed that evening I thanked the Lord for everything that He had done. "Oh give thanks to the Lord for He has done marvelous things!" God surely had seen us through all the way from beginning to the end. When God first spoke to me about doing this concert I had no idea we were going to go through all of the challenges that we did. In fact, I probably would have never started if I had known in the beginning. But isn't that just like God to only show you enough light for the next step. He wants us to trust Him all the way through our circumstances. Let go and let God! As my head hit the pillow, I fell instantly asleep dreaming about what wonderful things would happen tomorrow!

Chapter 26

THE FIRST CONCERT

The alarm clock went off sharply at 6:00 a.m. I groggily looked at the clock and realized that today was the big day! On one hand I was very excited, but on the other I was nervous as well. What happened if no one showed up! We needed at least 500 people to come to break even with paying all of the bills. We had never done anything before like this so it was new territory we were taking. I got my Bible from the table by the side of the bed and went downstairs for my quiet time. It is important that we take the first part of the day to come before the Lord. Jesus is our ultimate role model and it says in the Bible that He arose early and prayed. As I prayed and read the Bible, I once again felt the reassurance from the Lord that everything was going to be just fine. The Lord quietly spoke to me not to worry and to trust in Him.

As I fellowshipped with the Lord I felt a strength come over me that I didn't have when I first woke up. All of my little insecurities were now replaced with peace and a quiet strength from God. I had a fresh anticipation of what was going to take place tonight. But now it was time to go to work and get everything in order and prepared. I literally hit the ground running after my prayer time. I quickly showered and got ready. I woke up the children and got their breakfast ready and made their lunches. I then loaded them all in the car and dropped them all off at Stoneybrook Christian School. That is the school all of the children were enrolled at. It is a great school and I felt completely secure in the fact that they could pray and read the Bible in their classrooms. I drove away from the school and waved to the kids as they walked into the school. Now the real work was going to begin!

I picked up Robert Choate who was in town to film the event. He was going to help with the slide presentations as the music was playing. There were two large screens on the walls next to the stage. Robert's idea was to have pictures that go along with the music as it was playing. I was also going to be singing the song that Tim Miner had wrote for the event and he had the lyrics and was getting the appropriate pictures together for that as well.

We raced around to Kinko's to get the banners we had made for the ticket window. Juan Cassis was going to bring the wristbands, which would go around the kids' wrists when they paid to get in. This way we would know who had paid and who had not. Dorothy Johnson and some of the women on the Aglow Board were going to be handling all of the money as it came in. There was a side room where they could count the money away from the viewing public. It's not that we were interested in making any money. We hoped to break even! We wanted to see the gospel of the Lord go forth in a dramatic way and many new converts come into the Kingdom, but we had several thousands of dollars which needed to pay expenses and we believed God that all of the finances would come in to pay all of the expenditures.

The day flew by and before I knew it the time was almost 3:00 p.m. I had a friend go and pick up the kids from school. She was going to bring them to her house and then to the concert later on in the afternoon. Everyone else was going to meet at the Vineyard at 4:30 p.m. to get things in order for the concert. I arrived at the Vineyard a little before 4:00 p.m. I had a lot to do to get everything prepared. Robert Choate was with me and he helped me put the banners on the table and set up other pertinent details for the concert. Dorothy Johnson and her crew arrived shortly thereafter. We went over all of the details for the concert that night. She had ordered food for the bands, which was going to be arriving around 6:00 p.m. The doors were going to open up at 6:30 p.m. and we wanted the bands to be fed and ready for the concert by the time the doors were open.

The sound checks were going to begin at 5:00 and Juan Cassis was already in gear when I arrived. He was handling all of the bands check-in along with the stagehands. He had a crew with him and everything was in place as scheduled. I went over a brief overview with Juan shortly after I got there and everything seemed to be under control.

I had several friends come down who were going to volunteer taking the money at the door. Tracy Kemble, a good friend and founder of the Women in Need Foundation, was one of the first to show up. She was going to be heading up the ticket counter. Janet Walker and Elaine Rhodes showed up a little bit after Tracy. Everyone seemed to be coming in on time and as planned. My good friend, Kristen Barbato, was going to be heading up the prayer and counseling room. We had several women scheduled to be working with her. I had cards made up for the new converts to fill in and also get their prayer requests. We had some Bibles donated to us by the American Bible Society to give them as well. Kristen met with her team and went through the prayer room and got it all coordinated.

The time was now 5:30 p.m. and the bands had started to check in and were doing their first sound checks. The tables were set up at the front for the ticket booths. We had vendor booths for the bands to sell their t-shirts and other memorabilia. We also had a food vendor there on consignment, selling pizza slices and sodas.

I went through the venue and made a brief check on everything that was happening. We had rented walkie-talkies and everything seemed to be on track. The doors were going to open in another fifteen minutes. I was getting nervous! What if no one shows up? These are always the thoughts that will try to plague you when you step out by faith to do things for the Lord. I couldn't worry about that now. I just had to keep on going and trust that I have done everything God has wanted me to do!

Juan Cassis came up to me and told me that everyone who was not working with my crew needed to get out. We needed to do a sweep of the place before the doors were open. My crew was given a different color wristband so that we would know they were staff. After Juan had made a sweep of the place and everything looked secure, we checked our watches. It was time to open the doors in five minutes.

I looked out the front door and wanted to see what was happening outside. I had been so busy trying to get everything finalized on the inside that I was not paying any attention to what was going on outside! To my amazement, I saw hundreds of kids lined up outside the doors to get in and snaked around the parking lot! I couldn't believe my eyes! It seemed like there were hundreds. I was hoping for at least 500, but there were more than that waiting in line! I was so excited! Thank God we were going to break even!

Juan came to me and said that it was 6:00 p.m. He had all of the security guards in place who were going to do a brief pat down on the guys. They wanted to look in the girl's purses to make sure there was nothing in there that shouldn't be. Everyone was in place and Juan made the signal that the doors should be open. The doors were open and we had a mob of kids run in through the front doors of the Vineyard up to the ticket counter. Most of them didn't have tickets and were going to have to pay. Some had bought tickets at the

Vineyard bookstore right across the street at the parking lot. We also were selling them through ticketmaster and a few other Christian bookstores in the area.

There were several friends of mine taking money and tickets at the tables. There were lines stretched out into the parking lot. Janet Walker came up to me and said they were running out of change for twenty-dollar bills. Many of these kids were bringing in larger bills and they were running out of one-dollar bills and fives. As the kids would come in and pay they would then be searched and once they cleared the security they would be given a wristband. There were lines of kids snaking out into the parking lot. It was unbelievable how many kids just kept pouring into this venue. We kept running out of change for the people in line. We needed more ones and fives. God was truly outpouring His Spirit, and at the moment we were too busy to even notice what was going on.

I was running back and forth between the stage and the front area where the kids were pouring in. I had my walkie-talkie in my hand and was constantly getting new updates on various issues. Things were progressing quite smoothly in many respects and it would soon be time for the first band to go on. We opened the doors at 6:00 p.m. and the first band was slated to go on at 6:30 p.m.

I went backstage to check with Juan Cassis as to how things were progressing and if there was anything I could do. The food had just arrived from "Subway Sandwiches" shop. Dorothy had three giant foot long submarines made for all of the band members. She also had a variety of chips and sodas on hand for them to munch on. Some of the women from the local Aglow chapters made homemade cookies for desert. The bands were all set in regards to food. When I peeked my head into the room where all the meals were being set up, everyone was busily eating and enjoying themselves.

Juan told me that all of the bands had done their sound checks and we were all on schedule for the first band to come on at 6:30 p.m. That was another ten minutes or so and I told him I would do a final check around the premises and then come and open the show for the first band. I quickly made my way to the front again and found Dorothy trying to keep things in order. The crowds continued to grow and we were at the point that we would have to close the doors since we would not have adequate room for all of the people trying to get in! I thought to myself that this indeed was a good thing. We were worried that we would not have 500 people to cover expenses. Well now it looked like we might have 5,000. Look what the Lord has done!

After making a clean sweep of the premises, I saw that everything was under control. I went back and found Juan. "We are ready to start on schedule since it looks like everything else is going satisfactorily," I stated to Juan. The curtains were closed at this time on the stage. All of the band equipment was set up for the first band to come up and play. I got the guys on the stage with the group "D.O.G." ("Disciples of God"), and we all said a prayer together for the Lord to move in a powerful way as they played. Once the prayer was finished I told them I was going to open up the concert and greet the crowd. After that they were to go on stage and play their hearts out.

Now was the big moment of truth! It had taken several months of preparation to get to this point! We had many set backs and times where we never thought we would see this day. But now we had persevered through all of the storms and our dream was becoming a reality. I walked through the curtains and took my place in front of the microphone set right in the middle of the stage. The spotlight went on me and I heard the crowd silence for a moment. I took a deep breath and stepped up to the microphone and said, "Welcome to Youthwave '96, I hope you have a great time tonight. I want to welcome the first band who is going to perform tonight, D.O.G."

And with that short and brief announcement the music started blaring and the concert was off. The band started playing their first song and the crowd immediately reacted in a favorable way. Some of the kids ran down to the front of the stage and started to move to the beat of the music. D.O.G. was a punk band that had an unusual sound with a very quick tempo. They had only been a band for a few months, but had gotten very good from practice. I knew one of the guys in the band quite well named David Toste. I knew he walked with the Lord and saw the fruit of the Spirit evident in his life. Even though they were not too well known, they were called to play at this concert. After I introduced them, I walked backstage and took a deep breath. One down and two more to go.

I took another walk around the venue and saw the place was almost filled to capacity now. I walked over and talked to my head security guard. He said there were some kids he was keeping his eye on. They were clean when they were searched, but he was still watching them nonetheless. You don't understand the stress just in keeping everything running on track for an event like this. D.O.G. was completing their third song and I knew it was time to go back to the stage and introduce the next band, which was Valu Pac.

Valu Pac was another punk band that had been around for a few years. They even had some well-known hits in the community and nationally. As D.O.G. finished their last song, I saw Juan on the side of the stage motioning for them to cut the music in one minute. He was helping run the stage and Juan was keeping everything flowing in an orderly fashion so that we would be on time. D.O.G. came off the stage and their faces were beaming with satisfaction. They had never played a venue such as this one with as many people in attendance. I'm sure they felt like they had hit the big time. I was blessed to see that they had enjoyed themselves. The crowd was very enthusiastic to their performance and was clapping and calling for more. I thought this was indeed a very excellent sign.

I went back to the front of the stage again and started asking the crowd how they liked D.O.G. I heard a roar of approval from all of the kids present. "Would you like to hear another band?" I yelled out. I heard an overwhelming, "Yes!" Well, here's "Valu Pac," I shouted. The second band came onstage and started playing one of their most popular tunes. Everyone started jumping to their feet and you could see the front of the stage start to swell with young kids who wanted to start moshing. Moshing is where everyone gets in a large circle and starts bumping into each other. It's really hard to explain the dynamics of it, but at many of the concerts, whether it was Christian or secular, you would see a mosh pit.

I called the security guards over and told them to make sure that no one got hurt. I did not want to see anything happen which would put a damper on the evening. As Valu Pac kept playing, the crowd got more and more animated. It was totally amazing to see those kids on their feet and clapping for the Lord. It was exciting to watch everything transpire as quickly as it did. One of the youth pastor's from the Life Church was in the mosh pit keeping it under control. I watched him as he kept the kids in line and I had to silently laugh watching him. Jeremy was such a great guy and had a real heart for kids. He had brought the entire youth group down from Life Church where our family was attending church. Pastor Phil Munsey and his wife Jeannie were very supportive of Youthwave and our vision from the Lord.

Valu Pac was finished playing and now it was time for the headline band to be introduced. The Supertones were getting very popular with the kids in Orange County. They had been around for a few years but had recently released a new album, which was taking off in a big way. As Valu Pac walked off the stage there was a flurry of activity as the curtains closed. We needed to get all of Valu Pac's equipment off and put the Supertone's equipment on the stage. We had a stage crew moving gear quickly in preparation for the Supertones to come on.

Juan Cassis was busy handling the stage and I knew everything was under control in that department. As I scanned the audience I could see that the whole place was now packed out. There were kids literally everywhere! In my wildest imaginations I never thought that this concert would be this successful in terms of numbers of people present. But now I wanted to see the Spirit of God show up and touch these kids in a powerful way. We had a team of people praying in the prayer room. The intercessors that had prayed the last two months were also praying as well. Most of them could not attend the concert but had agreed to take that time to pray for the concert.

Finally, the Supertones were ready to go on! Juan had given me the signal and I walked up to the microphone. We had been given some t-shirts by the bands, which they said we could give away. I walked up to the microphone and yelled, "Who wants a free t-shirt?" The crowd went wild again and a few of the guys in the band started throwing out the t-shirts. It was really fun to watch as the kids scrambled to get these free shirts. "Are you ready for the Supertones?" I yelled out. "Yeeaaaahhhh!", the crowd roared in approval.

The father of Jason Carson, the drummer in the Supertones, had asked me earlier if he could introduce the band. So he stepped up to the microphone and yelled, "Orange County California, let's welcome the Supertones!" The curtain pulled back and the music started with a blast. Many of the kids tried to rush the stage and we had security people in the front of the stage all across the front. We did not want them climbing up on the stage and trying to stage dive. Stage diving is where someone will jump up on the stage and then dive into the crowd. Often the crowd will then pass that person on their hands over the crowd until he reaches the side. It is quite a sight to see!

The whole place was on their feet and moving with the music. The set seemed to go by very quickly. They were halfway through their songs when I noticed Steve Hage come into the room and stand off to the side. I had asked Steve to do the altar call for this event. A good friend of mine, Elaine Rhodes, recommended Steve to me. Steve was a pastor down in San Diego and was mightily used by God with youth. He himself had been in a gang growing up and was raised in Los Angeles. He was a very tough kid and ran the streets with some very hard-core gangs. God got a hold of him and changed his life dramatically several years prior. He had been a youth pastor at a large church in Los Angeles and the youth group had grown to several hundred kids.

He had recently moved to San Diego to pastor his own church. Steve agreed to drive up from San Diego and was going to take a few members of his staff. As I walked over and greeted him and their group, they stood dumbfounded looking at the crowd. "You did a good job, girl!" Steve replied in his normal laid-back style. I brought them back to where the green room was in the back of the stage. The green room is a term for where the bands and guests will hang out during a performance. No one was in there at the time because they all wanted to hear the Supertones perform their set. I told Steve that the Supertones would be done in another 20 minutes or so. I gave him the run down of what would transpire before he came up.

First of all the Supertones were going to do about four praise and worship songs after their set. Jason Carson, the drummer for the band, was also going to share a short testimony. Then I was going to sing a song that my friend, Tim Miner, wrote for this concert. Robert Choate was going to be doing a slide presentation while I sang with pictures that would be pertinent to the song. There were two big screens on each side of the stage. We had various pictures going on the whole time the bands were performing. Sometimes we had footage of the crowds that were there. I had hired two cameramen from the church and they were filming everything. The kids really got a kick out of seeing themselves on the screen as the cameramen randomly selected some of them.

After I was done with my song I would introduce Steve Hage to come up and share with those at the concert about what the Lord had put on his heart for that evening. Steve was a pro at sharing with kids in these types of situations. I knew God had chosen the right vessel and He would pour out His Spirit through Steve's message that night. We all held hands and said a short prayer. We prayed that the Spirit of God would move through Steve in a powerful way that evening.

We all went up to the side of the stage and watched the Supertones finish their set. I had talked to the band before they went on about doing some praise and worship songs at the end of their set. Jason, the drummer, looked at me and I gave him the cue. After the song ended, Jason got up from behind the drums and walked up to the microphone. The kids were screaming that they wanted another song. They were having such a great time and no one wanted it to be over with.

But we didn't put this concert on to just entertain them. God had ordained this concert because He wanted to bring forth His presence in a new dimension to these kids. Jason had a Bible in one hand and he brought forth a short word of exhortation. I had told Jason that we already had another minister to share the final message. Jason Carson is a mighty man of God and has been used at many concerts to bring forth the message of salvation. He shared for about five minutes about how God saved Him and what a difference Jesus had made in his life. I watched as the kids watched and listened to him in awe. They really listen intently when they hear someone they respect share about their experiences. Jason then thanked the crowd for listening and I walked up and grabbed the microphone.

I now was going to sing the song for the concert! Everything in me did not want to sing at that point. Here the kids had been listening to the Supertones! God had told me to do this and I had to be obedient. I explained to them about the song that was written especially for this event and about how God had told me to do this concert. I briefly told them that they should just listen intently because God wanted to speak to them through the song.

The music soundtrack came on and the lights in the house were dimmed. The spotlight went on me and I sang the song as Robert Choate had the images and pictures pertaining to the message in the song on the screens next to the stage. I had just gotten the song overnighted to my residence the day before. I hardly had time to practice, but I needed to be obedient and sing. I felt like I blew it in a few spots where I didn't hit the note correctly. I finished the song and the crowd let out a cheer of approval. It wasn't the roar that the Supertones were given, but it was a respectable acknowledgement.

"We have one other special guest which is going to briefly share with you before the Supertones come back and finish out with their most popular tune. Please give it up for Steve Hage."

Steve walked to the front of the stage and took the microphone from me. "Thank you, Meri."

I watched as Steve took the microphone and started sharing his heart with the kids present. It was almost a surreal moment and I felt as if I were suspended in space looking at what was happening. I know that may sound a little strange, but after spending so many months working towards this moment, it was such a moment of truth. God was bringing His truth forth from a young man who had seen it all. And Steve knew how to talk the lingo of these young people. He initially got some laughs from them, but eventually Steve started bringing it home towards the salvation message.

He asked for the young people to come forward who wanted Christ in their lives. He had shared some personal stories of what he had gone through. The kids had been impacted by the testimony and I could feel the power of the Holy Spirit surging through the audience. As Steve again made the altar call I started to see kids get up from their seats all over the auditorium and making their way down to the front. Steve is a master at knowing how to continue to press an issue. It wasn't like he was manipulating anything, but that he knew from past experiences that the devil was going to try to rip some of these young people off. Steve knew some would hesitate and he wanted to make sure that nobody would be left out who had wanted to come down. It took several minutes of Steve talking, but before we knew it hundreds of kids were flocking down to the front of the stage.

Since there was no room left in front of the stage, we had worked it out that the kids coming forward would actually come on the stage. So the stage was filling up with hundreds of kids. Many of them were crying and wiping their eyes. I was so overwhelmed with emotion! I was crying and could hardly believe what I was seeing. My good friend, Kristin Barbato, was next to me on the stage feverishly taking pictures of all of the things happening. She saw me crying and gave me a big hug. "It was worth it all, wasn't it?" I looked at her stunned as she said those words. And I realized that all of the trials and problems that had prevented us in the beginning from moving ahead were now all coming together. We had not given up and pressed forward in what God had said for us to do. And now we were seeing the fruit of our endeavors.

I looked at Kristen and replied, "It has been worth everything to see this." The kids kept piling onto the stage and finally there was a hush over the audience. A few very hard-looking young guys came up at last and everyone started clapping. Steve Hage turned around and saw them and told them to come to the microphone. "What is going on with you guys? What is happening here?" Steve asked inquisitively. "We were going to leave and thought this was just a joke at first, but then something got a hold of my heart and I knew I had to come down here," one of the young men told Steve.

Steve was able to share with them briefly about the love of God and lead them in the prayer of salvation. Everyone in the audience had a tear in their eye as the young men who came forward both hugged each other. You could sense the Holy Spirit in a most dramatic way at this moment.

Steve then turned to all of the young people on the stage and started sharing with them. "Some of you standing here have committed abortions. Some of you have been in gangs and wanted a family. Others of you have simply turned their back on God. But no matter what you have done, God loves you and sent His son Jesus to die for you. He has come to give you life and life in abundance." As Steve started sharing with them, you could see the young people on the stage hugging each other. Some were crying and hung their heads. We watched in unbelief as we saw these young people who hours before had been jumping and dancing now hanging their heads crying.

Steve asked them if they would pray a prayer that would invite the Lord Jesus Christ into their hearts. "The word of God says in Romans 10:9, *"That if you confess with your mouth, 'Jesus is Lord,' and believe in your heart that God raised him from the dead, you will be saved."* Steve went onto expound about the message of salvation for a few minutes. Then he told the young people to repeat this prayer after him. "Dear Jesus, I know that I am a sinner. Please come into my heart and cleanse me of all of my sin. Thank you Jesus!"

It was a very simple but powerful prayer. As the kids looked up from the prayer, I could see a change in their countenance. God had indeed made them new creatures in Christ as the gospel says. Old things are passed away and behold all things are made new. Steve then directed them to the back of the room where Kristen Barbato and her prayer team were ready to give them Bibles and pray over them individually.

They made their way down the stairs and everyone in the room started to clap. I could sense the angels of God in the room and they were also rejoicing. God was having a party in heaven over the fact that there were many new converts to the kingdom that day.

Kristin Barbato later told me that they did not have enough prayer counselors for the 500 or so kids that came forward. They only had about ten in their group for prayer. But it was a supernatural move of the Lord that took place. Out of the blue about 20 college students who attended Christian universities came to the back and told Kristin that God told them to come that night to help with the young people. There were just enough kids that came in the back to help counsel to make sure that everyone was prayed for.

Kristen later told me that it was a sight to see as the kids who accepted the Lord were ushered into the room. Many were still crying and under the power of the Lord. Kristen divided them up into groups of six and delegated the prayer counselors to the different groups. They were first told to fill out the information and prayer card. This way we could give a local youth pastor their name and information for further follow-up. So often people who come to accept Christ have no outside mentorship afterwards and fall by the wayside. We did not want that to happen and so I had partnered with many local churches to be a part of this event. Afterwards, we would send a list over of the kids in their areas. We would try to be fair to make sure each church was given the names of the people in their location.

The kids were filling out the prayer requests and then the prayer coordinator was able to pray with them individually for private requests. They were back there for a few hours after the event. Kristin and her staff told me they had never done anything as powerful as what had happened that night.

Meanwhile, I was back on the stage and the Supertones came back and did one more final song. The crowd all jumped to their feet as everyone rocked out to the music. When the last note played the crowd roared in approval and the stage curtain was drawn. The crowd wanted more but we were told to shut down by 10:00 p.m and it was after that time now. We still had to clean up and get everything broken down on the stage.

For the next few hours I made sure that everything was done. I went and checked with Dorothy Johnson and they were still counting all of the money that had come in that night from the masses. This indeed would pay all of the expenditures that we had incurred. I'm sure it would even leave a reserve for a future event. The counselors were praying with the last of the kids who had come forward. Everyone was tired, but so happy at what they had seen happen.

We had hired janitors to come in and clean the building. All of the bands had already packed up and had gone. I was doing the last walk through of the building and was very tired and ready to go home. As I walked to my car with my husband, I felt a sense of accomplishment. God had indeed done something so special words could not even express how I felt. As my head hit the pillow that night I smiled and thanked the Lord for coming through. He had never let me down to this point. In fact, He surpassed my greatest expectations!

That was the first Youthwave concert and will always be the most memorable. But there has been so much that has transpired since then. There will be an upcoming book devoted exclusively to chronicling the Youthwave Explosion. But in the meantime just know that since 1996 several more Youthwave concerts have taken place all over Southern California.

Youthwave has held concerts at San Diego State College in the Open Air Theatre where thousands attended and were touched by the Lord. Oceanside Amphitheatre again had several thousand where Grammy award nominees P.O.D. and other bands performed. Other venues where Youthwave concerts were held have been the "Jackie Robinson Stadium" in Compton, California; Calvary Chapel Church, and one of the most memorable concert was at Camp Pendleton to the Marines as they were preparing to go to Iraq. But no matter where the concerts are held the message is still the same. God is sending His wave to the young people of this nation. He is calling all the youth and God wants them to be a part of this new wave of revival. Come quickly Lord Jesus!

Chapter 27

NOW IS THE TIME

There are so many more things I could write to be a part of my first book. But the last chapter is very special to me. This is the chapter about how God birthed my television ministry. The word of the Lord says to not despise the days of small beginnings. Because that is where it literally started. With just a thought and a word from my husband. Let me briefly tell you the story.

I had been speaking up at a Full Gospel Businessmen's meeting in Los Angeles one night. My husband had come with me and listened intently as I shared a message of faith and courage to several hundred people present. After the message, the Lord used me to give the word of prophecy to many who were in attendance. Rick often will minister with me as well and that night was one of those nights. We both were up at the altar moving in the gifts of the spirit and it was wonderful to see people renewed and set free.

On the way home from the meeting Rick looked at me and said, "God wants you to start broadcasting on television." He spoke it very gently but to the point. I looked at him inquisitively and asked him why he would say that. Rick explained to me that as he was watching me share the message that night, he sensed the Lord speaking to him about getting me on television. I shrugged my shoulders and told him I would pray about it. We were both very tired and when we finally pulled into our driveway the thought about TV was far from my mind. All I wanted to do was hit the pillow since I felt exhausted.

The next morning I woke up and was making a cup of coffee in the kitchen. It was a Sunday morning and we were going to get ready for church soon. Rick came into the kitchen and the first thing that came out of his mouth was, "Well, have you thought more about the television program?"

I was still half asleep and I looked at him and couldn't believe he was pressing me on this issue so soon. "Honey, I haven't even given it a second thought! Let's continue to pray about it and wait upon the Lord." My husband smiled at me and told me he knew it was the Lord and was going to keep pestering me until I was obedient.

Well, I am a firm believer in moving out when God speaks to me. Over the years God had given me many things to do for the Kingdom. Once I knew it was the Lord nothing could stop me from doing His will. But I had to know as well. It was a very good sign that Rick was saying this to me. I sensed that indeed God wanted me to move in this direction. But I am also a firm believer in waiting on the Lord and praying over major issues before you start to move in that direction.

So for the next few months that is what I did. I prayed and waited upon the Lord for an answer about the television ministry. In the meantime, every day Rick would continue to ask me about getting on television. I had been married to Rick for over twenty years and never before had I seen him so persistent about an issue involving me in ministry. As I prayed, I sensed a peace from the Lord about television, but it wasn't any great revelation.

When I had moved to California several years prior I had taken many voice-over and acting classes up in Los Angeles at various times. I had auditioned for some parts and gotten them, but for the most part nothing opened up for me in acting. I did sense that I was suppose to take these on-camera classes and it really helped me in honing my skills in front of a camera. But as I was thinking back over the years now, I was beginning to see the plan that God was shaping. Maybe God had me taking these classes because He was getting me ready for television? I pondered this again in my heart for another few months.

Finally, after about six months of waiting and listening to my husband asking when I was going to go on television, I made a decision. I felt God was telling me to step out by faith and do a television taping of one of my meetings. When I saw Rick later that day I told him the news and he was exuberant! "Finally!" he stated enthusiastically. "You should have listened to me the first day I told you!" There's nothing like hearing "I told you so". I just looked at Rick and smiled. I had long ago learned when to shut my mouth and just let him savor in victory.

So we started planning the first television production. I had met a young man named Romeo Carrey who had a film production studio in Los Angeles. I called him up and we set an appointment to meet and go over all of the details. The following week I was sitting in Romeo's office and I told him the vision and purpose of the show. It was to be a Christian television show where I will speak at venues where I will minister and other times I will interview various guests with a message of courage and hope. We went over prices and dates and finally came to a conclusion as to the format of this show. As I left, I thanked Romeo and told him I would be getting back to him with projected dates for this show.

In the meantime, I needed to find a great venue to tape my first show. A good friend of mine had asked me to speak at her church for a women's conference they were putting on. I had spoken at the church - Impact Community Church - the month prior and it was a beautifully designed church with great staging and lighting as well. I called Janece and asked her if I could possibly use the church for a taping. She told me she would get back to me later in the day. I went about my normal routine when the phone rang later in the day. "Pastor Scott Turner told me that you could use the Church for the taping," Janece blurted out in excitement. "Praise God!" I shouted and we were off running again.

We set a date for the taping the following month on the first Saturday. This would give me time to mail out invitations and to confirm with Romeo Carrey that he would be able to film that day. When I called Romeo he was available and it was scheduled. Now I was busy getting all the preparations made for the event. I called a good friend of mine, Sandy Casanelli, who was very talented and creative in set design. I told her about the taping and she got very excited. "Of course I will be there and help you with the set design," Sandy replied after I asked her if she could design a set. Basically, I was going to be preaching and sharing from the pulpit. It wasn't as if we were going to have to do a lot of improvement on what was already there. But there are factors with lighting and color that needed to be addressed.

There was one last detail I needed to wrap up. I needed to have a great worship team to bring forth praise and worship for the event. I called another friend named Mike Gyminates who had played with Kim Clement often on his worship team. Mike lived a few hours away and when I asked him to come, after looking at his schedule he said yes. He would bring his family who played in their band. Now it was all set!

Invitations went out to my local ministry mailing list. I started preparing my message for the program and went into fasting and prayer. I met with Romeo several times to go over the details with the filming. I found a great Christian make-up artist and hairdresser for the show as well. Everything was set and ready to go.

The alarm clock woke me up suddenly! I looked at the clock and it was 5:00 a.m. on Saturday. It was the big day for my first television taping. I went down and spent some time with the Lord. I asked the Lord to bless the taping and to give me the strength to do what He called me to do. I had never done something like this before and it was a leap of faith for me. As I was praying I heard the Lord speak to me, "Meri, now is the time when I am going to bring forth my church into a new dimension of my power. When you speak today, walk in My authority and boldness. I will be with you and give you great strength to deliver a message from Me. Now is the appointed time!" As I listened to the Lord, all of a sudden I realized something very dramatic. I had been praying as to what I would call the show, but had not gotten anything from the Lord. "Now is the time!" That would be the new name for my television show: "Now is the Time."

I was so excited that I quickly jumped up and ran upstairs. I needed to be at the church at 7:00 a.m. because Toni Spicer, the make-up artist, was going to meet me there to do my hair and make-up. Television is very different from normal settings and it is important that the right make-up be applied so that you don't look washed out on the camera. Toni had expertise in this from working on various commercials and television productions. We had already gone over a run through when she had done my make up the week before and I was pleased with the outcome.

I had a few different outfits I brought with me and I packed everything in the car and was on my way. My husband Rick was still asleep but was going to come to the church for the beginning of the taping. I had many friends who were going to attend who had already told me they were coming. As I drove to the church I felt like this was the beginning of something great God was going to do through me. I'm not trying to be boastful here. I just sensed that this was my destiny and purpose. When you finally start walking in what you were created to do there is a natural excitement and anticipation that comes. That is why the Lord says, "He will give you the desires of your heart." God wants you to enjoy what you are doing. There will be times when you may have to do things you normally would not want to do out of obedience. But for the most part, it is God's will for you to be happy and fulfilled in your calling.

I sense that some of you reading this book are not satisfied where you are now in life. That is a normal thing to be happening at certain periods in your life. The Lord may be trying to get your attention and telling you to start looking in other directions. I understand that you have bills to pay and responsibilities. But too many people play it safe doing things that they hate. It's never to late to change careers in your life. If you are in the ministry and you don't like where you are, maybe God is calling you to the market place. God is raising up many men and women in His Kingdom to bring forth great finances for His purposes. So often projects don't go forth because of lack of funding. So today, just step out of the boat if you are in that place. Believe that God is going to give you the desires of your heart and start walking in the direction of your dreams.

I pulled up to the church and met Toni at the front door. She had just pulled in at the same time and had her make-up kit and bag with her. Janece had already opened up the door to the church and we walked into the sanctuary. It was very quiet and dark! Suddenly a light was switched on and the whole place was bright. Isn't that just like God to brighten up darkened places, I thought to myself.

We got started immediately on my hair and make-up. It was going to take over an hour and I had other things to attend to as well before the taping would begin at 9:30 a.m. There was a team of people who arrived early to get all of the preparations for the show ready. Sandy Casanelli drove up from San Marcos and started working with the set design. She was moving trees and decorations on the stage to where they would get the most benefit. By the time I walked into the sanctuary, after having my make-up and hair done, the place looked like a professional set. "Wow, what a difference an hour makes!" I exclaimed.

Romeo Carrey had already arrived and was setting up the camera equipment. Mike Gymnates and his family were already there as well and getting all of their equipment sound checked for the worship.

People were starting to show up for the taping. I had been very specific that people should show up on time for the taping. I didn't want there to be any interruptions once we started! I did a sound check with the microphone and everything was ready to go.

I had typed out all of my notes for my sermon, but I did not want to have to rely on them. I had been studying and memorizing my lines for the last few weeks. I had gotten very prepared in the message God had given me.

Romeo came up to me and said they were ready to start. I told him I would be ready in a few minutes after I talked with my team. I called together my main core of people helping and we had a moment of prayer before the taping would begin. As we gathered around in a circle, we could feel the power of the Holy Spirit in a very unique and dynamic way. I was not in the least bit nervous, and I knew that had to be the Lord. I am used to speaking in front of people, but when you have to film something, that is a different story. When you start branching out into a new arena it can often be intimidating. That is why so few people will step out and do something new or unique. We can become creatures of habit and don't like change. But we have to be ready to do whatever

God is telling us by His Spirit. It is a time to step out of the boat and walk by faith in the purposes God has for you.

There are some people reading this book who have been straddling the fence for many years. You can't have it both ways; you either need to get on one side or the other. You can't please everyone. If you try to please everyone you will please no one. The only one that we need to be worried about pleasing in the first place is the Lord anyway. So get off the fence, get out of the boat and start making decisions that are going to change your life. So what if you make a mistake - you will see what not to do the next time. Quit being so indecisive and start walking in the authority God has given you. God wants you to have dominion over your problems and circumstances. Take the authority and start moving out by faith and watch and see the mountains God will move.

It was now time to start the first taping and I walked to the podium and welcomed all of the people who had come to the meeting that day. There were several hundred present and I could sense anticipation in the room of what was about to happen. After we opened in prayer I called up Mike and his family to do the worship. It was an awesome time of worship with the Lord for the next fifteen minutes or so. I only had hired the film crew for so many hours so we could not worship for a long time. But the anointing was truly there and we were all blessed by the worship.

Now it was time for the show to really get going! I came up and gave a few brief instructions about turning off cell phones, trying not to leave in the middle of the message unless it was an emergency, and a few other bits of information pertinent to the meeting. Then I said a quick prayer and I was off. Romeo gave me the count down from behind the camera and I started my first show.

I was planning on filming for at least a few hours and hopefully get at least three shows for the television series out of it. The message flowed and I could sense the prophetic anointing flowing from me in a very powerful way. God was having me speak a message of where the church was today but how He was transitioning the church to cross over Jordan and come into the Promised Land. As I was preaching I felt the spirit of prophesy come upon me and I started to prophesy to the audience under the power of the Holy Spirit. "It's not business as usual anymore. Things are going to start changing very dramatically. Trust in Me during these times coming upon this nation. I have given you My Son. But what have you done with My Son? I gave you everything, but some of you have overlooked my son. What have you done with My Son? I gave you My best and now I want yours." That was just a short part of the prophecy that came forth that day. I was flabbergasted as I heard the Spirit of the Lord speak through me saying, "What have you done with my Son?" There is nothing like the Lord to cut right through and get to the heart of the matter.

God had sent His only begotten Son that whosoever should believe in Him would not perish but have everlasting life. But so many people have overlooked what Jesus did for them. God wants us all to come to the knowledge that Jesus Christ is the only begotten Son of God who died for us to give all of us life. Life and life more abundantly. Oh to know the Lord is so glorious!

I then presented the Gospel of the Lord Jesus Christ and the plan of salvation on the taping. I spoke with authority and led those listening in a prayer of salvation to know the Lord. As I closed the sermon I then started calling up some for prayer. The cameras were still filming at this time and for the next few hours the Lord moved in a powerful prophetic anointing. Finally, it was time to go and film the last few sequences outside. I needed to do introductions to the programs as well as closings. There is so much to do sometimes for these television shows that sometimes you don't realize all of the work that goes into it.

I had brought another change of clothes for the openings and closings. I quickly changed and then went outside to finish the filming. I had brought some cue cards to read for the openings. That took another hour or so and finally it was a wrap. I took a deep breath and sighed in relief. This is just the beginning of a new journey. I took the first step today in answering the call that God commissioned me to walk. I had no clue where the journey would eventually lead, but one thing I did know: God would be with me every step of the way.

Since that first day of filming the journey has continued for the past three years while we have prepared for the launch of the program.

A wonderfully talented friend, and annointed singer, Teresa Taylor, wrote and sang the theme song to the show.

God opened several doors through my good friends at deepercalling media, who arranged both the broadcasting of my show, and the publishing of my first book.

To date, "Now Is The Time" has been picked up for broadcast by several US Christian Networks, local cable stations and the Australian Christian Channel. As this book goes to press, we have just completed construction of a new studio, taking the show to the next level. The show is continuing to expand and I'm formulating some new television programs for the future as well.

One thing that I can say about my journey with the Lord is that God has always been with me. "Where He leads I will follow" has always been one of my favorite scripture verses. On this journey with the Lord it may sometimes lead us to mountaintops. Often it will lead us to valleys. But whether it is mountaintops or valleys God is always with us.

Where is your journey leading you today? God has an exciting walk for you with Him. But you need to follow Him and listen to His voice when He speaks. God will speak to you and show you the paths He has called you on. It may not be an easy path, but it will be rewarding if you learn to follow. That is where He had called me. When God spoke I followed Him. And it has been a glorious walk every single day. I don't know the paths God will continue to have me walk down, but one thing I do know, I don't want to miss out on anything God has for me. And so I will continue on with my journeys with God and continue to let God speak to me. When God speaks, I listen. He leads me in paths of righteousness for His names sake. My cup runs over. Surely goodness and mercy shall follow me all the days of my life and I will dwell in the house of the Lord forever, Amen (Psalms 23).

About The Author

Meri Crouley

Meri Crouley

Author Biography

Meri Crouley is a sought after speaker, singer and author, who speaks at various venues and churches throughout the United States and Internationally. Her television program "Now Is The Time" is launching on television channels and networks throughout the United States, and via satellite to countries around the globe.

Founder of Meri Crouley Ministries (www.mericrouley.com), a non-profit Christian organization, she is also President and Director of Youthwave Explosion Foundation based in Southern California. Youthwave is a dynamic evangelistic organization, with events that have brought thousands of young people to the Lord.

Through Meri's personal testimony and life experiences she imparts a fresh revelation on how to find God's purpose for your life. "Find your Purpose and you'll find your Passion" is one of her key life phrases. Her ministry is to challenge and encourage the Body of Christ through the gifts of the Holy Spirit and the teaching of God's Word.

Meri has been married for over 23 years to her husband Rick, and has three children, Christina, Jeremy and Jason. She resides in Laguna Niguel, California.

For more information regarding Meri Crouley Ministries, YouthWave Explosion Foundation, or the "Now Is The Time" television program, visit Meri on the web at www.mericrouley.com

For details on additional authors and ministries represented by deepercalling media, visit us on the web at www.deepercalling.com